PSYCHIATRIC HELP 5¢
MODERN METHODS
SCHULZ

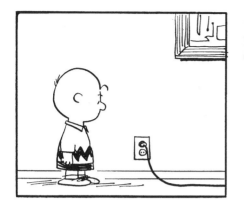

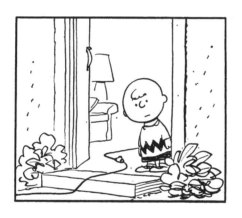

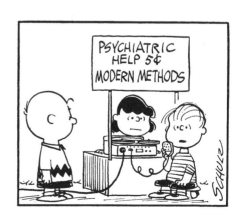

Books by Charles M. Schulz

Peanuts

More Peanuts

Good Grief, Charlie Brown!

Good Ol' Charlie Brown

Snoopy

You're Out of Your Mind, Charlie Brown

But We Love You, Charlie Brown

Peanuts Revisited

Go Fly a Kite, Charlie Brown

Peanuts Every Sunday

Snoopy, Come Home

Sunday's Fun Day, Charlie Brown

It's a Dog's Life, Charlie Brown

And a Woodstock in a Birch Tree

Here's To You, Charlie Brown

Charles M. Schulz

TITAN COMICS

HERE'S TO YOU, CHARLIE BROWN
ISBN: 9781787742697

COPYRIGHT© 2024, 1960, 1961, 1962 BY UNITED FEATURE SYNDICATE, INC.
ALL RIGHTS RESERVED, INCLUDING THE RIGHT TO REPRODUCE THIS BOOK
OR PORTIONS THEREOF IN ANY FORM.

ORIGINALLY PUBLISHED FAWCETT CREST PRINTING, MAY 1969.

FACSIMILE EDITION PUBLISHED JUNE 2024 BY TITAN COMICS,
A DIVISION OF TITAN PUBLISHING GROUP, LTD.
144 SOUTHWARK STREET, LONDON SE1 0UP.
TITAN COMICS IS A REGISTERED TRADEMARK OF
TITAN PUBLISHING GROUP, LTD.
ALL RIGHTS RESERVED.

COPYRIGHT © 2024 BY PEANUTS WORLDWIDE LLC.

FIRST EDITION

PRINTED IN INDIA

10 9 8 7 6 5 4 3 2 1

WWW.TITAN-COMICS.COM
WWW.PEANUTS.COM

A CIP CATALOGUE RECORD FOR THIS TITLE
IS AVAILABLE FROM THE BRITISH LIBRARY.

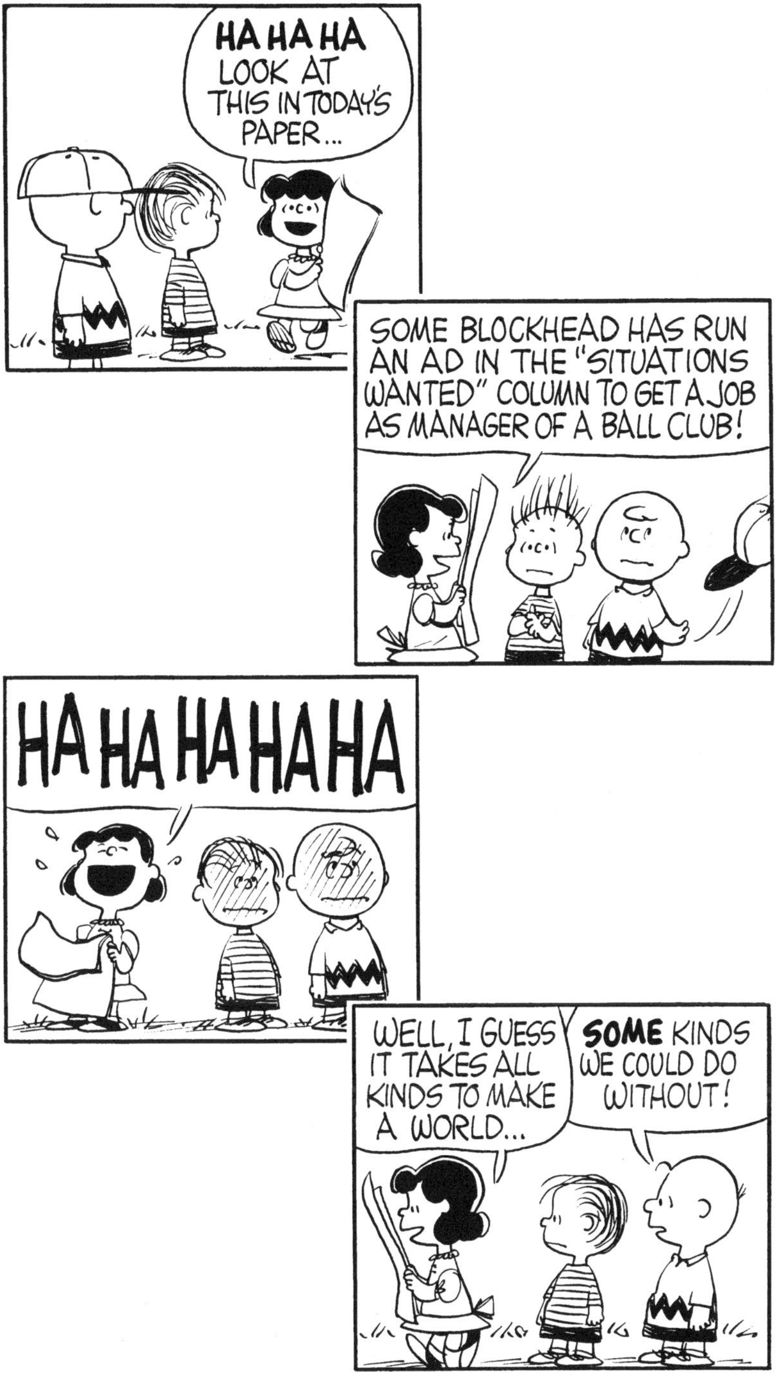
HA HA HA
LOOK AT THIS IN TODAY'S PAPER...
SOME BLOCKHEAD HAS RUN AN AD IN THE "SITUATIONS WANTED" COLUMN TO GET A JOB AS MANAGER OF A BALL CLUB!
HA HA HA HA HA
WELL, I GUESS IT TAKES ALL KINDS TO MAKE A WORLD...
SOME KINDS WE COULD DO WITHOUT!

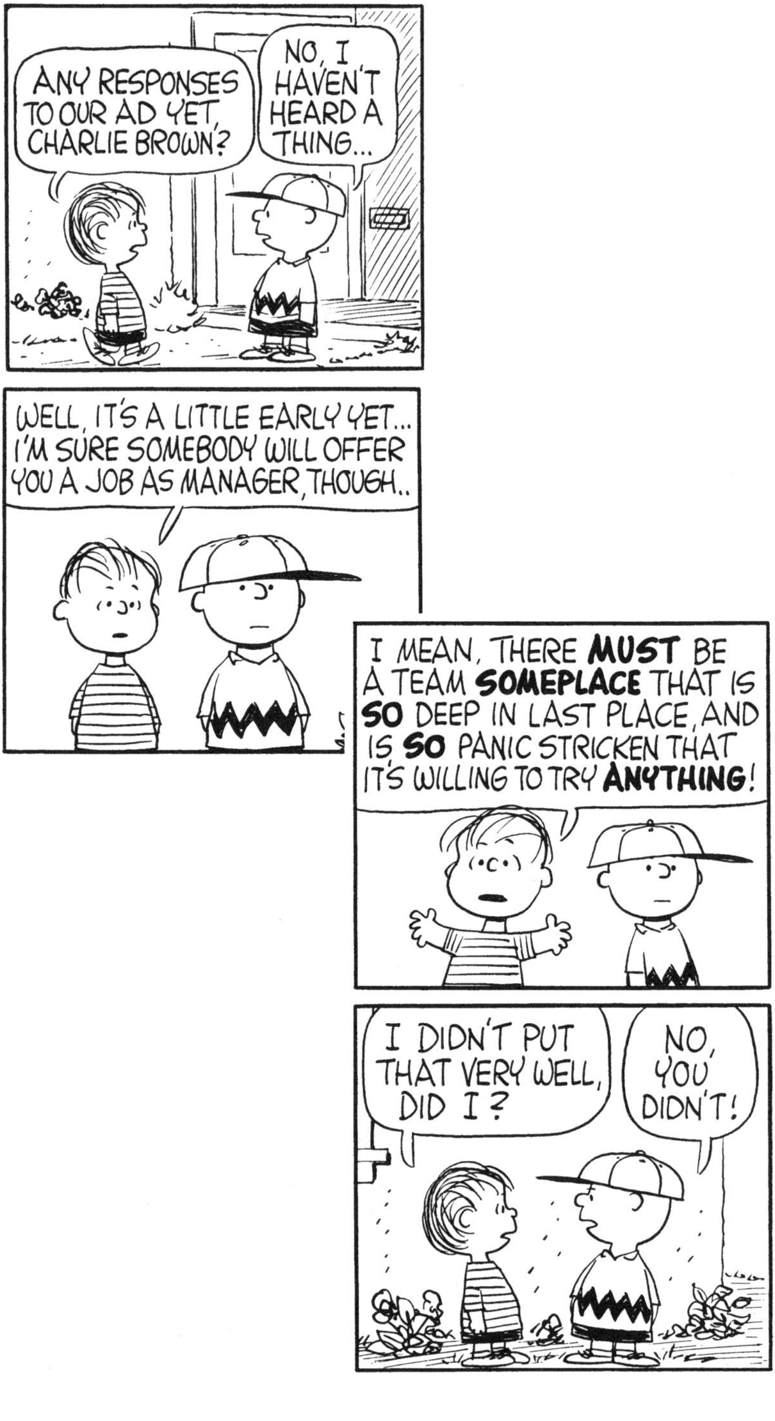
ANY RESPONSES TO OUR AD YET, CHARLIE BROWN?
NO, I HAVEN'T HEARD A THING...
WELL, IT'S A LITTLE EARLY YET... I'M SURE SOMEBODY WILL OFFER YOU A JOB AS MANAGER, THOUGH..
I MEAN, THERE **MUST** BE A TEAM **SOMEPLACE** THAT IS **SO** DEEP IN LAST PLACE, AND IS **SO** PANIC STRICKEN THAT IT'S WILLING TO TRY **ANYTHING**!
I DIDN'T PUT THAT VERY WELL, DID I?
NO, YOU DIDN'T!

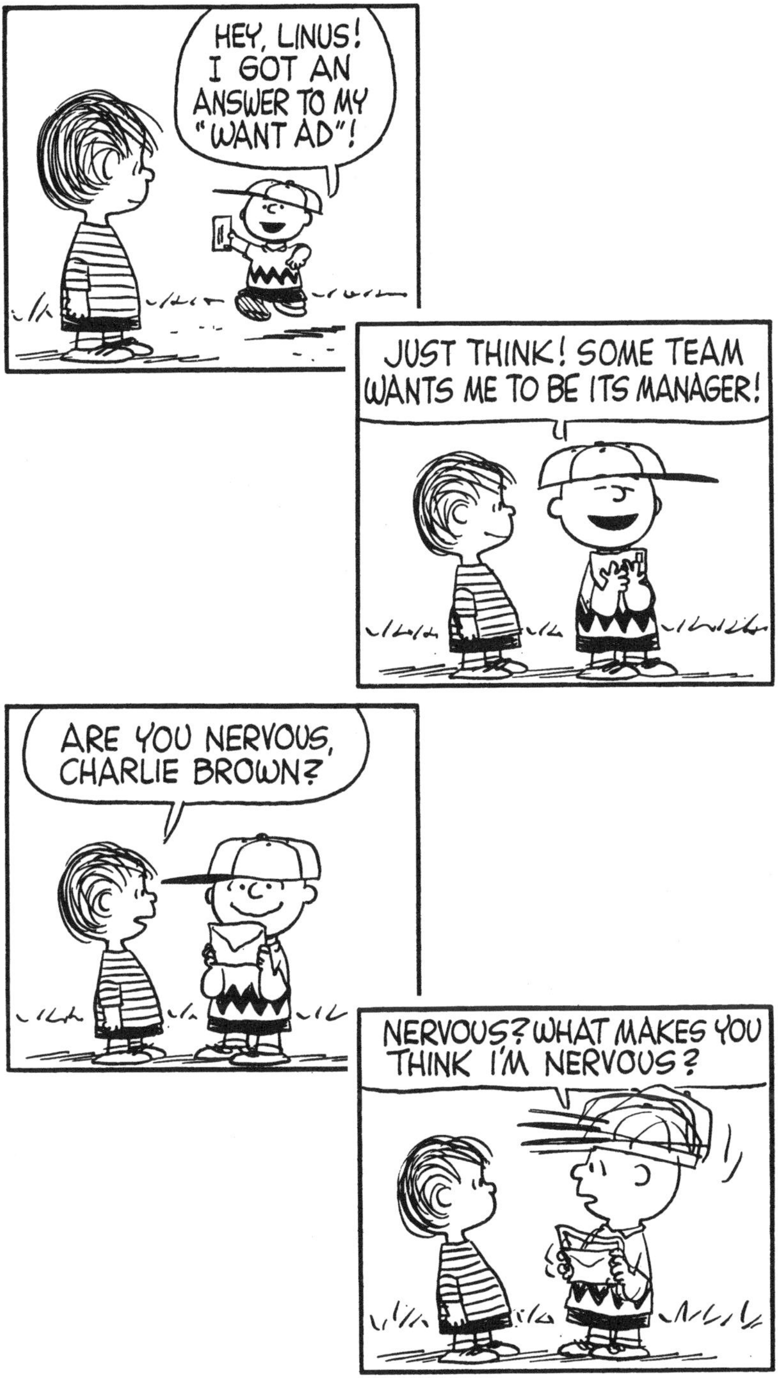
HEY, LINUS! I GOT AN ANSWER TO MY "WANT AD"!
JUST THINK! SOME TEAM WANTS ME TO BE ITS MANAGER!
ARE YOU NERVOUS, CHARLIE BROWN?
NERVOUS? WHAT MAKES YOU THINK I'M NERVOUS?

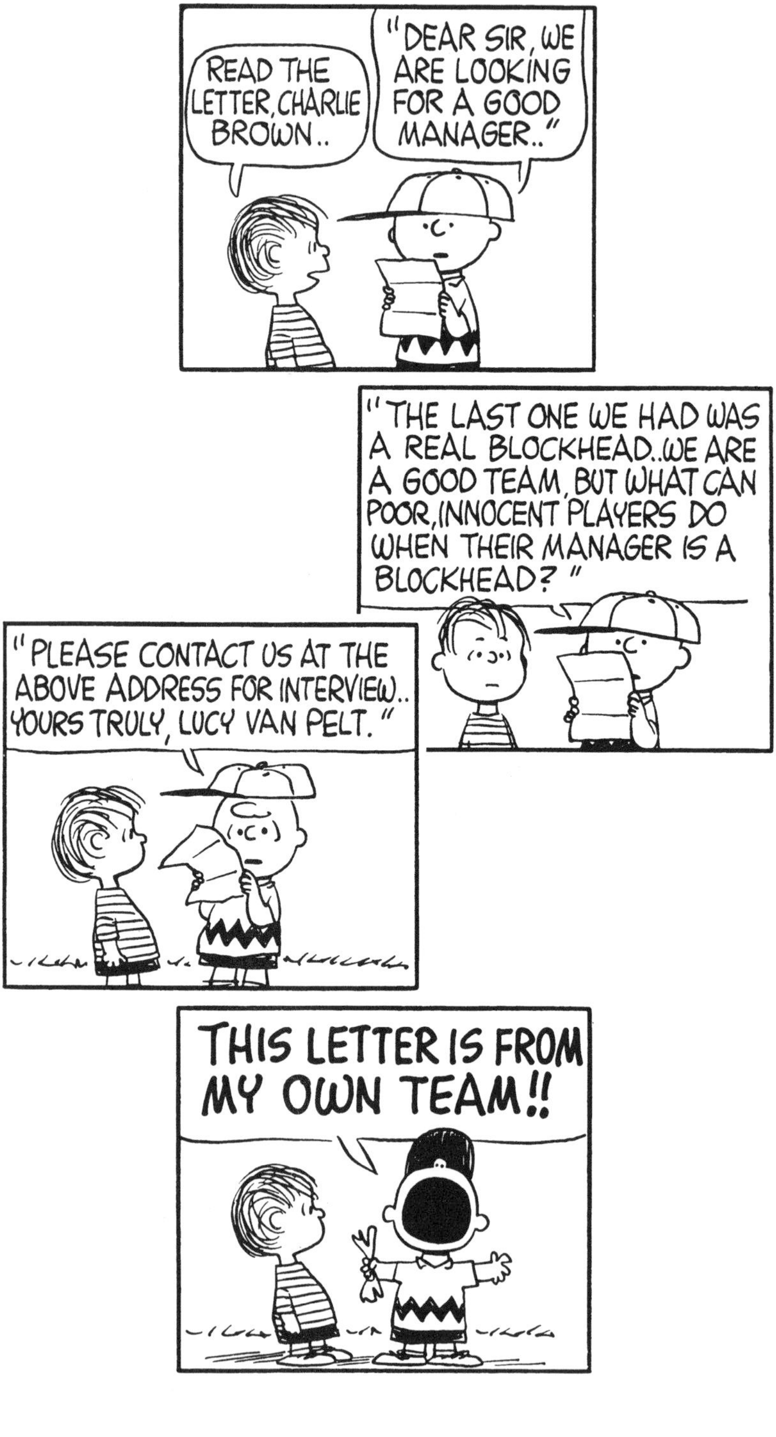
READ THE LETTER, CHARLIE BROWN..
"DEAR SIR, WE ARE LOOKING FOR A GOOD MANAGER.."
"THE LAST ONE WE HAD WAS A REAL BLOCKHEAD..WE ARE A GOOD TEAM, BUT WHAT CAN POOR, INNOCENT PLAYERS DO WHEN THEIR MANAGER IS A BLOCKHEAD?"
"PLEASE CONTACT US AT THE ABOVE ADDRESS FOR INTERVIEW.. YOURS TRULY, LUCY VAN PELT."
THIS LETTER IS FROM MY OWN TEAM!!

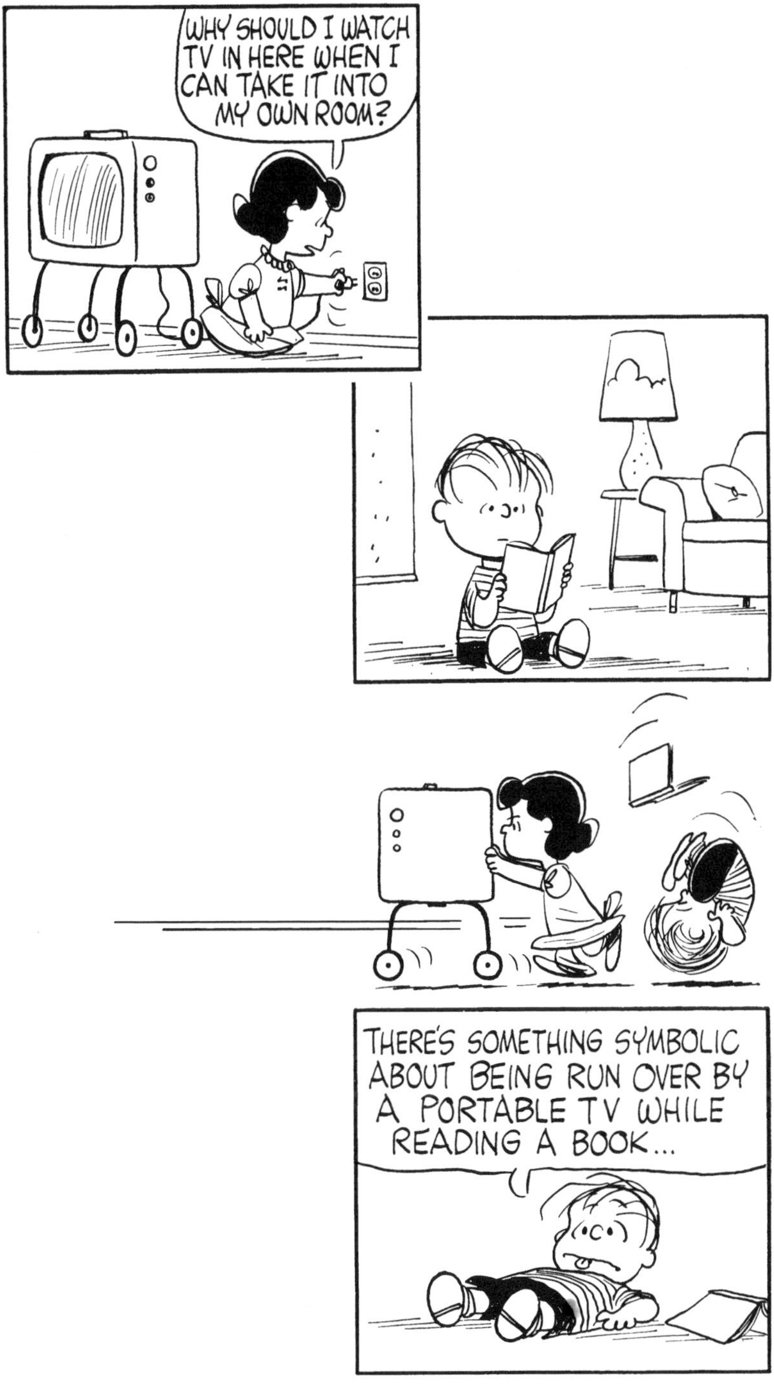

WHY SHOULD I WATCH TV IN HERE WHEN I CAN TAKE IT INTO MY OWN ROOM?
THERE'S SOMETHING SYMBOLIC ABOUT BEING RUN OVER BY A PORTABLE TV WHILE READING A BOOK...

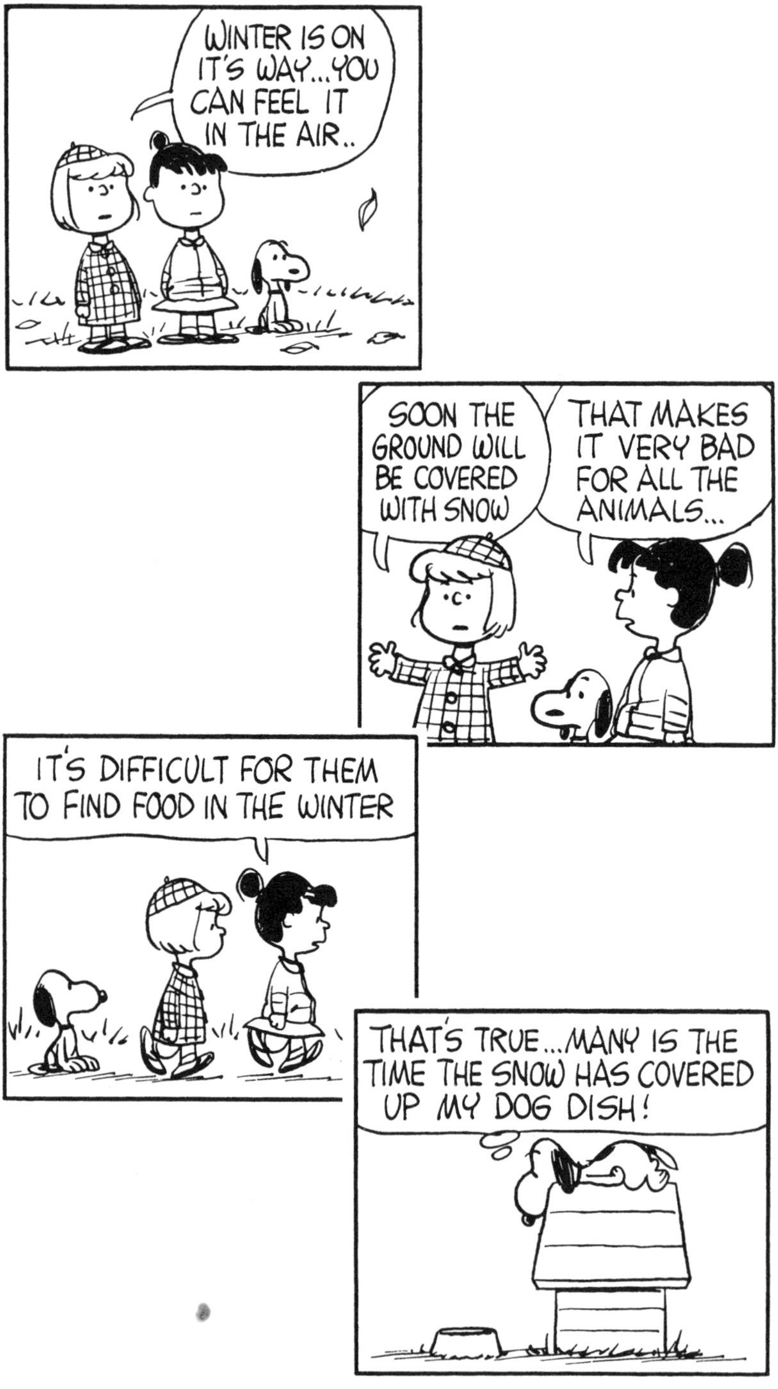
WINTER IS ON IT'S WAY...YOU CAN FEEL IT IN THE AIR..
SOON THE GROUND WILL BE COVERED WITH SNOW
THAT MAKES IT VERY BAD FOR ALL THE ANIMALS...
IT'S DIFFICULT FOR THEM TO FIND FOOD IN THE WINTER
THAT'S TRUE...MANY IS THE TIME THE SNOW HAS COVERED UP MY DOG DISH!

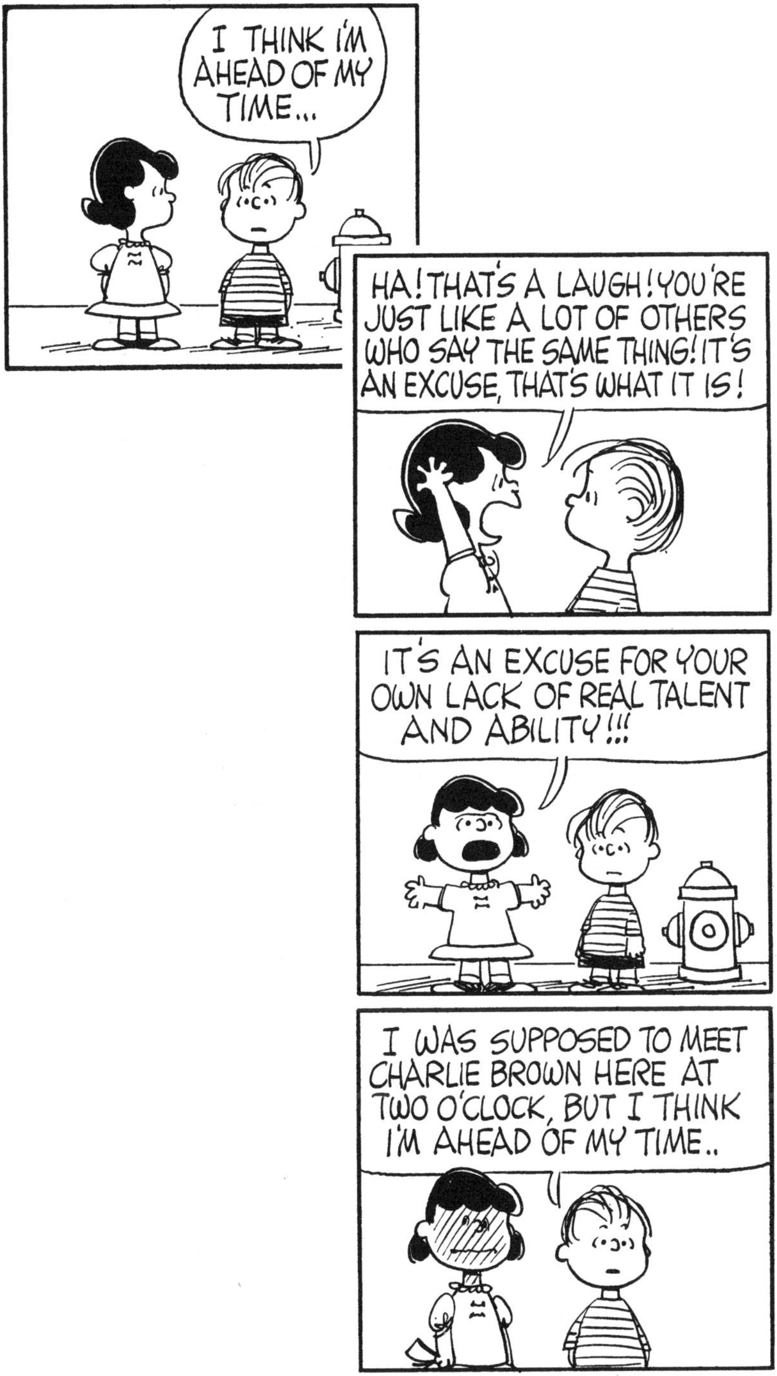
I THINK I'M AHEAD OF MY TIME...
HA! THAT'S A LAUGH! YOU'RE JUST LIKE A LOT OF OTHERS WHO SAY THE SAME THING! IT'S AN EXCUSE, THAT'S WHAT IT IS!
IT'S AN EXCUSE FOR YOUR OWN LACK OF REAL TALENT AND ABILITY!!!
I WAS SUPPOSED TO MEET CHARLIE BROWN HERE AT TWO O'CLOCK, BUT I THINK I'M AHEAD OF MY TIME..

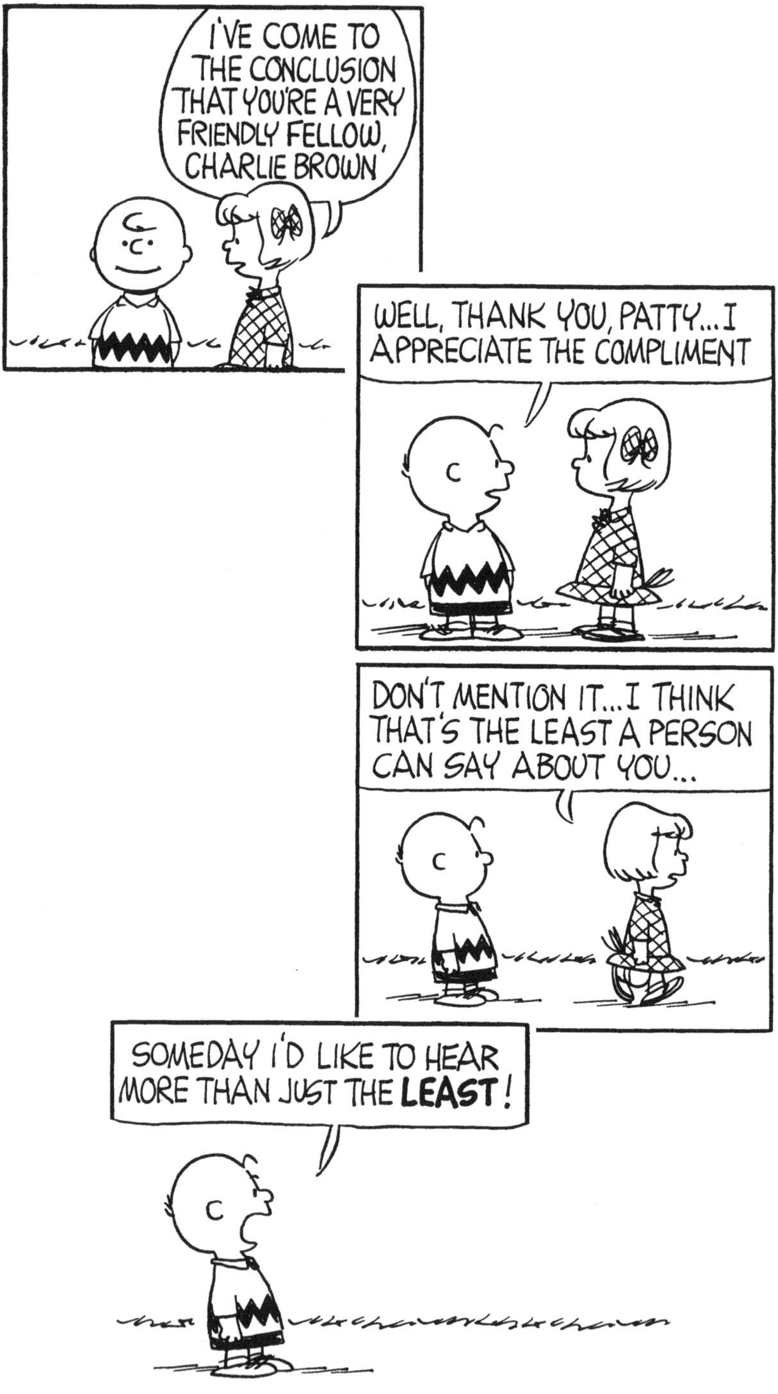
I'VE COME TO THE CONCLUSION THAT YOU'RE A VERY FRIENDLY FELLOW, CHARLIE BROWN
WELL, THANK YOU, PATTY...I APPRECIATE THE COMPLIMENT
DON'T MENTION IT...I THINK THAT'S THE LEAST A PERSON CAN SAY ABOUT YOU...
SOMEDAY I'D LIKE TO HEAR MORE THAN JUST THE **LEAST**!

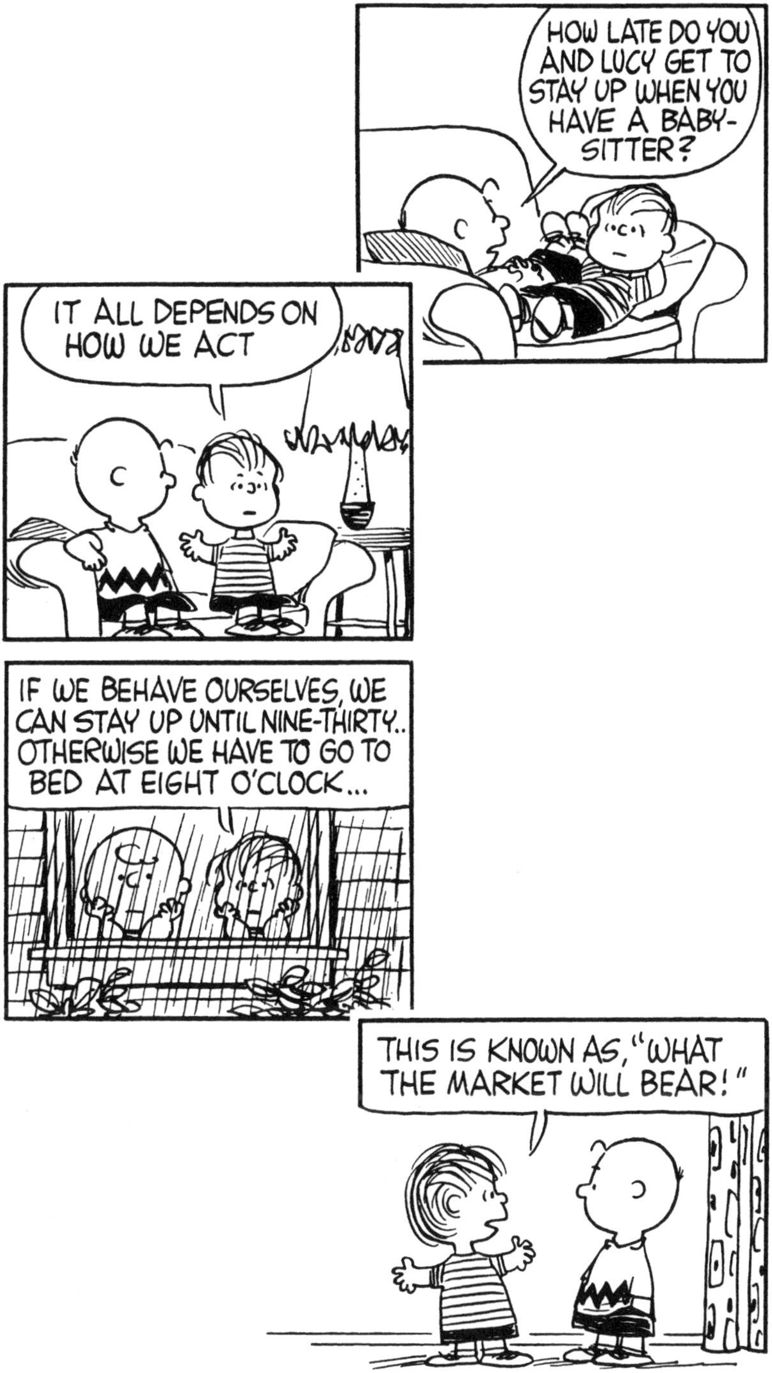
HOW LATE DO YOU AND LUCY GET TO STAY UP WHEN YOU HAVE A BABY-SITTER?
IT ALL DEPENDS ON HOW WE ACT
IF WE BEHAVE OURSELVES, WE CAN STAY UP UNTIL NINE-THIRTY.. OTHERWISE WE HAVE TO GO TO BED AT EIGHT O'CLOCK...
THIS IS KNOWN AS, "WHAT THE MARKET WILL BEAR!"

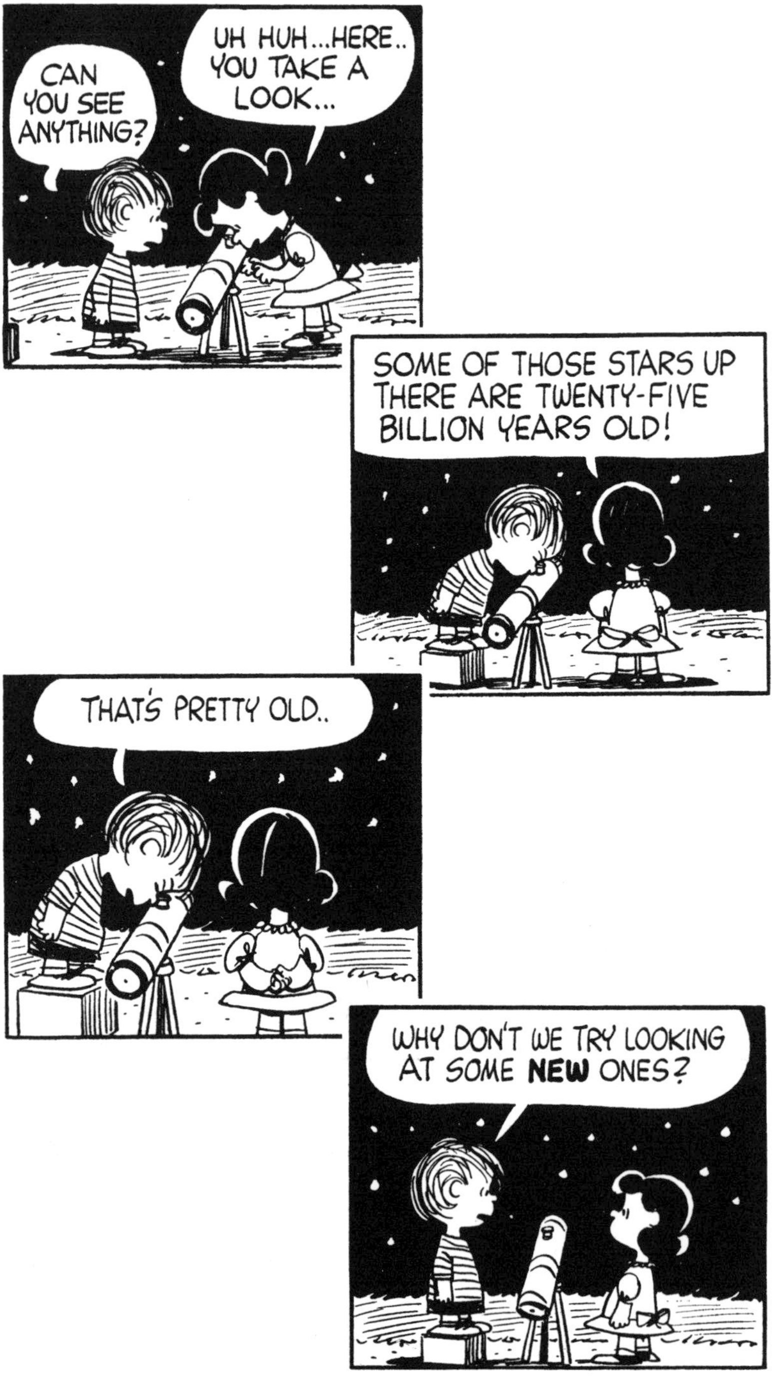
CAN YOU SEE ANYTHING?
UH HUH...HERE.. YOU TAKE A LOOK...
SOME OF THOSE STARS UP THERE ARE TWENTY-FIVE BILLION YEARS OLD!
THAT'S PRETTY OLD..
WHY DON'T WE TRY LOOKING AT SOME **NEW** ONES?

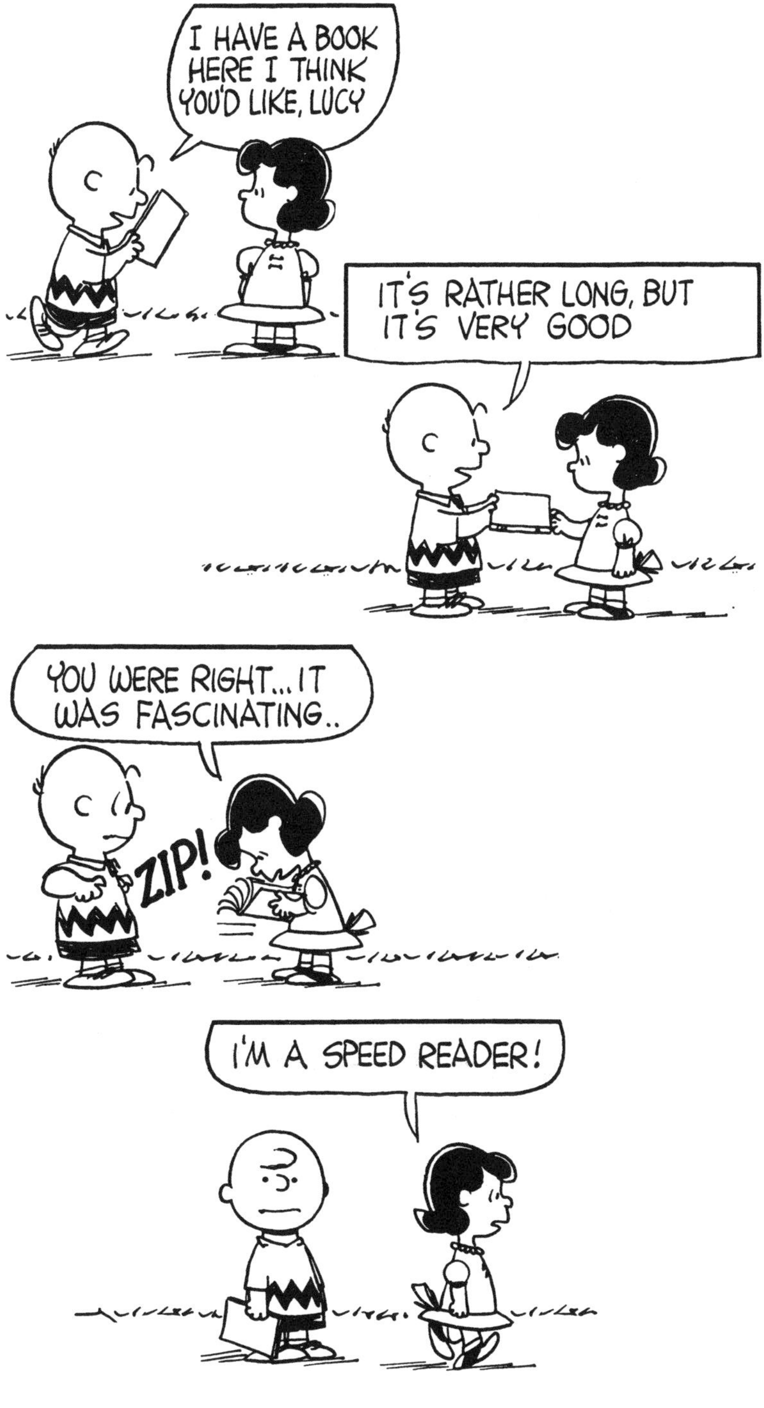
I HAVE A BOOK HERE I THINK YOU'D LIKE, LUCY
IT'S RATHER LONG, BUT IT'S VERY GOOD
YOU WERE RIGHT... IT WAS FASCINATING..
ZIP!
I'M A SPEED READER!

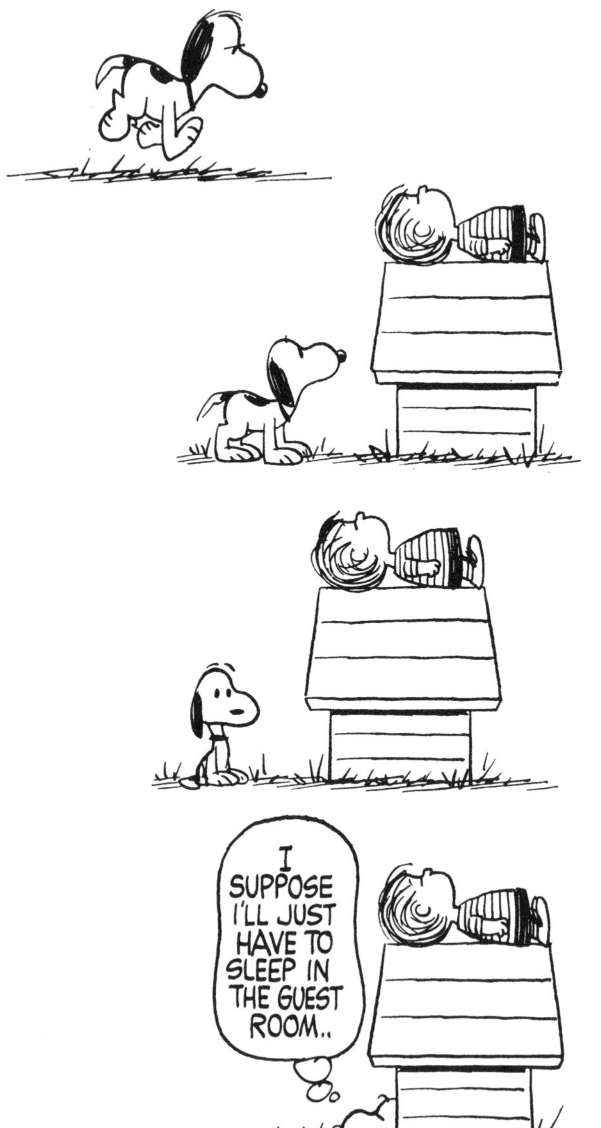
I SUPPOSE I'LL JUST HAVE TO SLEEP IN THE GUEST ROOM..

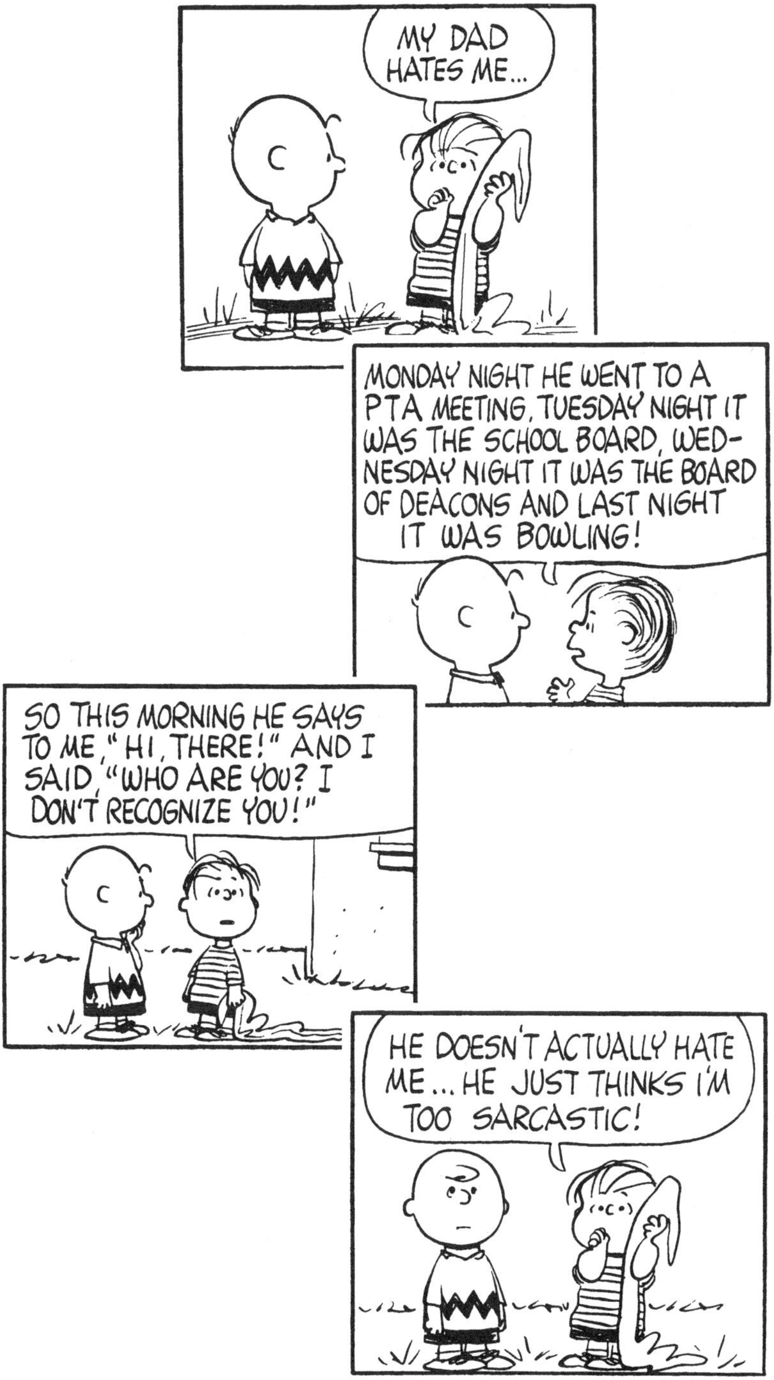
MY DAD HATES ME...
MONDAY NIGHT HE WENT TO A PTA MEETING, TUESDAY NIGHT IT WAS THE SCHOOL BOARD, WEDNESDAY NIGHT IT WAS THE BOARD OF DEACONS AND LAST NIGHT IT WAS BOWLING!
SO THIS MORNING HE SAYS TO ME, "HI, THERE!" AND I SAID, "WHO ARE YOU? I DON'T RECOGNIZE YOU!"
HE DOESN'T ACTUALLY HATE ME... HE JUST THINKS I'M TOO SARCASTIC!

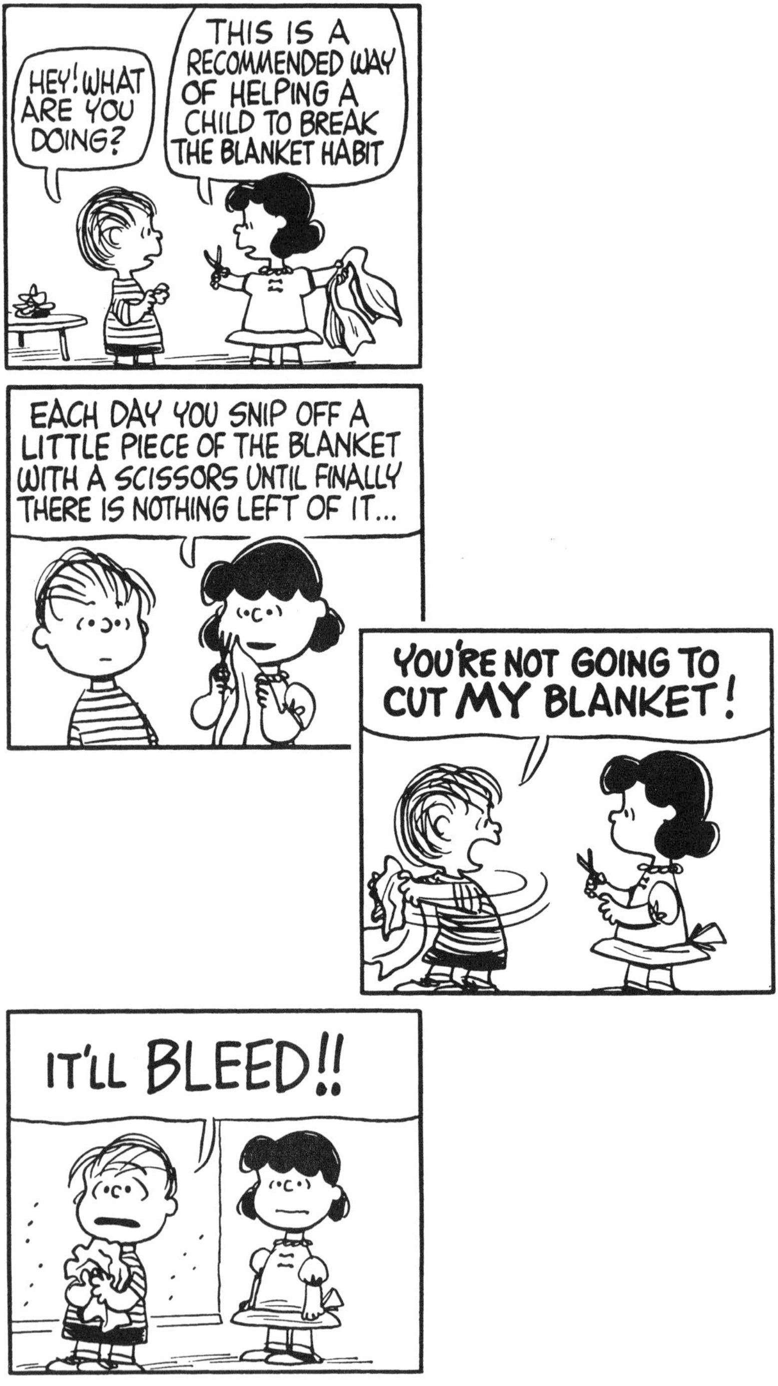
HEY! WHAT ARE YOU DOING?
THIS IS A RECOMMENDED WAY OF HELPING A CHILD TO BREAK THE BLANKET HABIT
EACH DAY YOU SNIP OFF A LITTLE PIECE OF THE BLANKET WITH A SCISSORS UNTIL FINALLY THERE IS NOTHING LEFT OF IT...
YOU'RE NOT GOING TO CUT MY BLANKET!
IT'LL BLEED!!

DEAR SNICKER SNACK CEREAL COMPANY,

I APPRECIATE YOUR OFFER OF ONE HUNDRED REVOLUTIONARY WAR SOLDIERS FOR FIFTEEN CENTS.

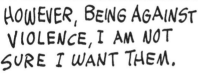

HOWEVER, BEING AGAINST VIOLENCE, I AM NOT SURE I WANT THEM.

INSTEAD, COULD I PLEASE HAVE A SET OF PEACE-TIME CIVILIANS?

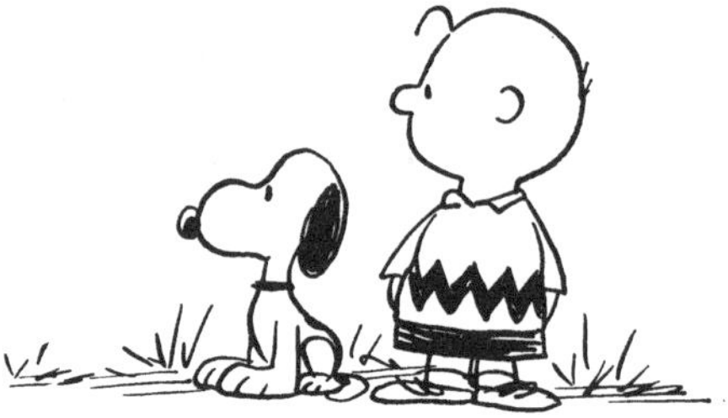

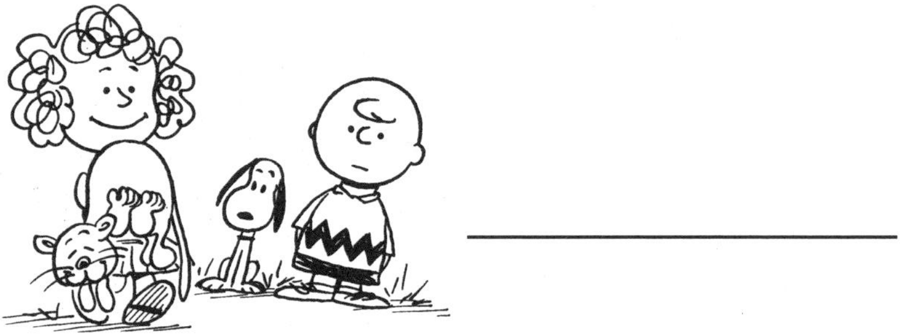

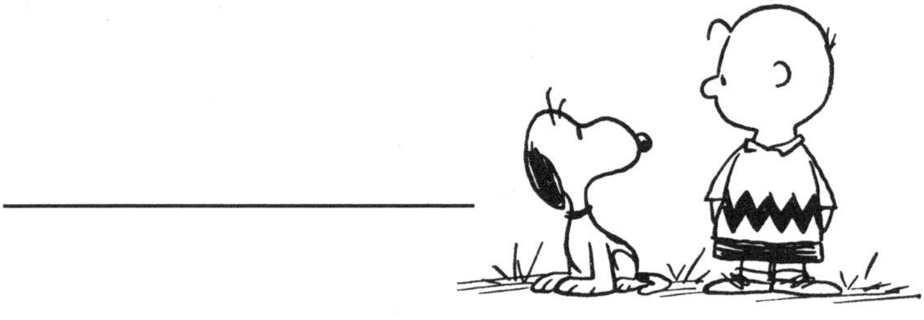

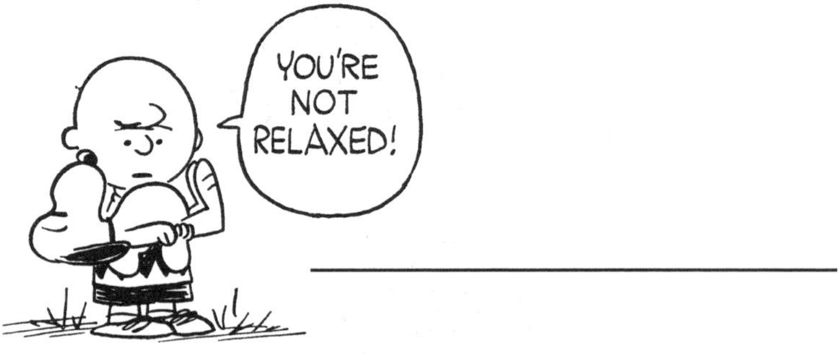
YOU'RE NOT RELAXED!

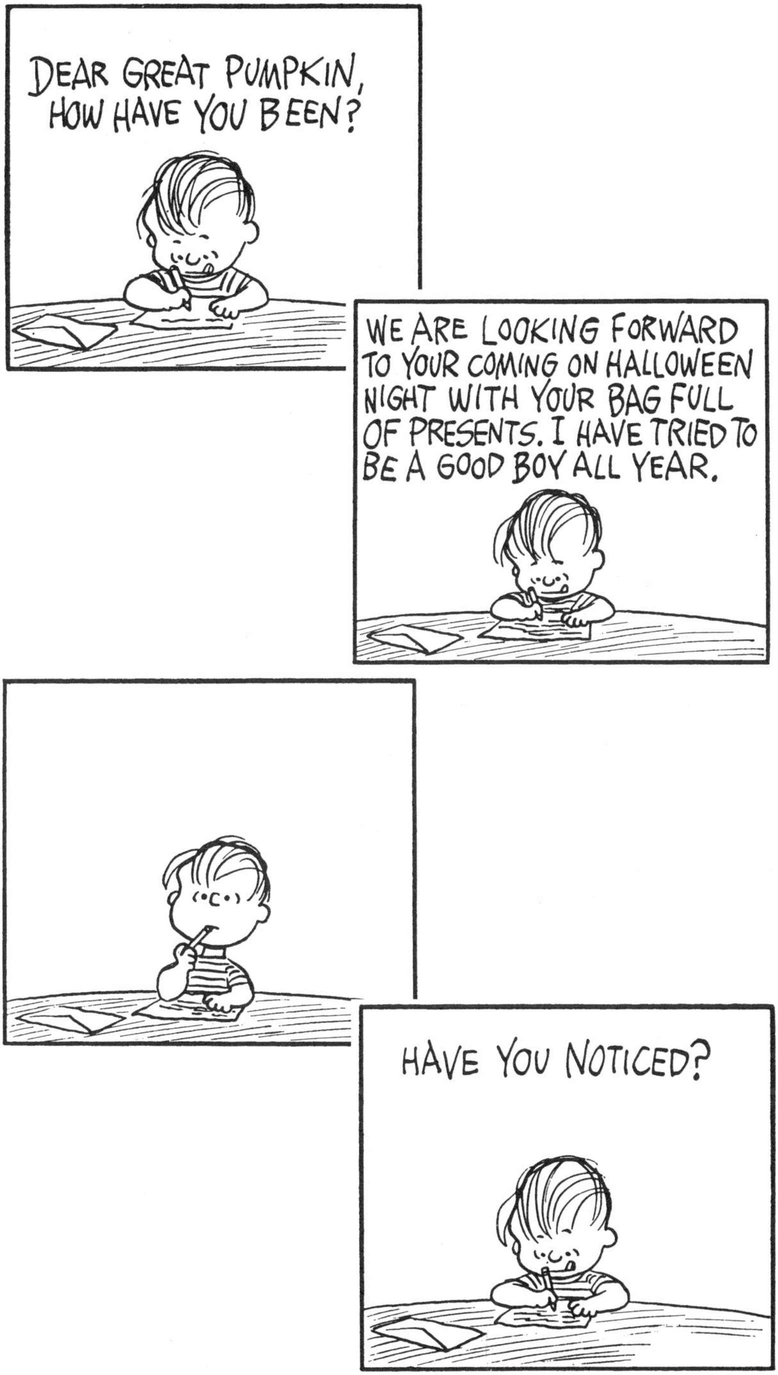
DEAR GREAT PUMPKIN, HOW HAVE YOU BEEN?
WE ARE LOOKING FORWARD TO YOUR COMING ON HALLOWEEN NIGHT WITH YOUR BAG FULL OF PRESENTS. I HAVE TRIED TO BE A GOOD BOY ALL YEAR.
HAVE YOU NOTICED?

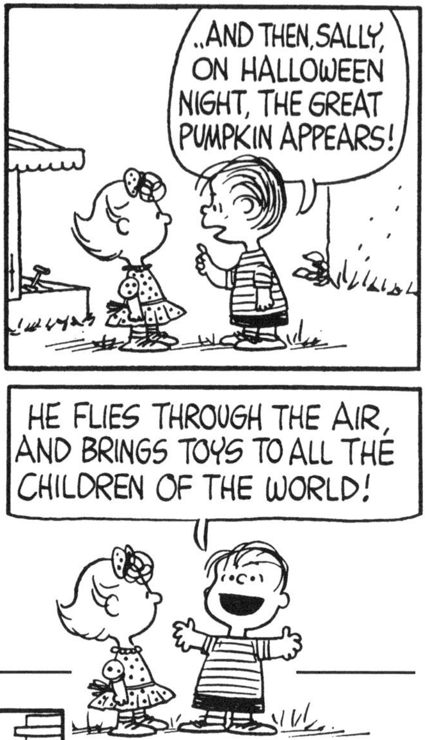
..AND THEN, SALLY, ON HALLOWEEN NIGHT, THE GREAT PUMPKIN APPEARS!
HE FLIES THROUGH THE AIR, AND BRINGS TOYS TO ALL THE CHILDREN OF THE WORLD!

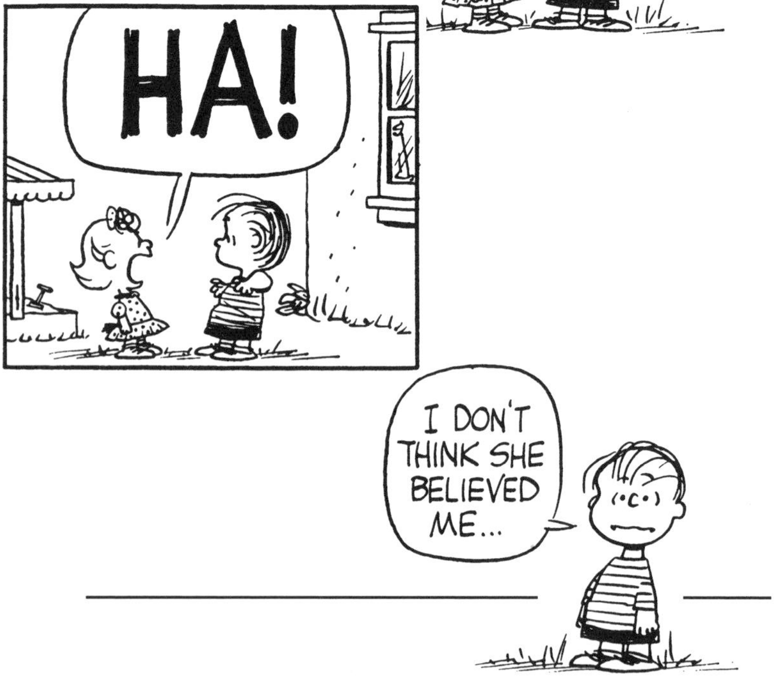
HA!
I DON'T THINK SHE BELIEVED ME...

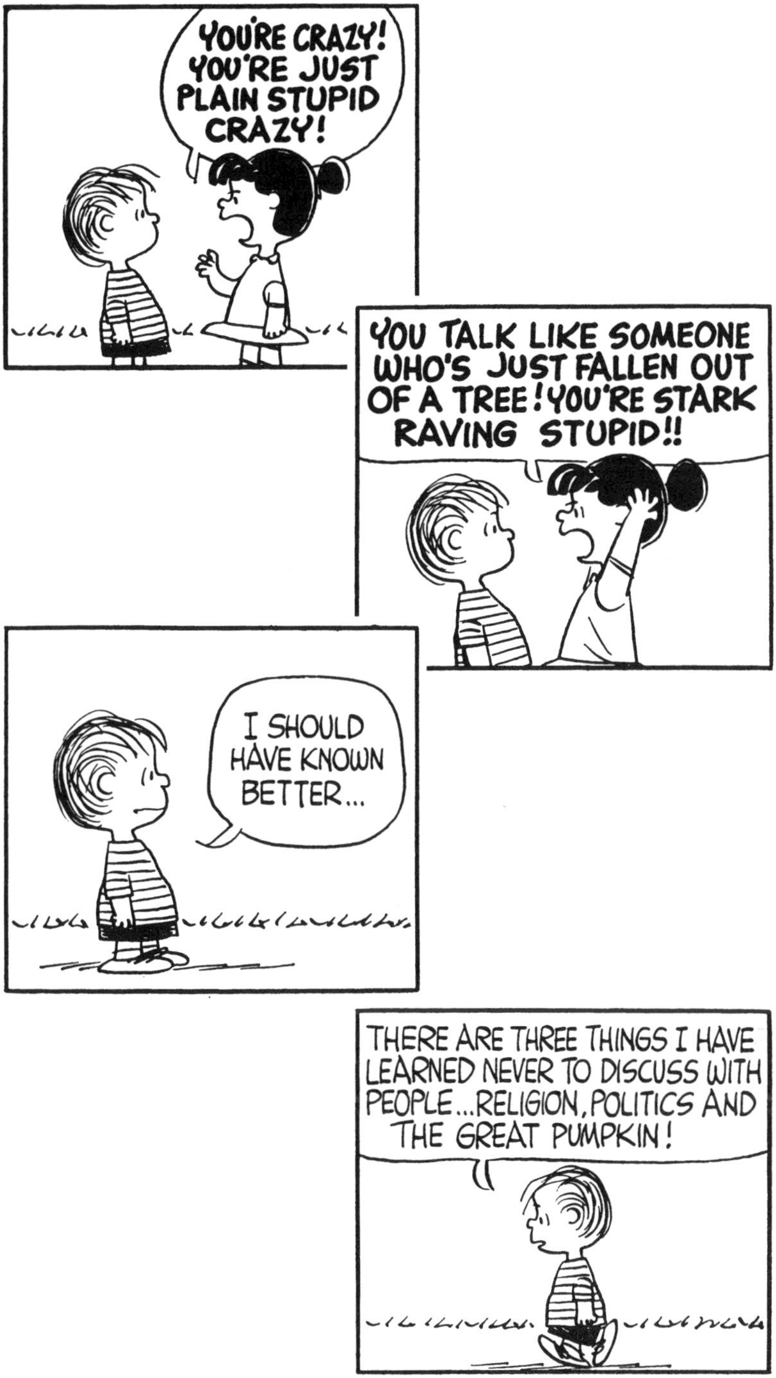
YOU'RE CRAZY! YOU'RE JUST PLAIN STUPID CRAZY!
YOU TALK LIKE SOMEONE WHO'S JUST FALLEN OUT OF A TREE! YOU'RE STARK RAVING STUPID!!
I SHOULD HAVE KNOWN BETTER...
THERE ARE THREE THINGS I HAVE LEARNED NEVER TO DISCUSS WITH PEOPLE...RELIGION, POLITICS AND THE GREAT PUMPKIN!

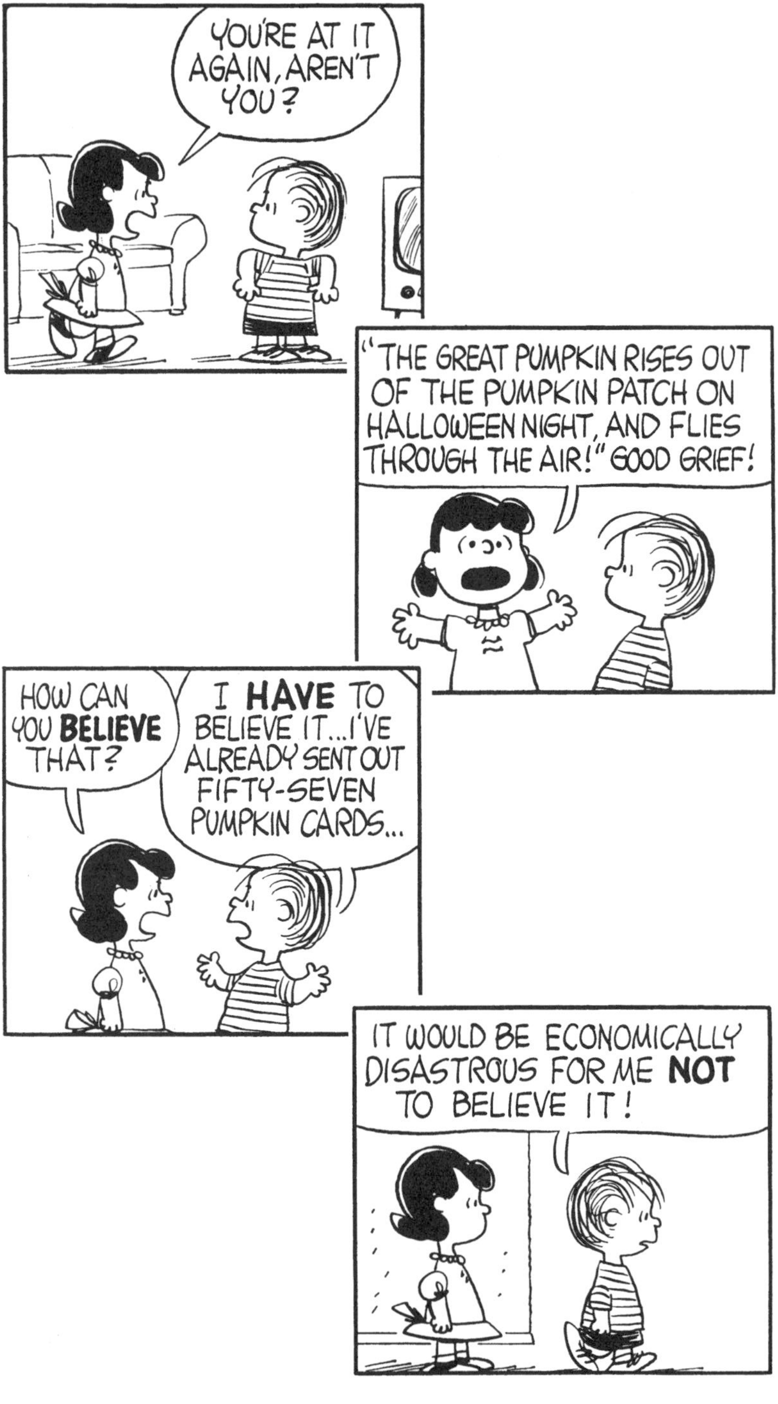
YOU'RE AT IT AGAIN, AREN'T YOU?
"THE GREAT PUMPKIN RISES OUT OF THE PUMPKIN PATCH ON HALLOWEEN NIGHT, AND FLIES THROUGH THE AIR!" GOOD GRIEF!
HOW CAN YOU **BELIEVE** THAT?
I **HAVE** TO BELIEVE IT...I'VE ALREADY SENT OUT FIFTY-SEVEN PUMPKIN CARDS...
IT WOULD BE ECONOMICALLY DISASTROUS FOR ME **NOT** TO BELIEVE IT!

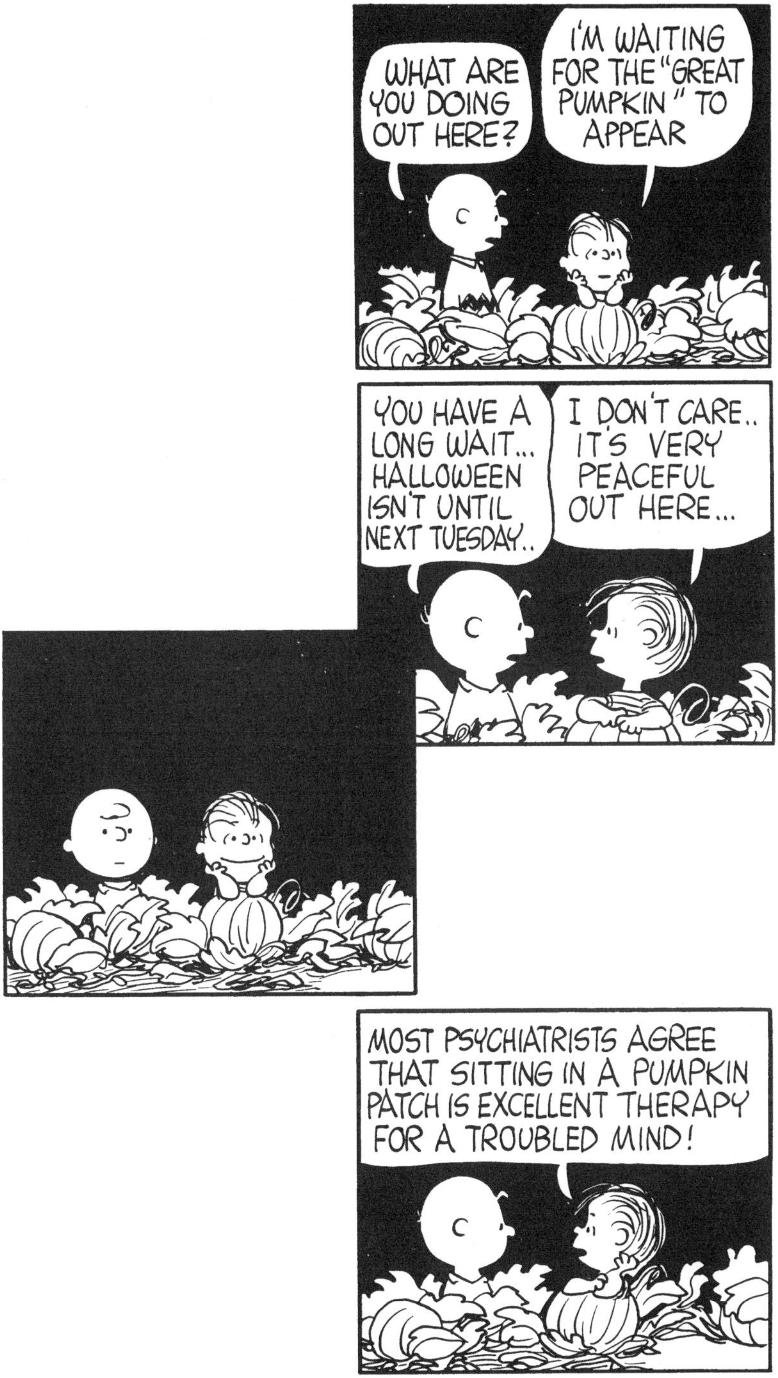
WHAT ARE YOU DOING OUT HERE?
I'M WAITING FOR THE "GREAT PUMPKIN" TO APPEAR
YOU HAVE A LONG WAIT... HALLOWEEN ISN'T UNTIL NEXT TUESDAY..
I DON'T CARE.. IT'S VERY PEACEFUL OUT HERE...
MOST PSYCHIATRISTS AGREE THAT SITTING IN A PUMPKIN PATCH IS EXCELLENT THERAPY FOR A TROUBLED MIND!

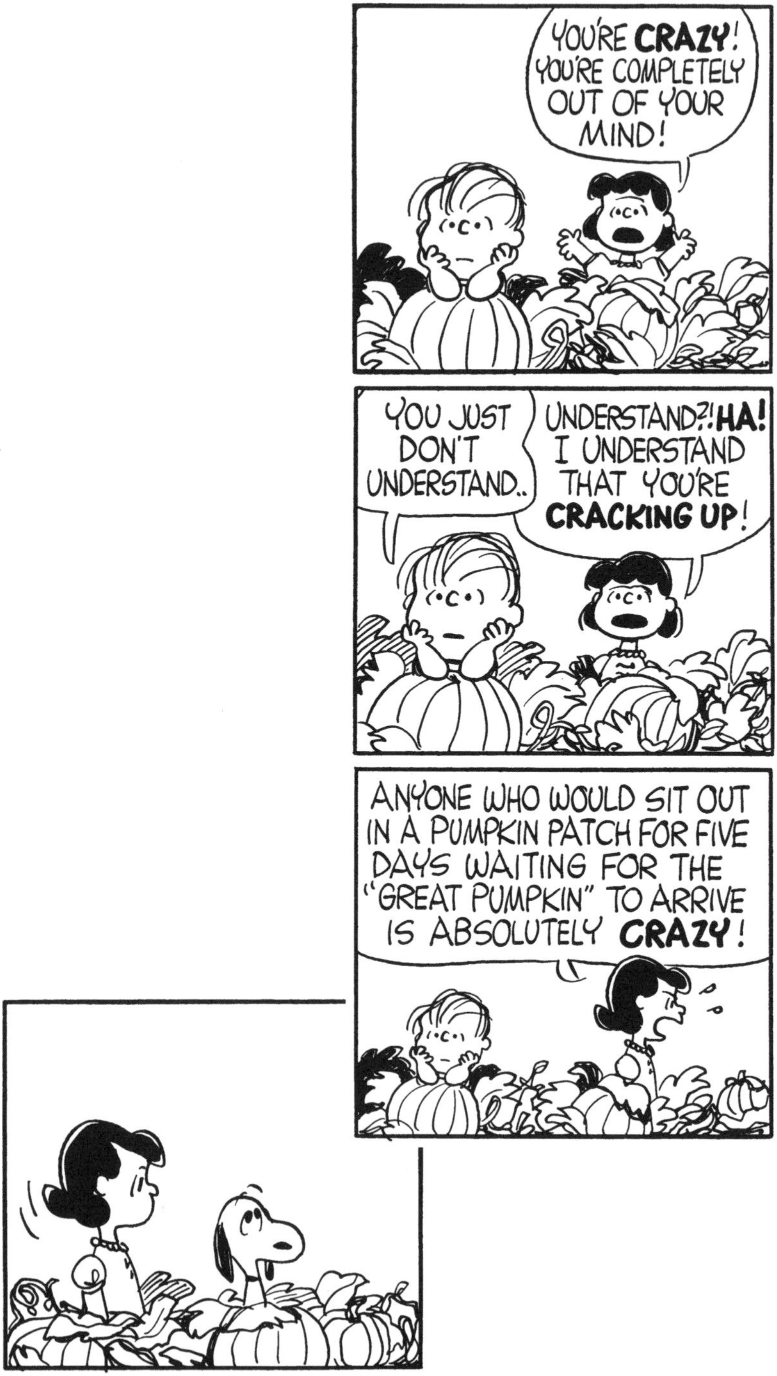
YOU'RE CRAZY! YOU'RE COMPLETELY OUT OF YOUR MIND!
YOU JUST DON'T UNDERSTAND..
UNDERSTAND?! HA! I UNDERSTAND THAT YOU'RE CRACKING UP!
ANYONE WHO WOULD SIT OUT IN A PUMPKIN PATCH FOR FIVE DAYS WAITING FOR THE "GREAT PUMPKIN" TO ARRIVE IS ABSOLUTELY CRAZY!

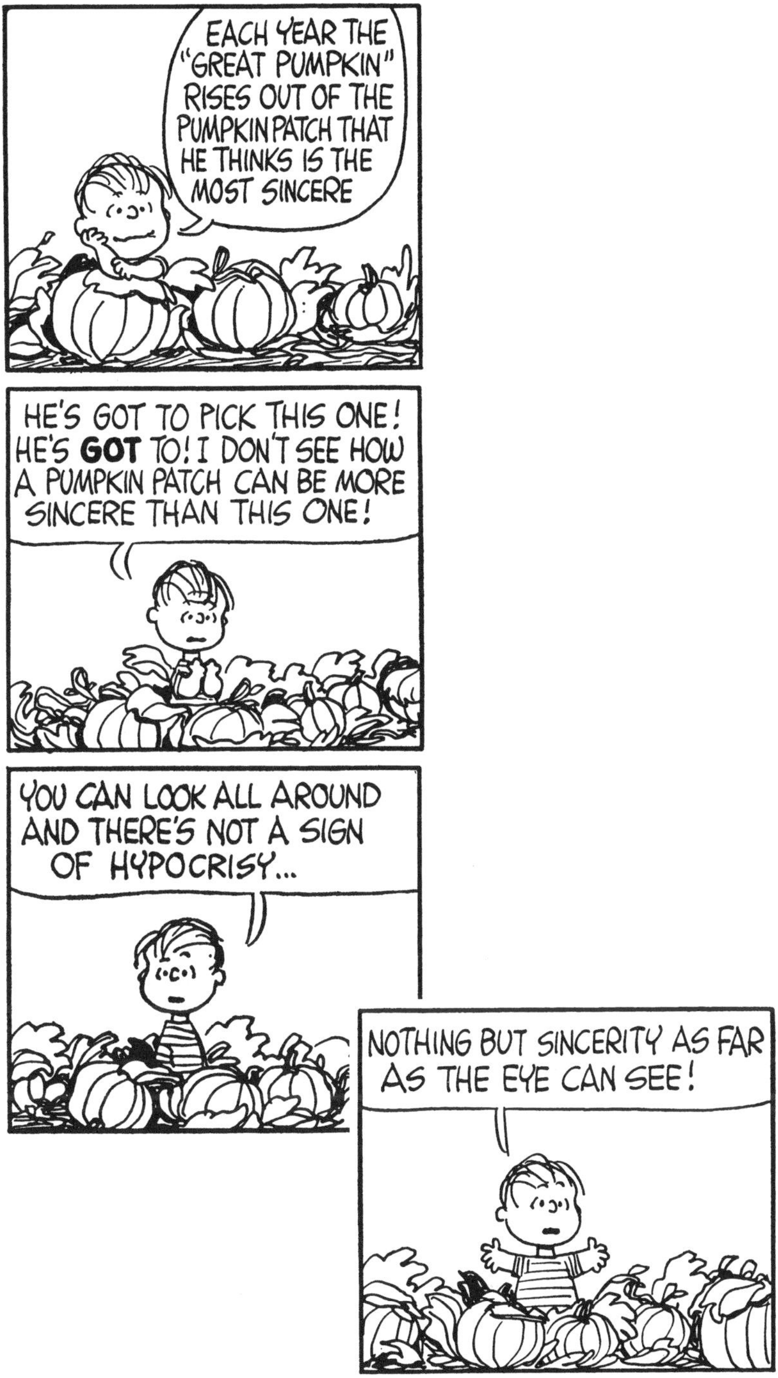
EACH YEAR THE "GREAT PUMPKIN" RISES OUT OF THE PUMPKIN PATCH THAT HE THINKS IS THE MOST SINCERE
HE'S GOT TO PICK THIS ONE! HE'S **GOT** TO! I DON'T SEE HOW A PUMPKIN PATCH CAN BE MORE SINCERE THAN THIS ONE!
YOU CAN LOOK ALL AROUND AND THERE'S NOT A SIGN OF HYPOCRISY...
NOTHING BUT SINCERITY AS FAR AS THE EYE CAN SEE!

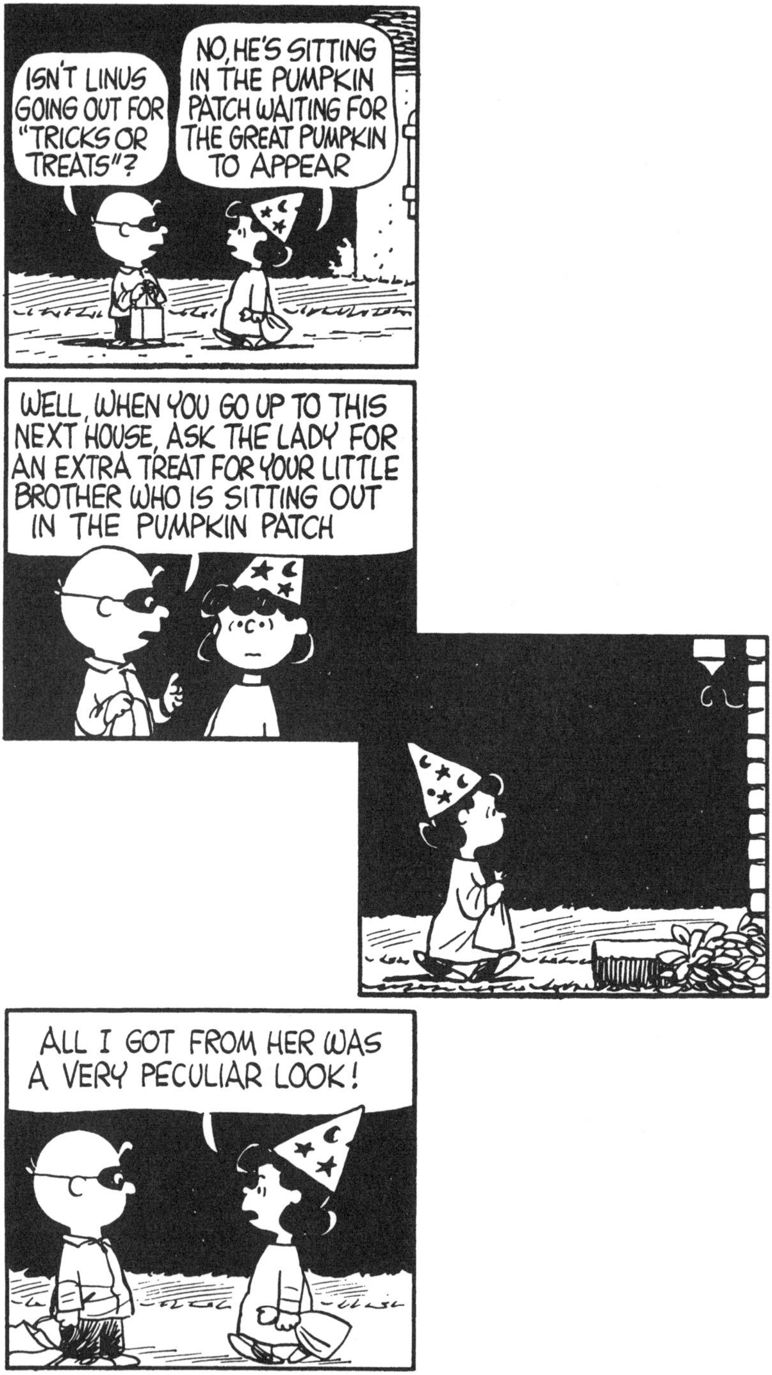

ISN'T LINUS GOING OUT FOR "TRICKS OR TREATS"?
NO, HE'S SITTING IN THE PUMPKIN PATCH WAITING FOR THE GREAT PUMPKIN TO APPEAR
WELL, WHEN YOU GO UP TO THIS NEXT HOUSE, ASK THE LADY FOR AN EXTRA TREAT FOR YOUR LITTLE BROTHER WHO IS SITTING OUT IN THE PUMPKIN PATCH
ALL I GOT FROM HER WAS A VERY PECULIAR LOOK!

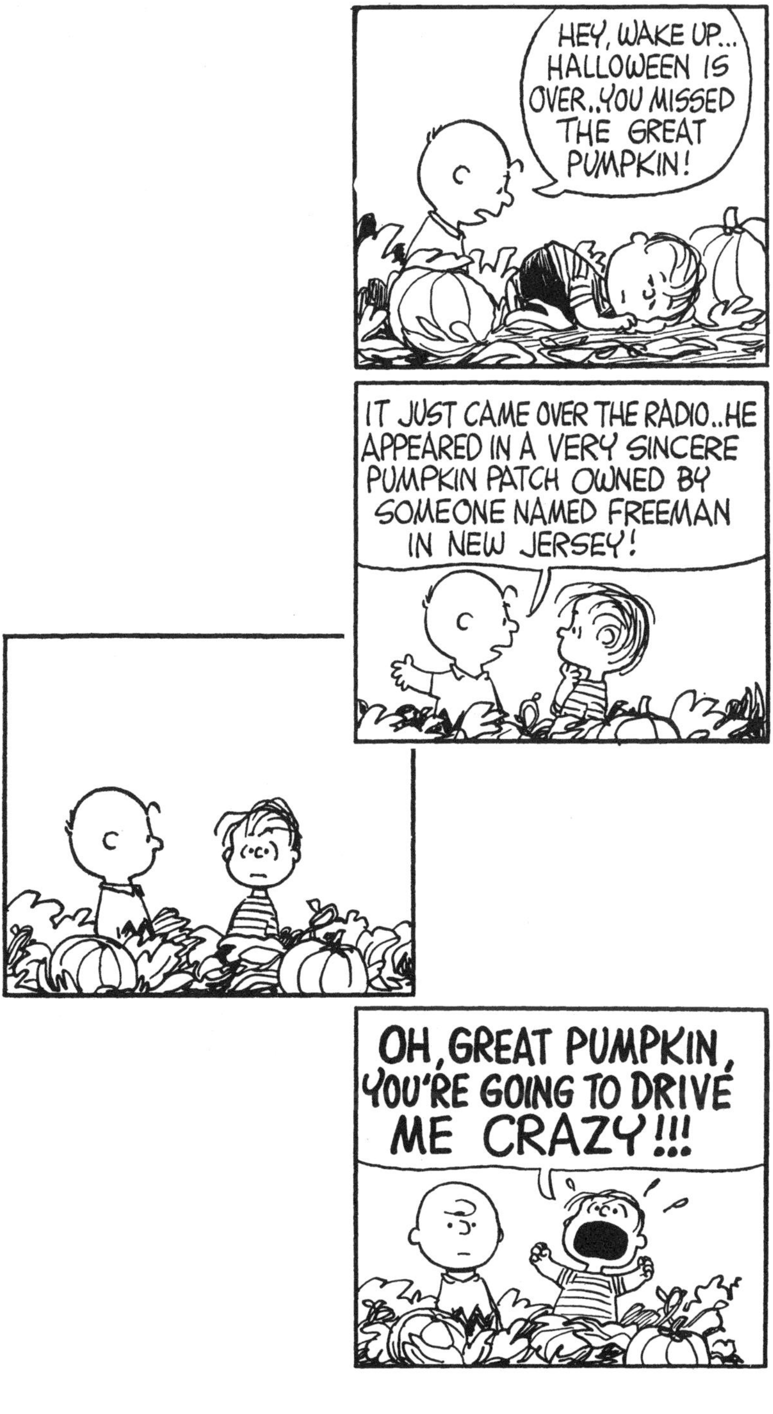
HEY, WAKE UP... HALLOWEEN IS OVER..YOU MISSED THE GREAT PUMPKIN!
IT JUST CAME OVER THE RADIO..HE APPEARED IN A VERY SINCERE PUMPKIN PATCH OWNED BY SOMEONE NAMED FREEMAN IN NEW JERSEY!
OH, GREAT PUMPKIN, YOU'RE GOING TO DRIVE ME CRAZY!!!

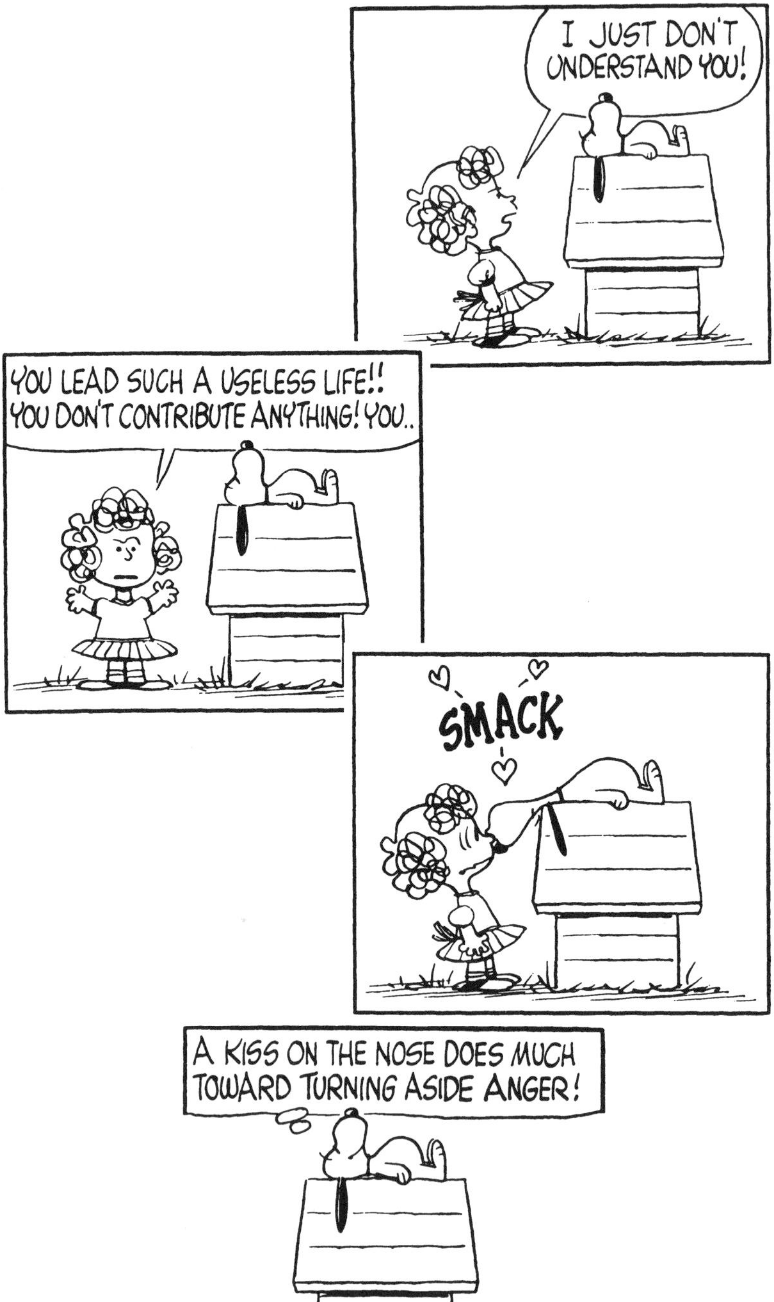
I JUST DON'T UNDERSTAND YOU!
YOU LEAD SUCH A USELESS LIFE!! YOU DON'T CONTRIBUTE ANYTHING! YOU..
SMACK
A KISS ON THE NOSE DOES MUCH TOWARD TURNING ASIDE ANGER!

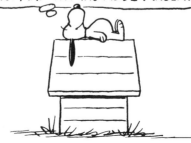

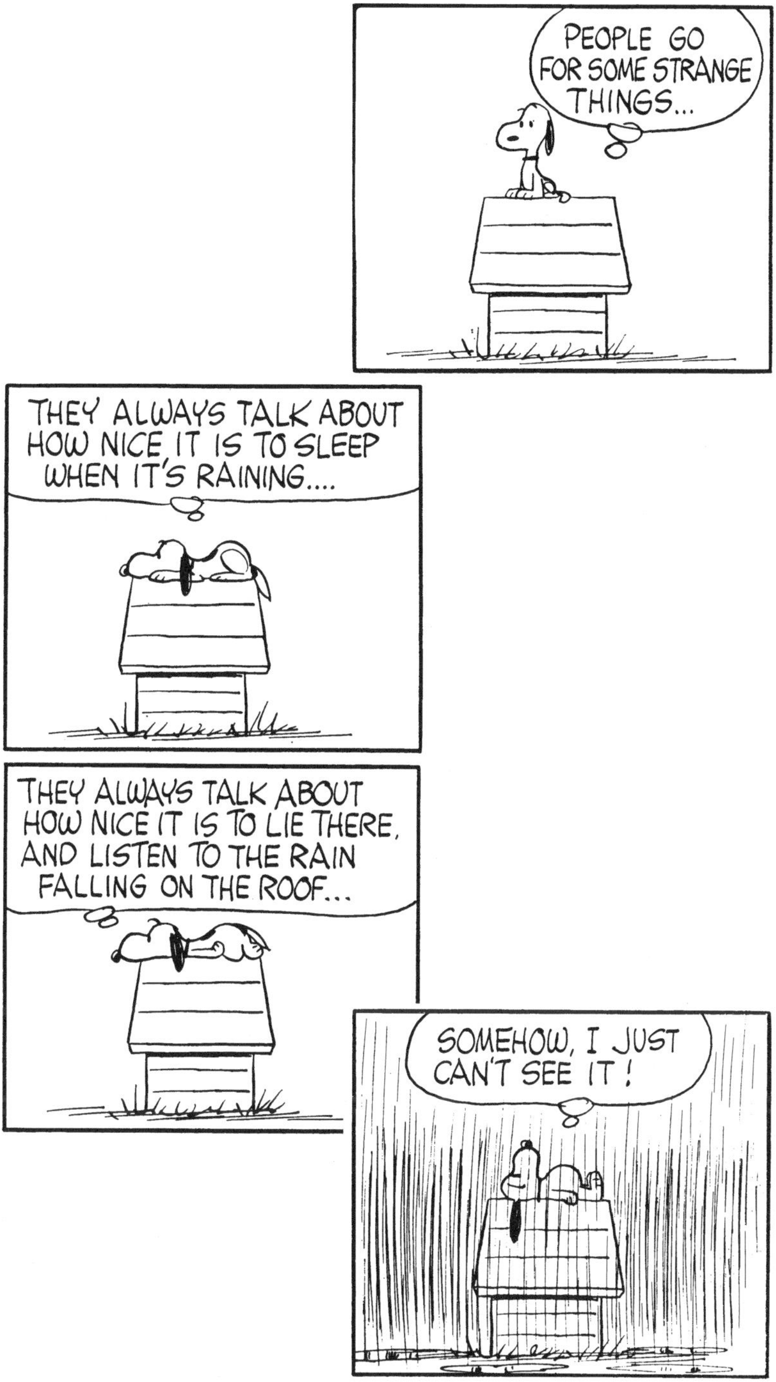
PEOPLE GO FOR SOME STRANGE THINGS...
THEY ALWAYS TALK ABOUT HOW NICE IT IS TO SLEEP WHEN IT'S RAINING....
THEY ALWAYS TALK ABOUT HOW NICE IT IS TO LIE THERE, AND LISTEN TO THE RAIN FALLING ON THE ROOF...
SOMEHOW, I JUST CAN'T SEE IT!

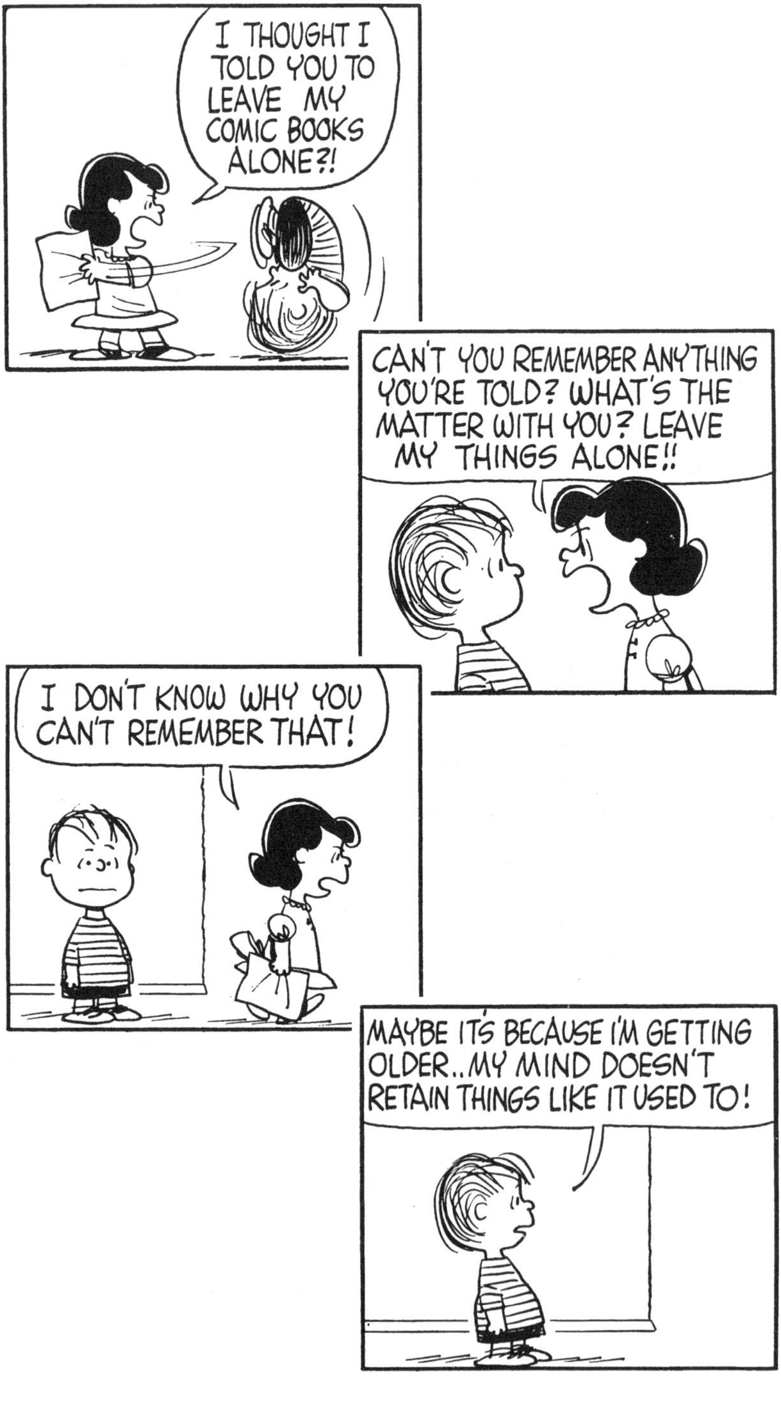
I THOUGHT I TOLD YOU TO LEAVE MY COMIC BOOKS ALONE?!
CAN'T YOU REMEMBER ANYTHING YOU'RE TOLD? WHAT'S THE MATTER WITH YOU? LEAVE MY THINGS ALONE!!
I DON'T KNOW WHY YOU CAN'T REMEMBER THAT!
MAYBE IT'S BECAUSE I'M GETTING OLDER..MY MIND DOESN'T RETAIN THINGS LIKE IT USED TO!

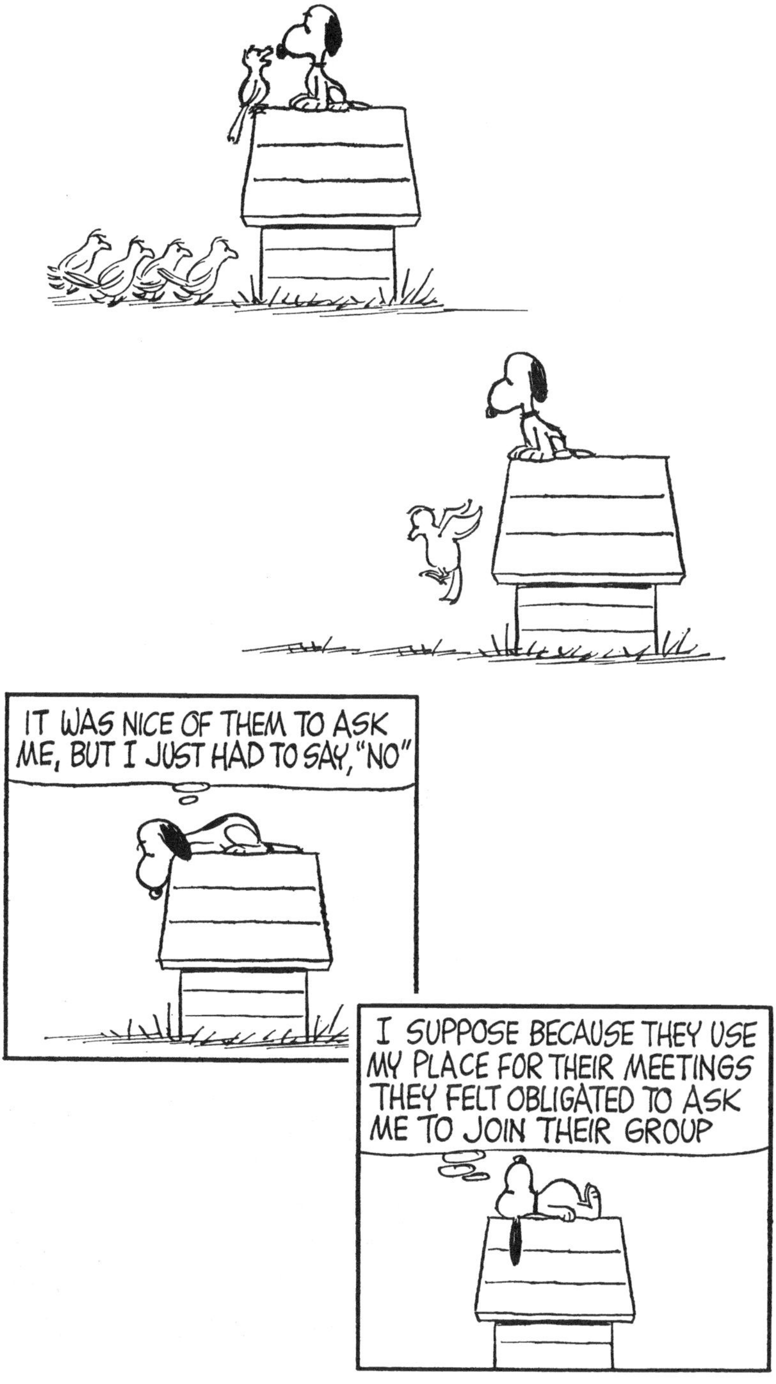
IT WAS NICE OF THEM TO ASK ME, BUT I JUST HAD TO SAY, "NO"
I SUPPOSE BECAUSE THEY USE MY PLACE FOR THEIR MEETINGS THEY FELT OBLIGATED TO ASK ME TO JOIN THEIR GROUP

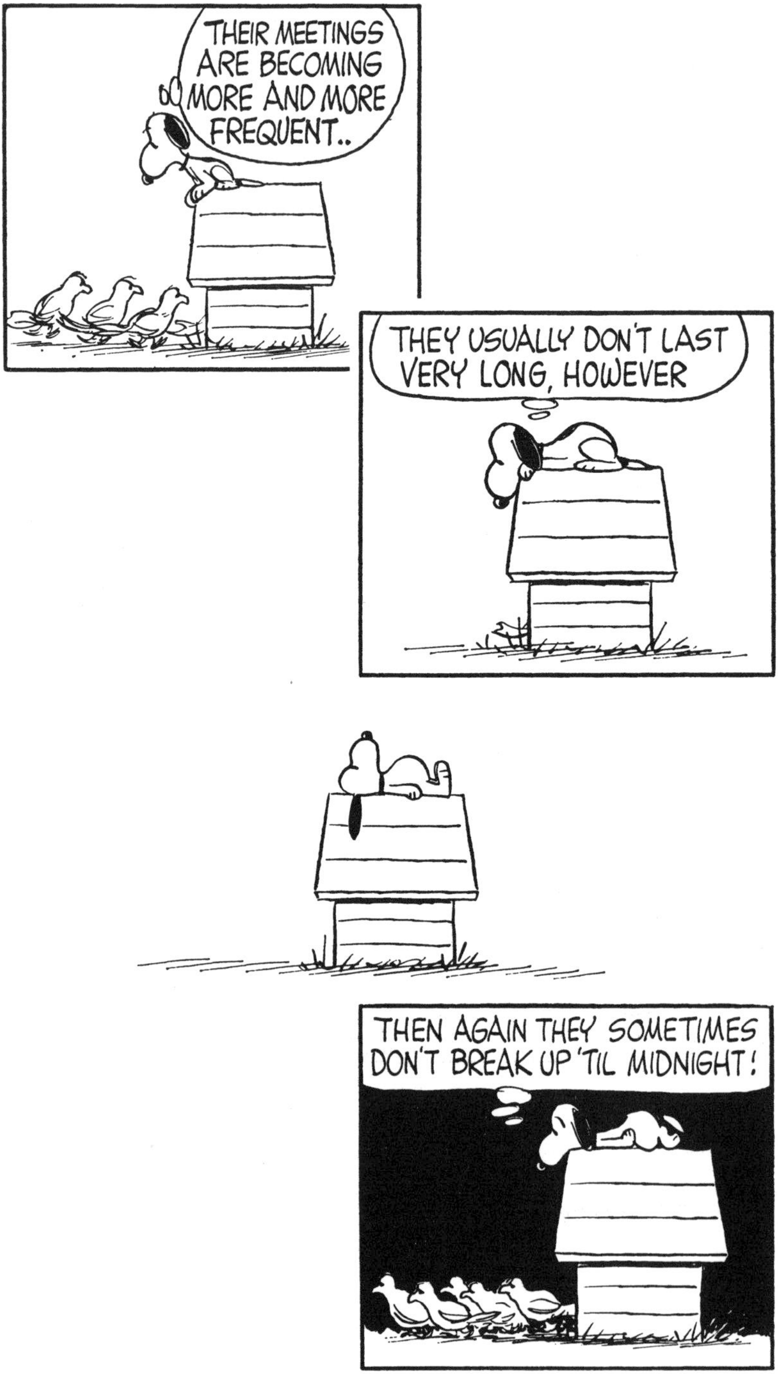
THEIR MEETINGS ARE BECOMING MORE AND MORE FREQUENT..
THEY USUALLY DON'T LAST VERY LONG, HOWEVER
THEN AGAIN THEY SOMETIMES DON'T BREAK UP 'TIL MIDNIGHT!

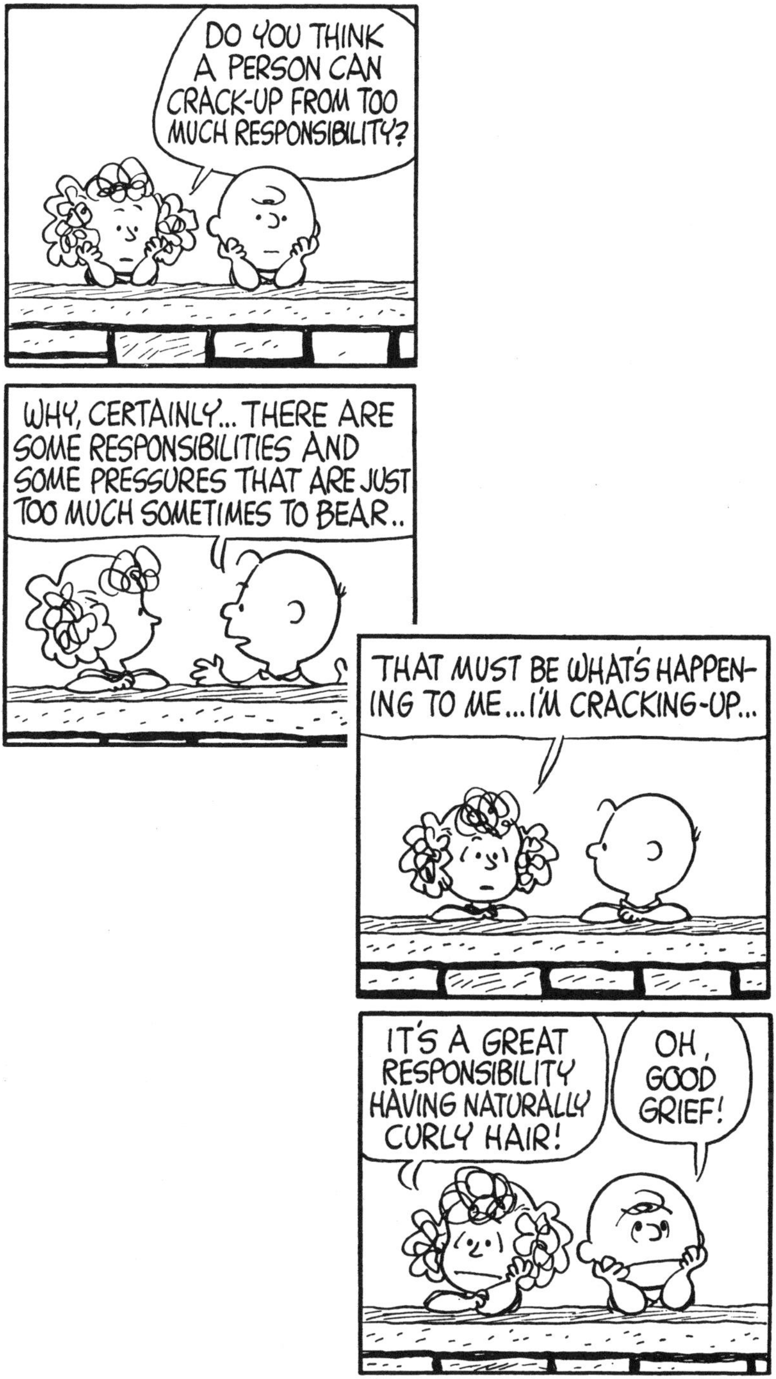
DO YOU THINK A PERSON CAN CRACK-UP FROM TOO MUCH RESPONSIBILITY?
WHY, CERTAINLY... THERE ARE SOME RESPONSIBILITIES AND SOME PRESSURES THAT ARE JUST TOO MUCH SOMETIMES TO BEAR..
THAT MUST BE WHAT'S HAPPENING TO ME...I'M CRACKING-UP...
IT'S A GREAT RESPONSIBILITY HAVING NATURALLY CURLY HAIR!
OH, GOOD GRIEF!

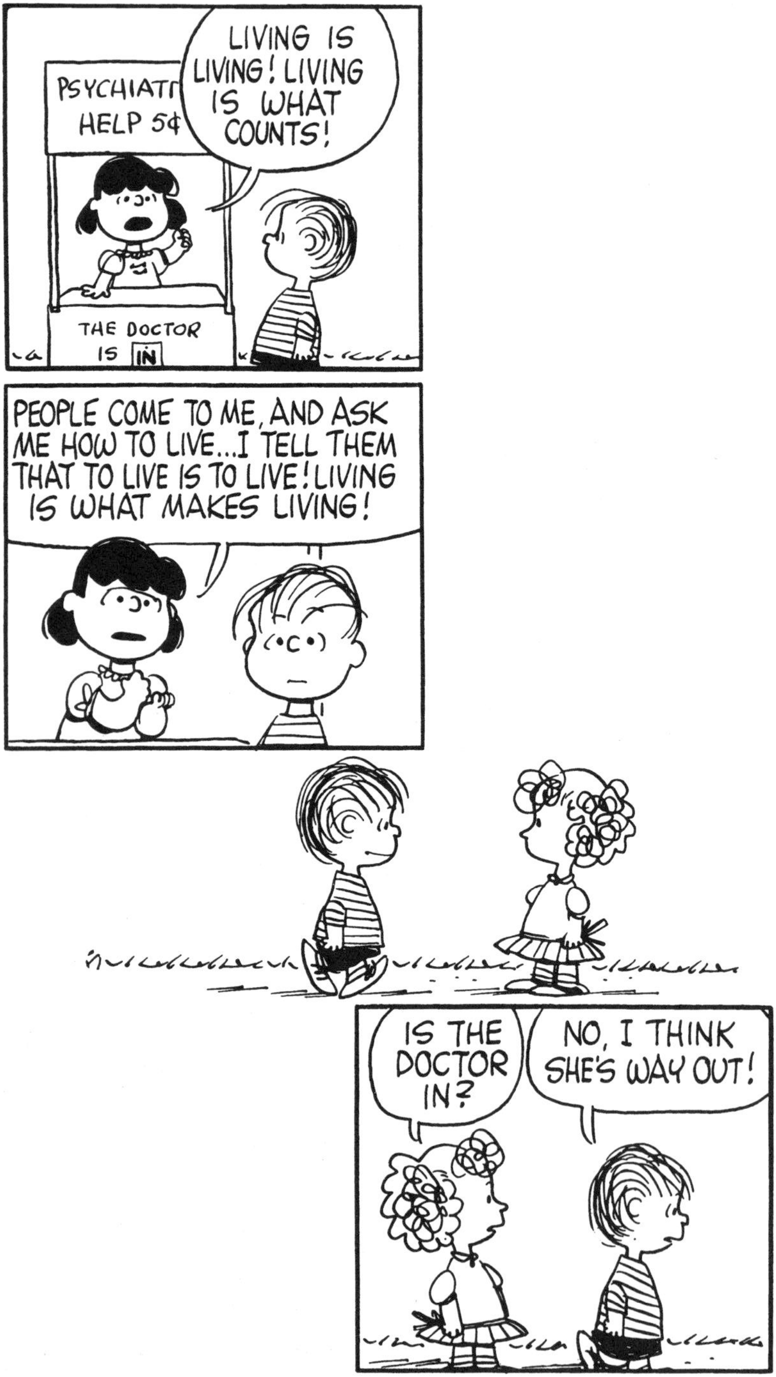
PSYCHIATR
HELP 5¢
THE DOCTOR IS IN
LIVING IS LIVING! LIVING IS WHAT COUNTS!
PEOPLE COME TO ME, AND ASK ME HOW TO LIVE...I TELL THEM THAT TO LIVE IS TO LIVE! LIVING IS WHAT MAKES LIVING!
IS THE DOCTOR IN?
NO, I THINK SHE'S WAY OUT!

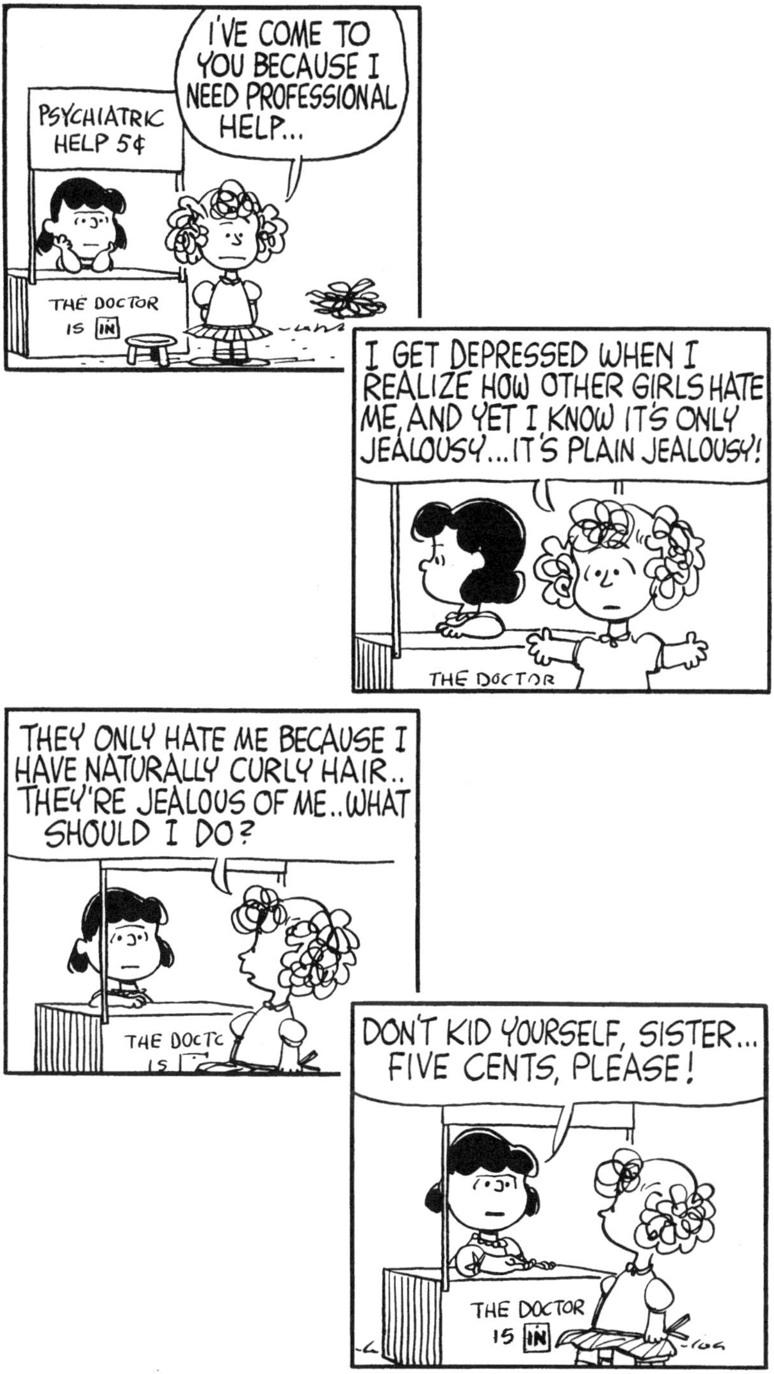
PSYCHIATRIC HELP 5¢
THE DOCTOR IS IN
I'VE COME TO YOU BECAUSE I NEED PROFESSIONAL HELP...
I GET DEPRESSED WHEN I REALIZE HOW OTHER GIRLS HATE ME, AND YET I KNOW IT'S ONLY JEALOUSY...IT'S PLAIN JEALOUSY!
THE DOCTOR
THEY ONLY HATE ME BECAUSE I HAVE NATURALLY CURLY HAIR.. THEY'RE JEALOUS OF ME..WHAT SHOULD I DO?
DON'T KID YOURSELF, SISTER... FIVE CENTS, PLEASE!
THE DOCTOR IS IN

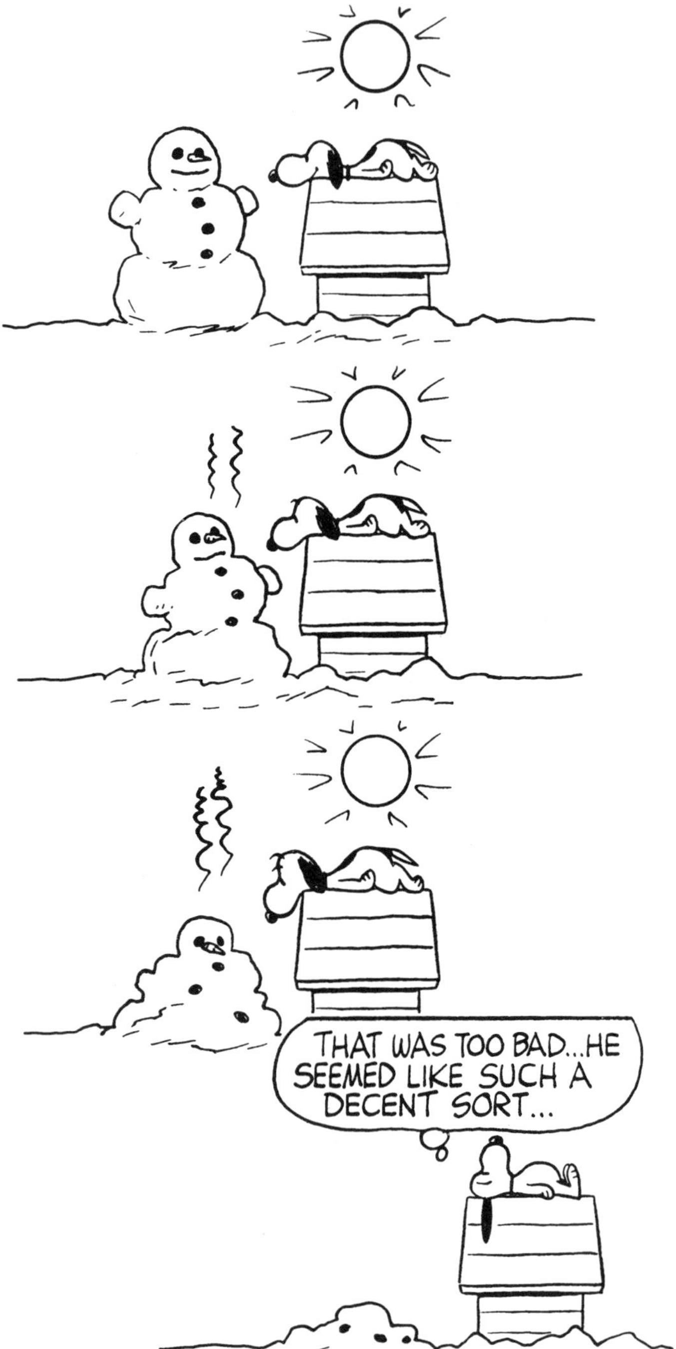
THAT WAS TOO BAD...HE SEEMED LIKE SUCH A DECENT SORT...

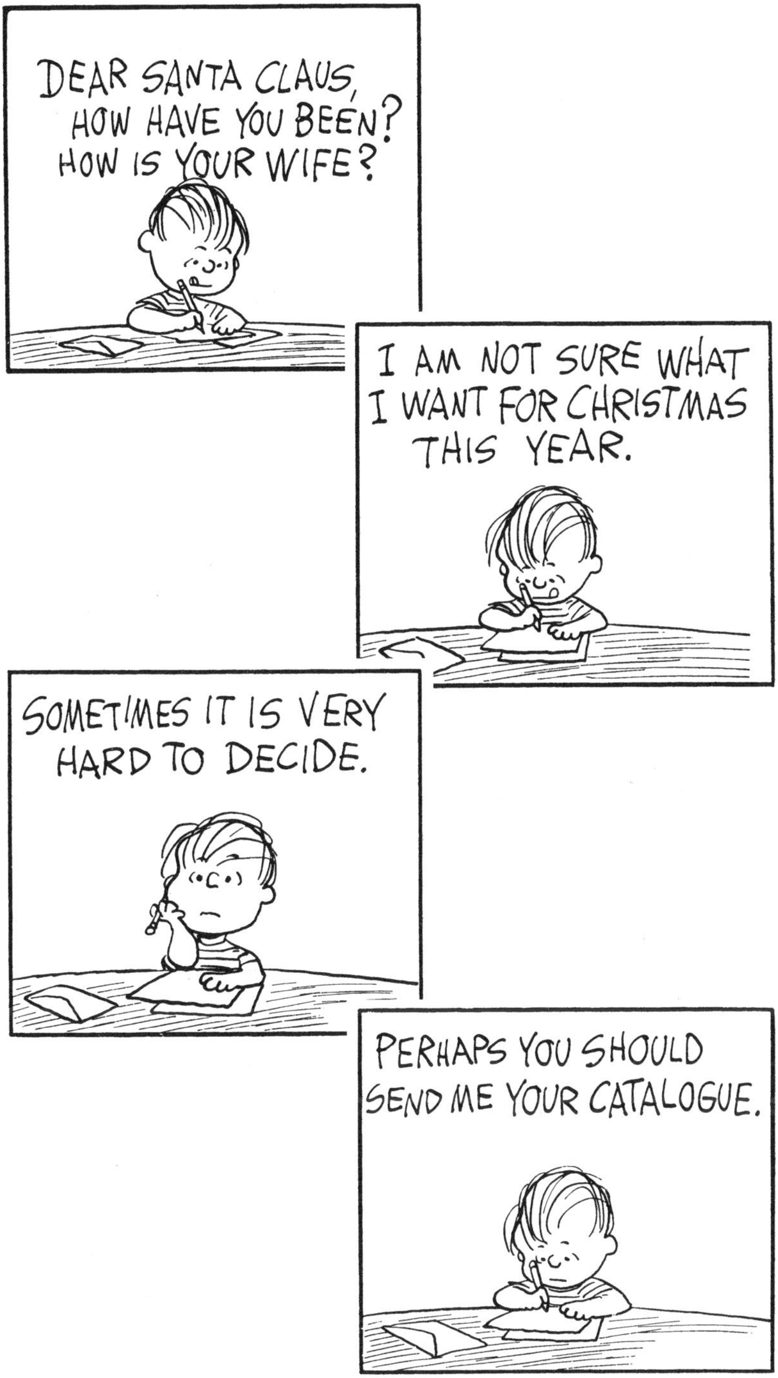
DEAR SANTA CLAUS,
HOW HAVE YOU BEEN?
HOW IS YOUR WIFE?
I AM NOT SURE WHAT I WANT FOR CHRISTMAS THIS YEAR.
SOMETIMES IT IS VERY HARD TO DECIDE.
PERHAPS YOU SHOULD SEND ME YOUR CATALOGUE.

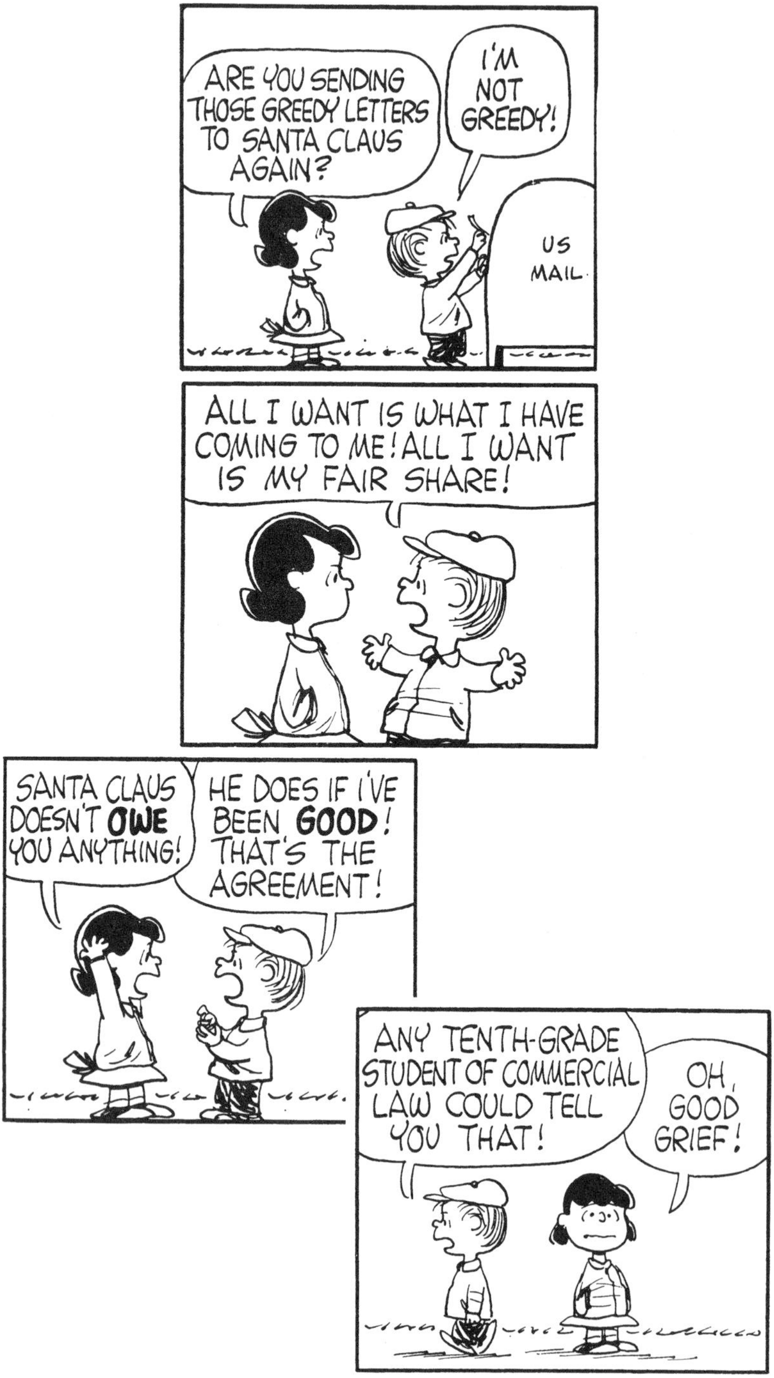
ARE YOU SENDING THOSE GREEDY LETTERS TO SANTA CLAUS AGAIN?
I'M NOT GREEDY!
US MAIL
ALL I WANT IS WHAT I HAVE COMING TO ME! ALL I WANT IS MY FAIR SHARE!
SANTA CLAUS DOESN'T **OWE** YOU ANYTHING!
HE DOES IF I'VE BEEN **GOOD**! THAT'S THE AGREEMENT!
ANY TENTH-GRADE STUDENT OF COMMERCIAL LAW COULD TELL YOU THAT!
OH, GOOD GRIEF!

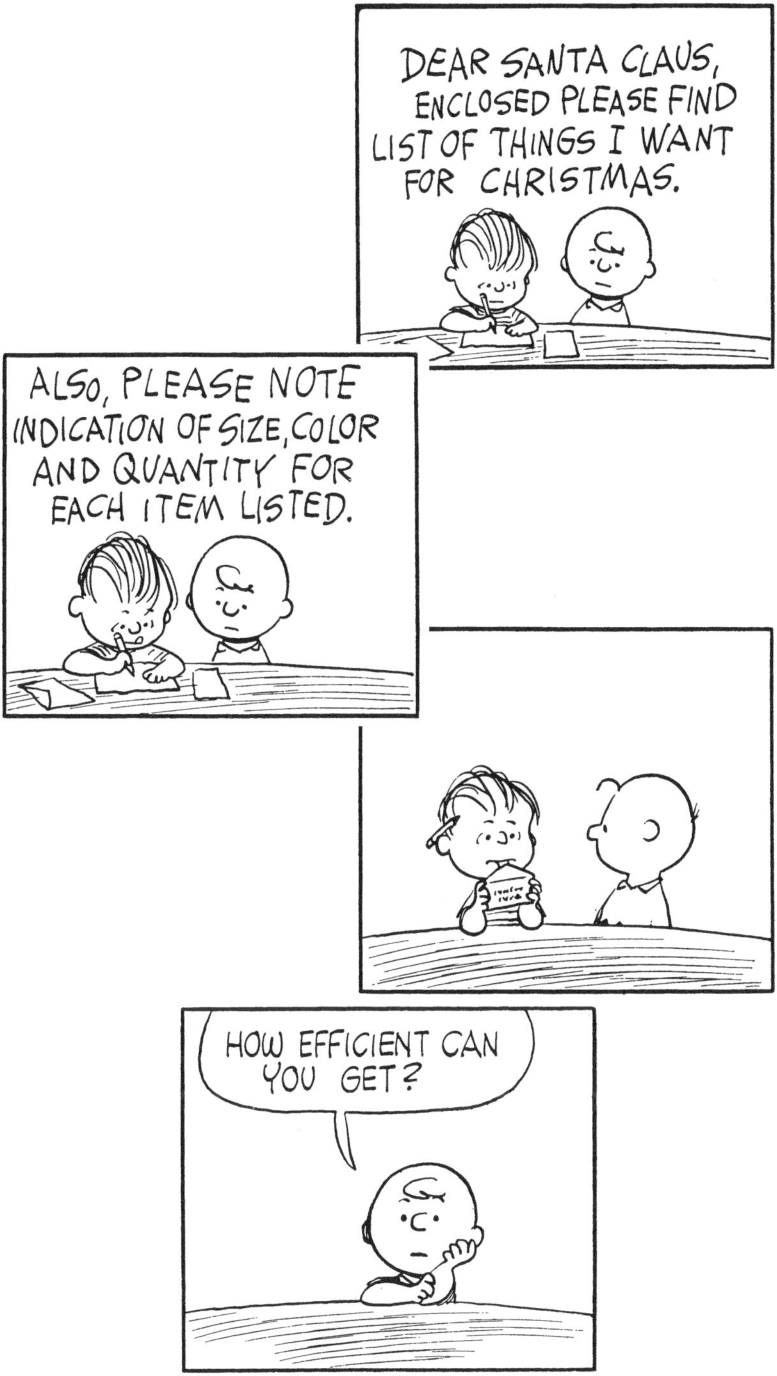
DEAR SANTA CLAUS, ENCLOSED PLEASE FIND LIST OF THINGS I WANT FOR CHRISTMAS.
ALSO, PLEASE NOTE INDICATION OF SIZE, COLOR AND QUANTITY FOR EACH ITEM LISTED.
HOW EFFICIENT CAN YOU GET?

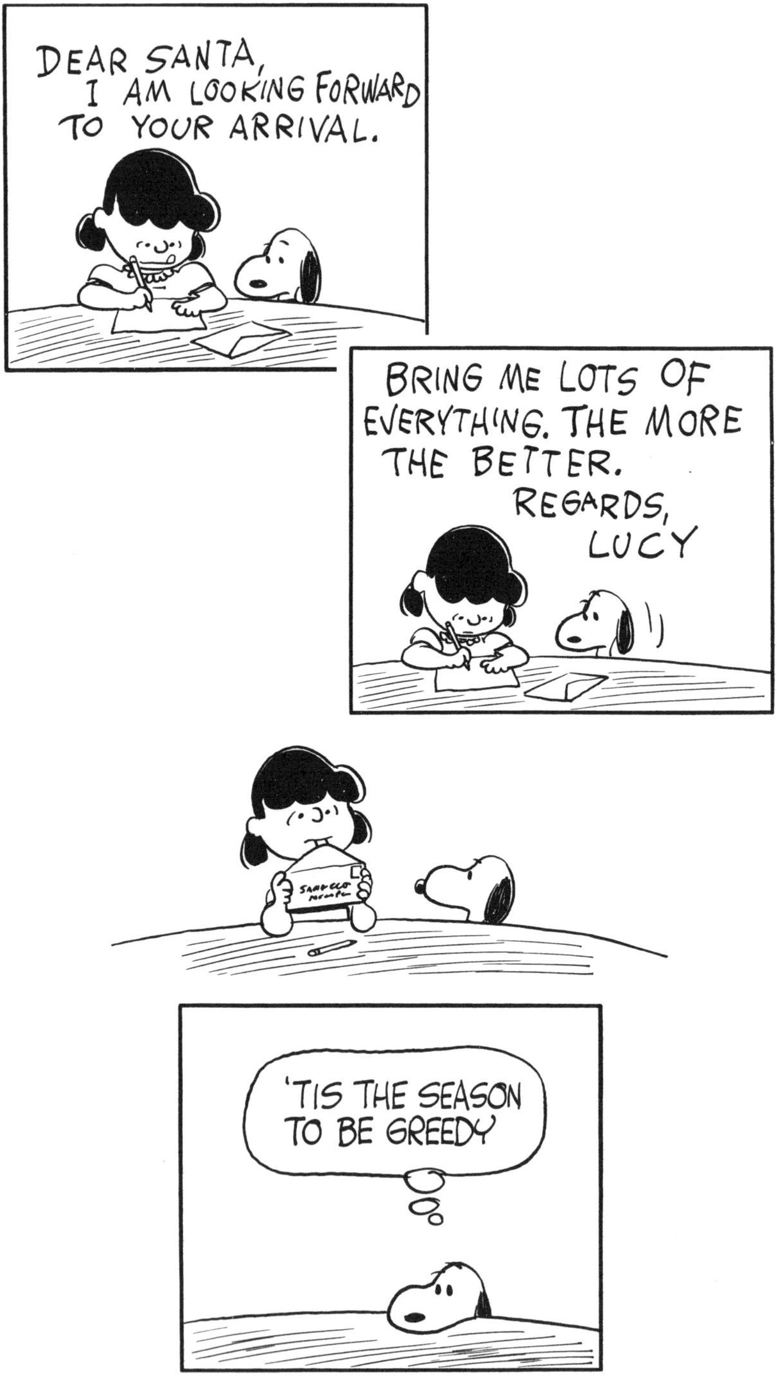
DEAR SANTA,
I AM LOOKING FORWARD TO YOUR ARRIVAL.
BRING ME LOTS OF EVERYTHING. THE MORE THE BETTER.
REGARDS,
LUCY
'TIS THE SEASON TO BE GREEDY

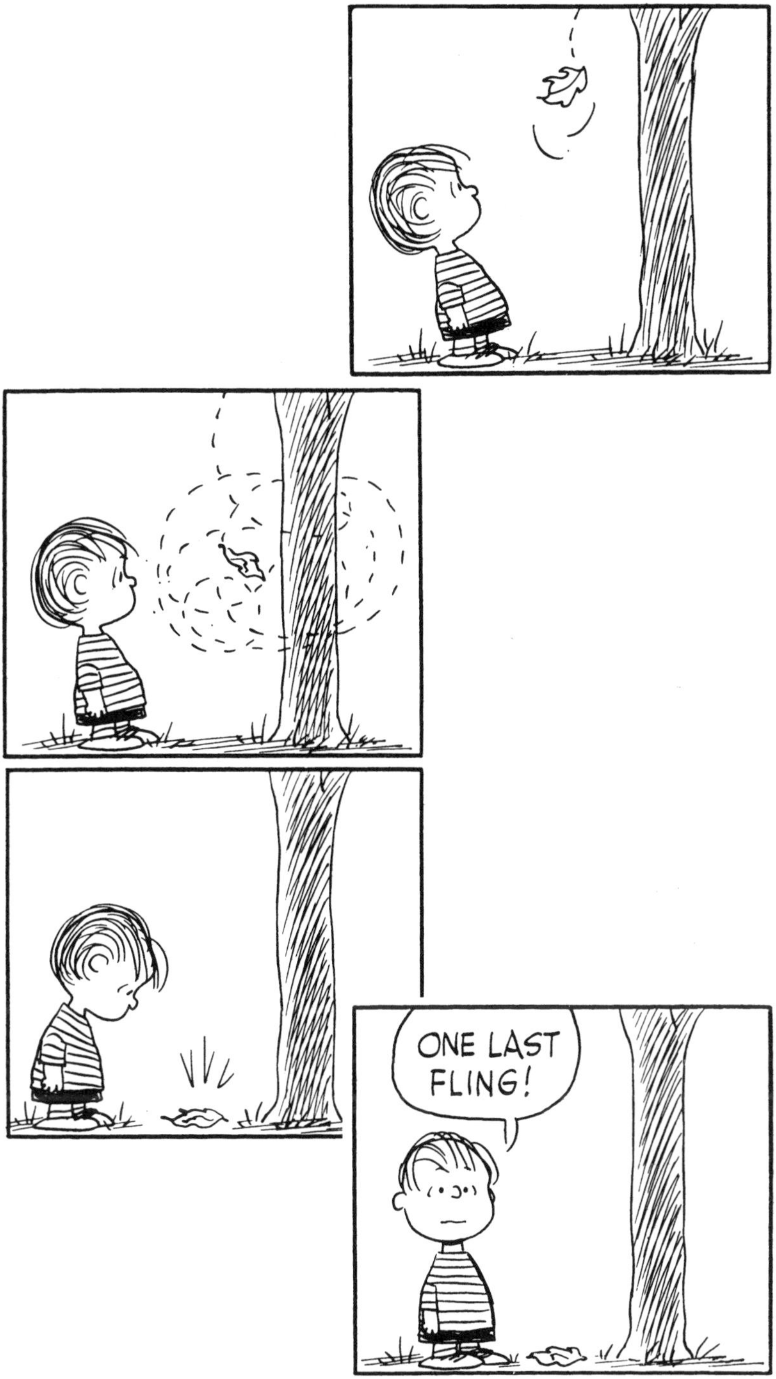
ONE LAST FLING!

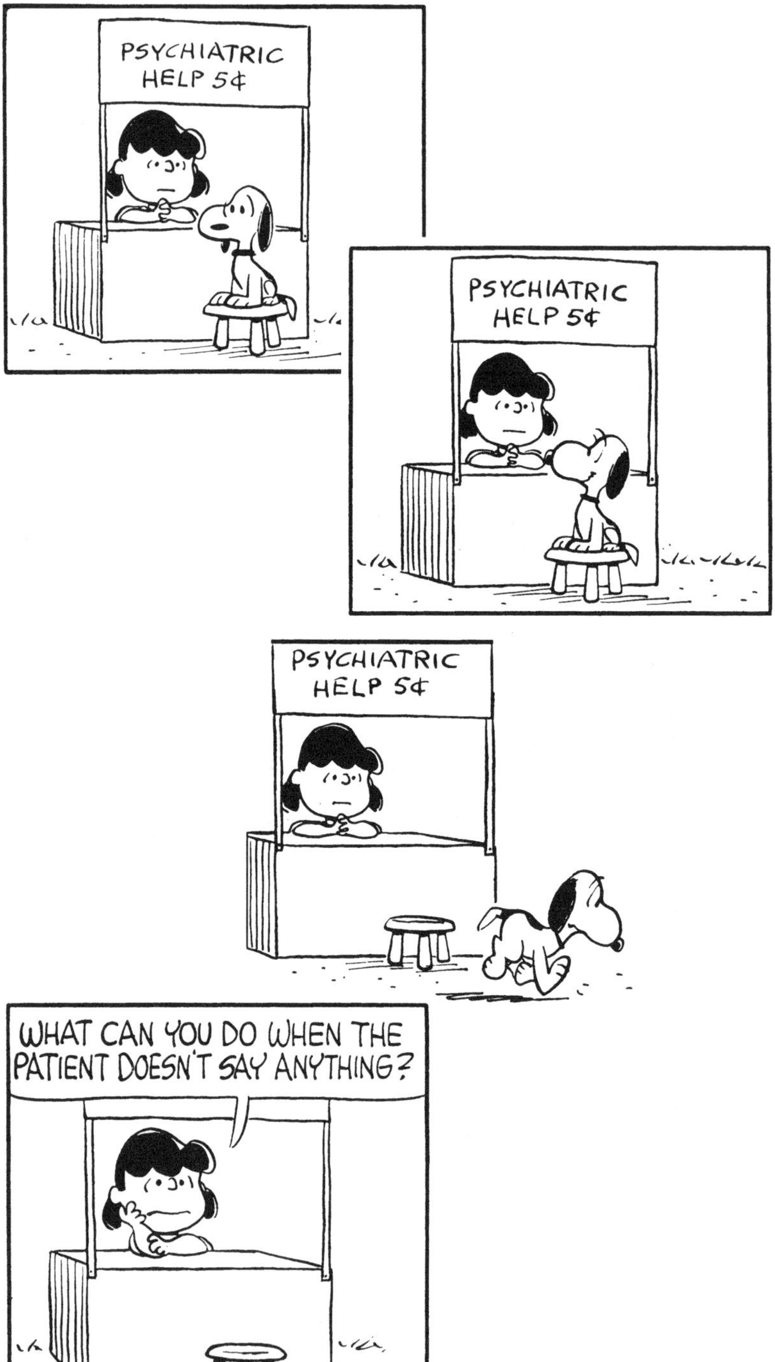
PSYCHIATRIC HELP 5¢
PSYCHIATRIC HELP 5¢
PSYCHIATRIC HELP 5¢
WHAT CAN YOU DO WHEN THE PATIENT DOESN'T SAY ANYTHING?

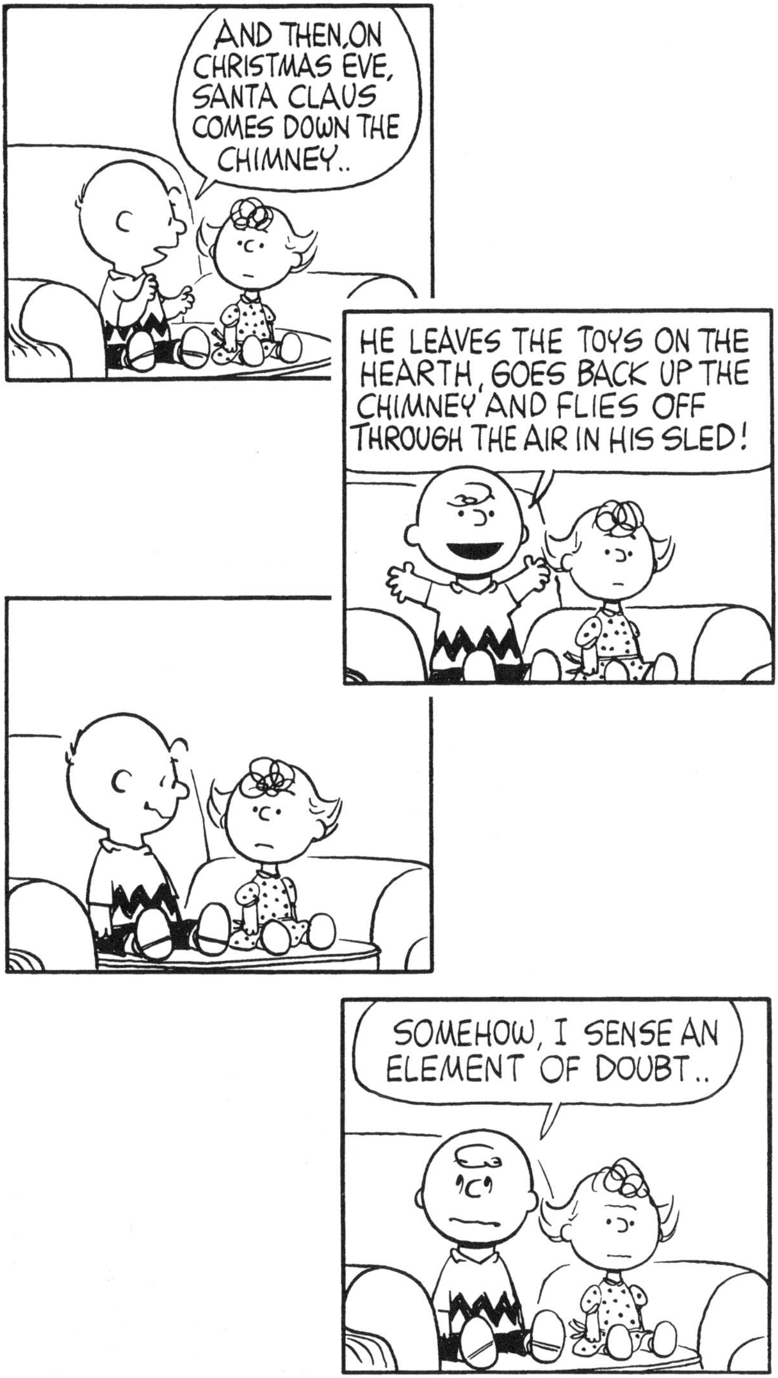
AND THEN, ON CHRISTMAS EVE, SANTA CLAUS COMES DOWN THE CHIMNEY..
HE LEAVES THE TOYS ON THE HEARTH, GOES BACK UP THE CHIMNEY AND FLIES OFF THROUGH THE AIR IN HIS SLED!
SOMEHOW, I SENSE AN ELEMENT OF DOUBT..

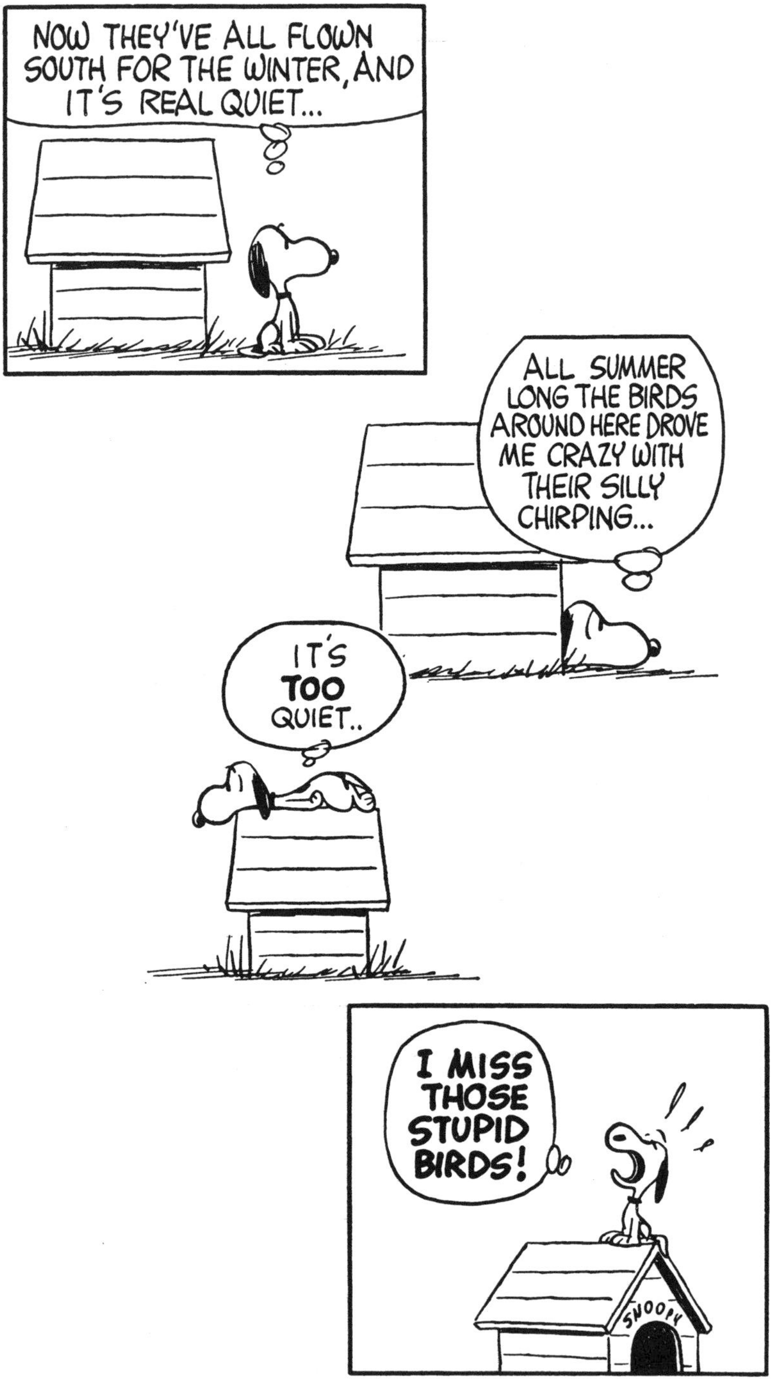
NOW THEY'VE ALL FLOWN SOUTH FOR THE WINTER, AND IT'S REAL QUIET...
ALL SUMMER LONG THE BIRDS AROUND HERE DROVE ME CRAZY WITH THEIR SILLY CHIRPING...
IT'S **TOO** QUIET..
I MISS THOSE STUPID BIRDS!
SNOOPY

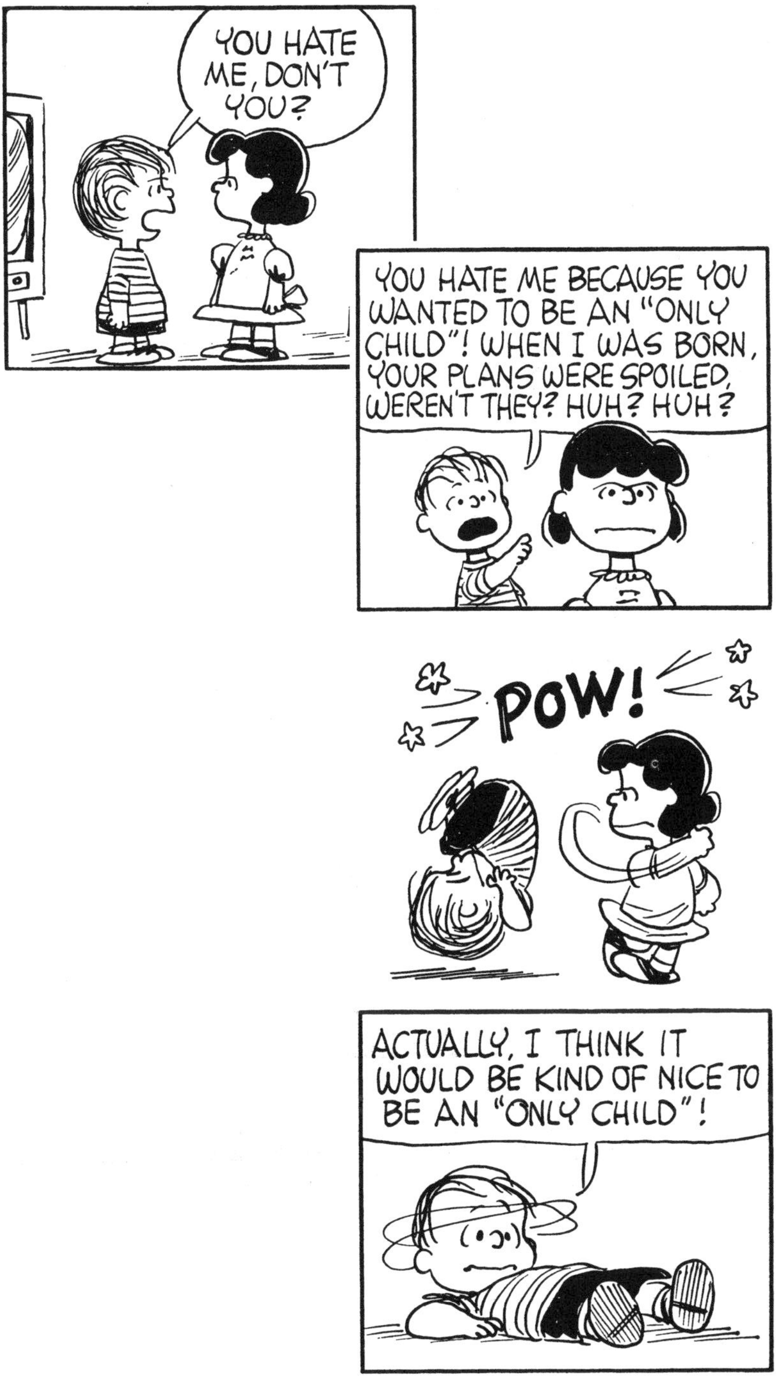
YOU HATE ME, DON'T YOU?
YOU HATE ME BECAUSE YOU WANTED TO BE AN "ONLY CHILD"! WHEN I WAS BORN, YOUR PLANS WERE SPOILED, WEREN'T THEY? HUH? HUH?
POW!
ACTUALLY, I THINK IT WOULD BE KIND OF NICE TO BE AN "ONLY CHILD"!

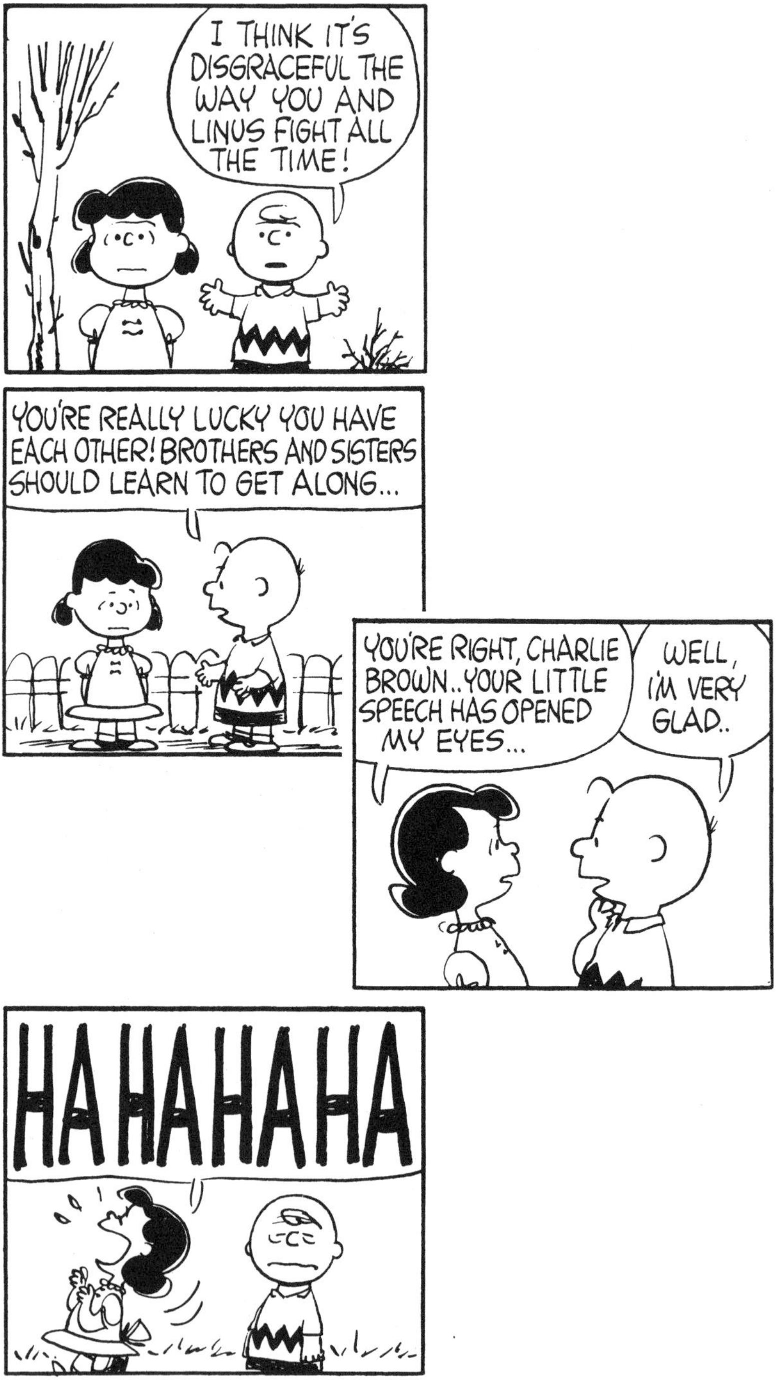
I THINK IT'S DISGRACEFUL THE WAY YOU AND LINUS FIGHT ALL THE TIME!
YOU'RE REALLY LUCKY YOU HAVE EACH OTHER! BROTHERS AND SISTERS SHOULD LEARN TO GET ALONG...
YOU'RE RIGHT, CHARLIE BROWN..YOUR LITTLE SPEECH HAS OPENED MY EYES...
WELL, I'M VERY GLAD..
HAHAHAHAHA

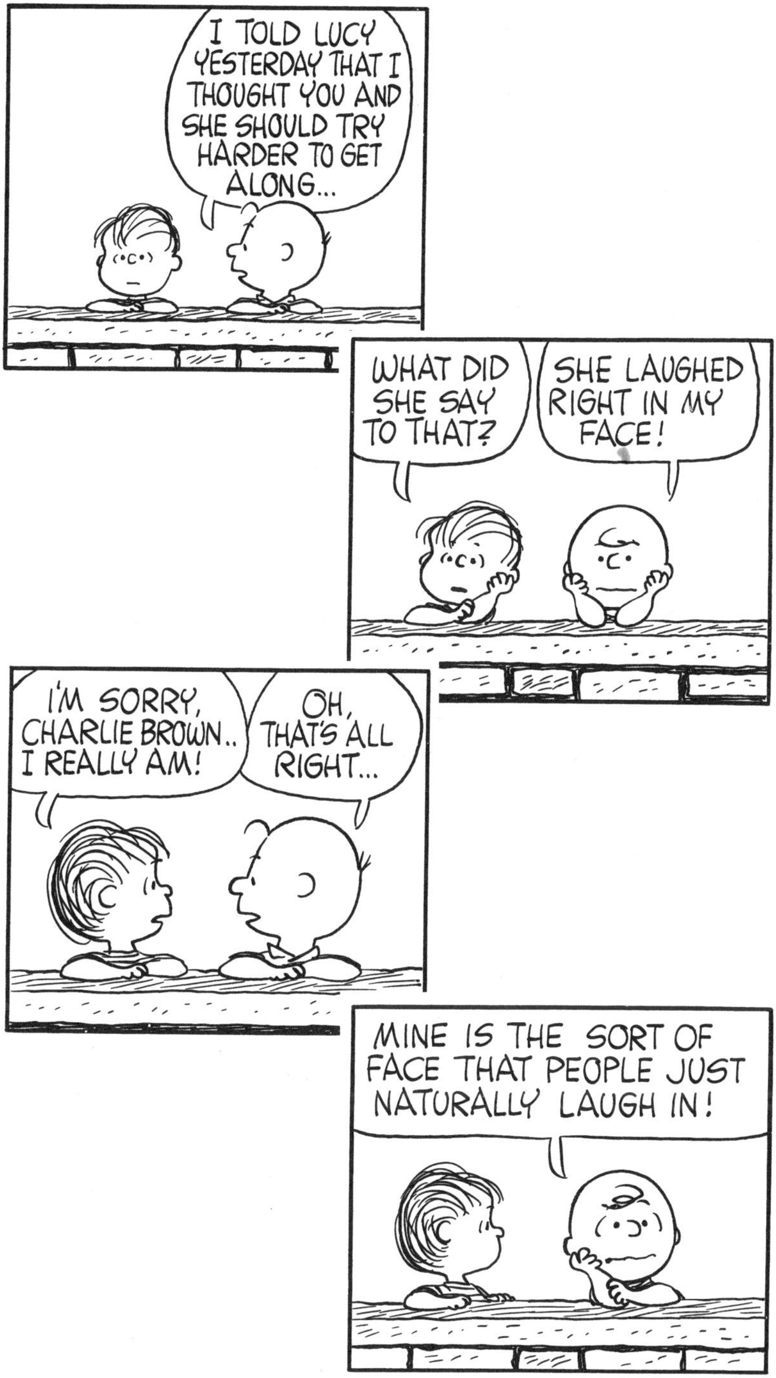
I TOLD LUCY YESTERDAY THAT I THOUGHT YOU AND SHE SHOULD TRY HARDER TO GET ALONG...
WHAT DID SHE SAY TO THAT?
SHE LAUGHED RIGHT IN MY FACE!
I'M SORRY, CHARLIE BROWN.. I REALLY AM!
OH, THAT'S ALL RIGHT...
MINE IS THE SORT OF FACE THAT PEOPLE JUST NATURALLY LAUGH IN!

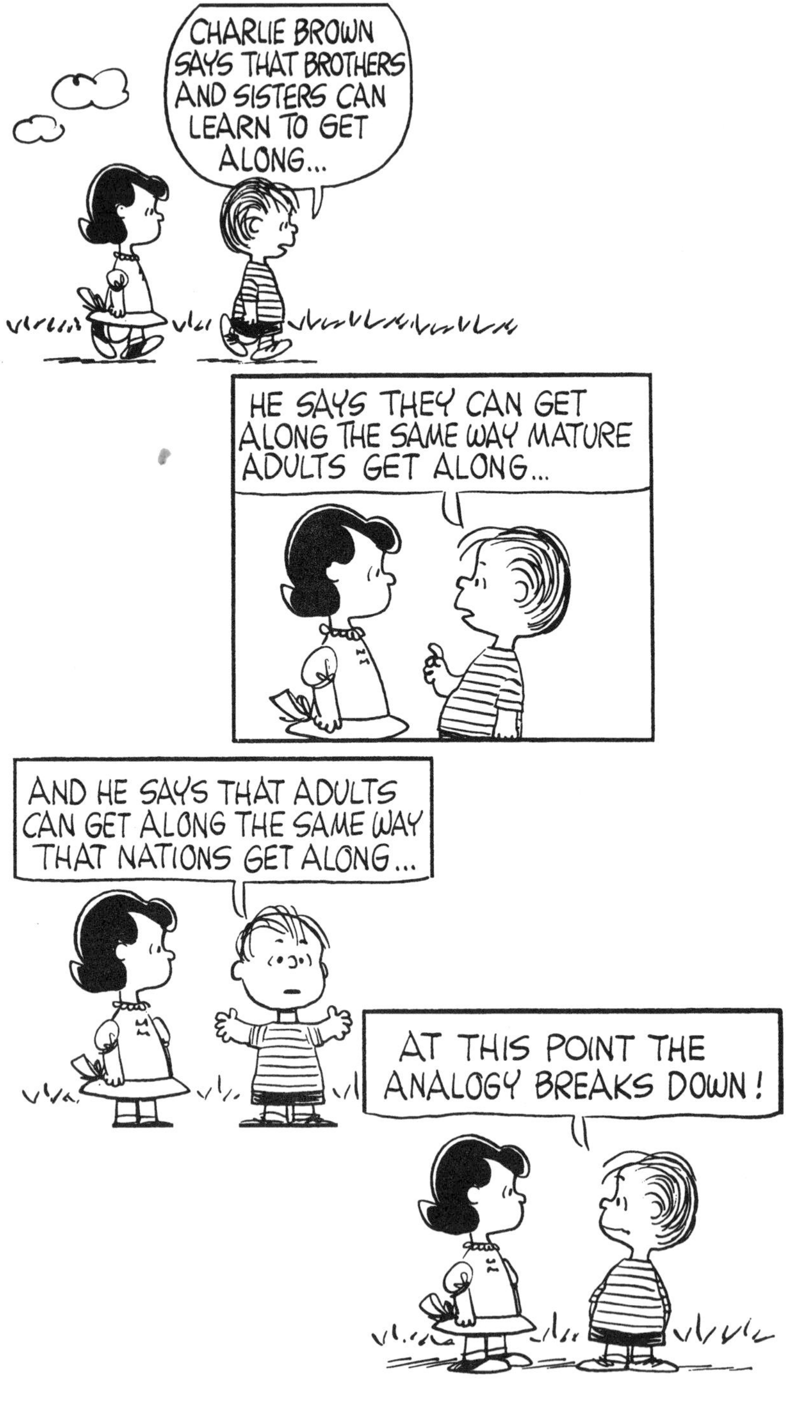
CHARLIE BROWN SAYS THAT BROTHERS AND SISTERS CAN LEARN TO GET ALONG...
HE SAYS THEY CAN GET ALONG THE SAME WAY MATURE ADULTS GET ALONG...
AND HE SAYS THAT ADULTS CAN GET ALONG THE SAME WAY THAT NATIONS GET ALONG...
AT THIS POINT THE ANALOGY BREAKS DOWN!

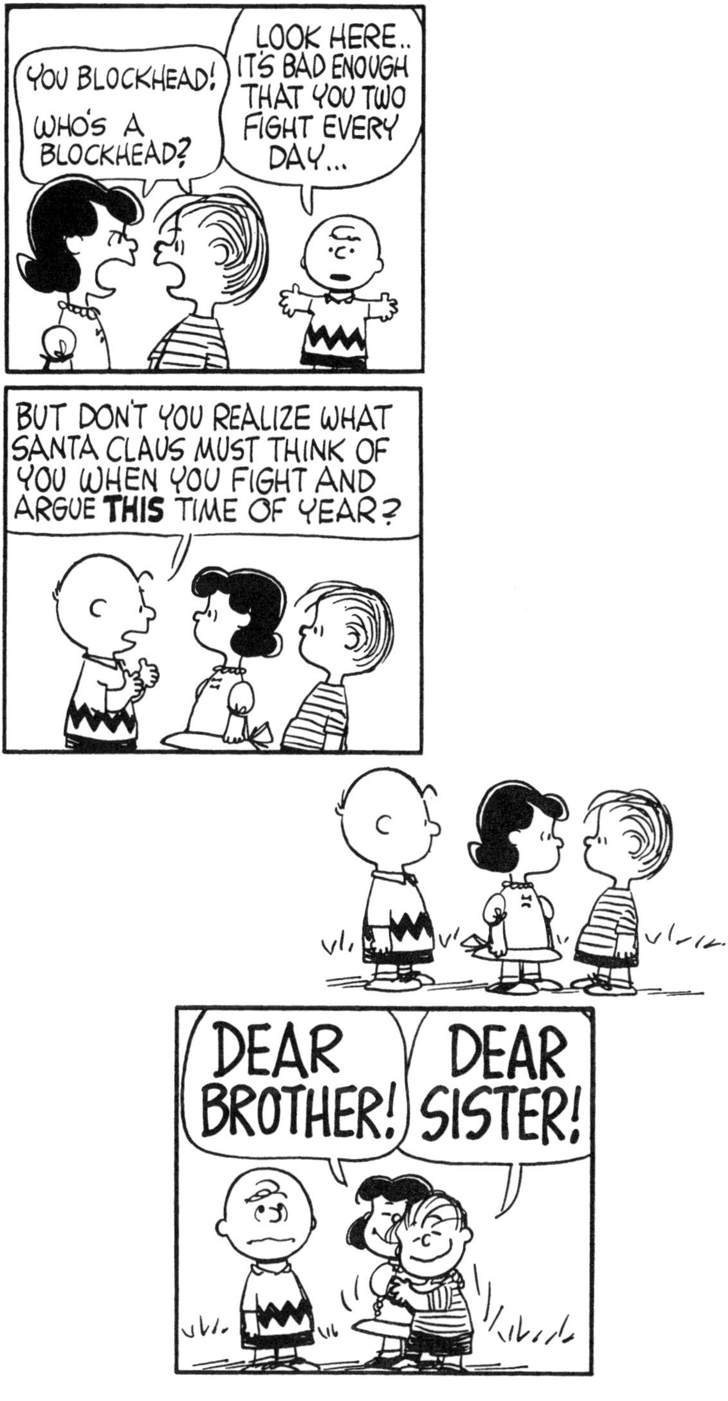
YOU BLOCKHEAD!
WHO'S A BLOCKHEAD?
LOOK HERE.. IT'S BAD ENOUGH THAT YOU TWO FIGHT EVERY DAY...
BUT DON'T YOU REALIZE WHAT SANTA CLAUS MUST THINK OF YOU WHEN YOU FIGHT AND ARGUE THIS TIME OF YEAR?
DEAR BROTHER!
DEAR SISTER!

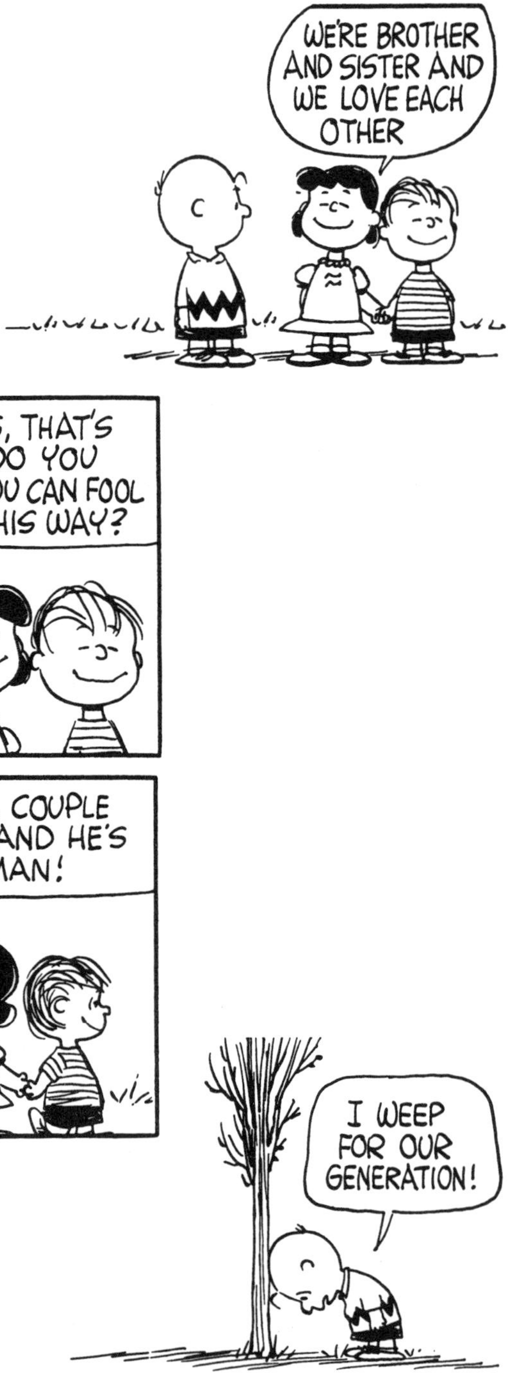

WE'RE BROTHER AND SISTER AND WE LOVE EACH OTHER
YOU'RE HYPOCRITES, THAT'S WHAT YOU ARE! DO YOU REALLY THINK YOU CAN FOOL SANTA CLAUS THIS WAY?
WHY NOT? WE'RE A COUPLE OF SHARP KIDS, AND HE'S JUST AN OLD MAN!
I WEEP FOR OUR GENERATION!

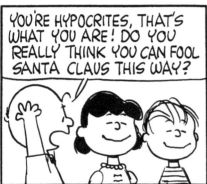

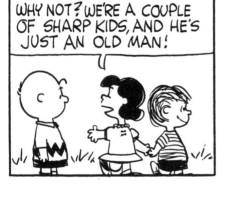

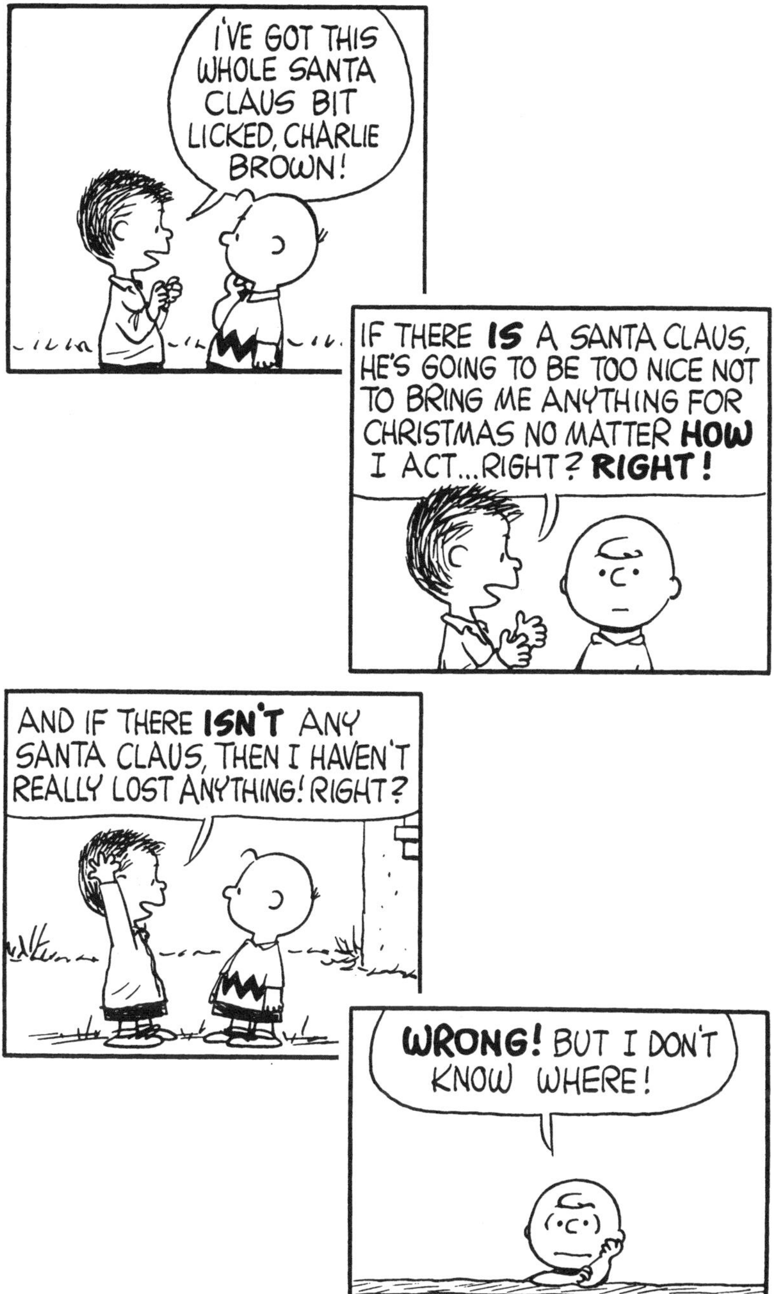

I'VE GOT THIS WHOLE SANTA CLAUS BIT LICKED, CHARLIE BROWN!
IF THERE **IS** A SANTA CLAUS, HE'S GOING TO BE TOO NICE NOT TO BRING ME ANYTHING FOR CHRISTMAS NO MATTER **HOW** I ACT...RIGHT? **RIGHT!**
AND IF THERE **ISN'T** ANY SANTA CLAUS, THEN I HAVEN'T REALLY LOST ANYTHING! RIGHT?
WRONG! BUT I DON'T KNOW WHERE!

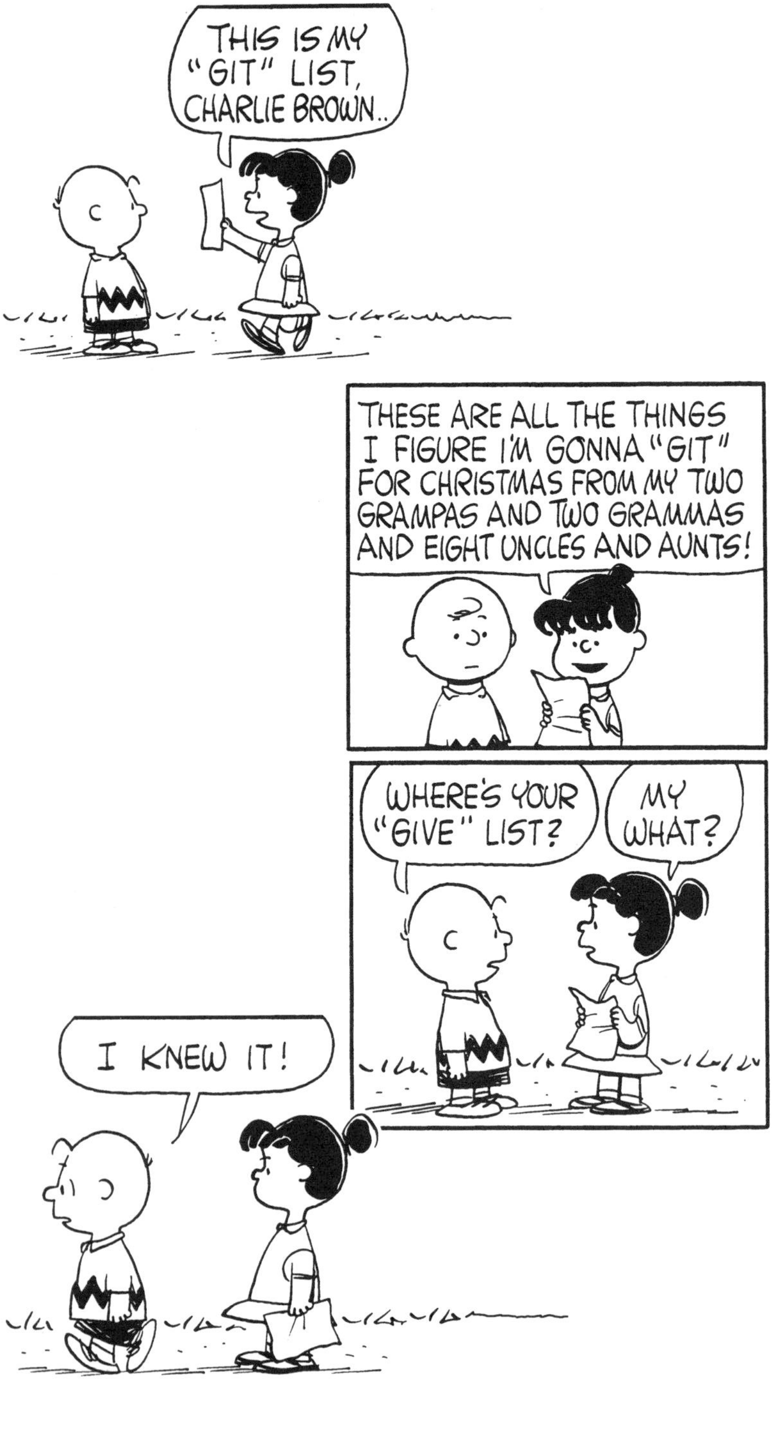
THIS IS MY "GIT" LIST, CHARLIE BROWN..
THESE ARE ALL THE THINGS I FIGURE I'M GONNA "GIT" FOR CHRISTMAS FROM MY TWO GRAMPAS AND TWO GRAMMAS AND EIGHT UNCLES AND AUNTS!
WHERE'S YOUR "GIVE" LIST?
MY WHAT?
I KNEW IT!

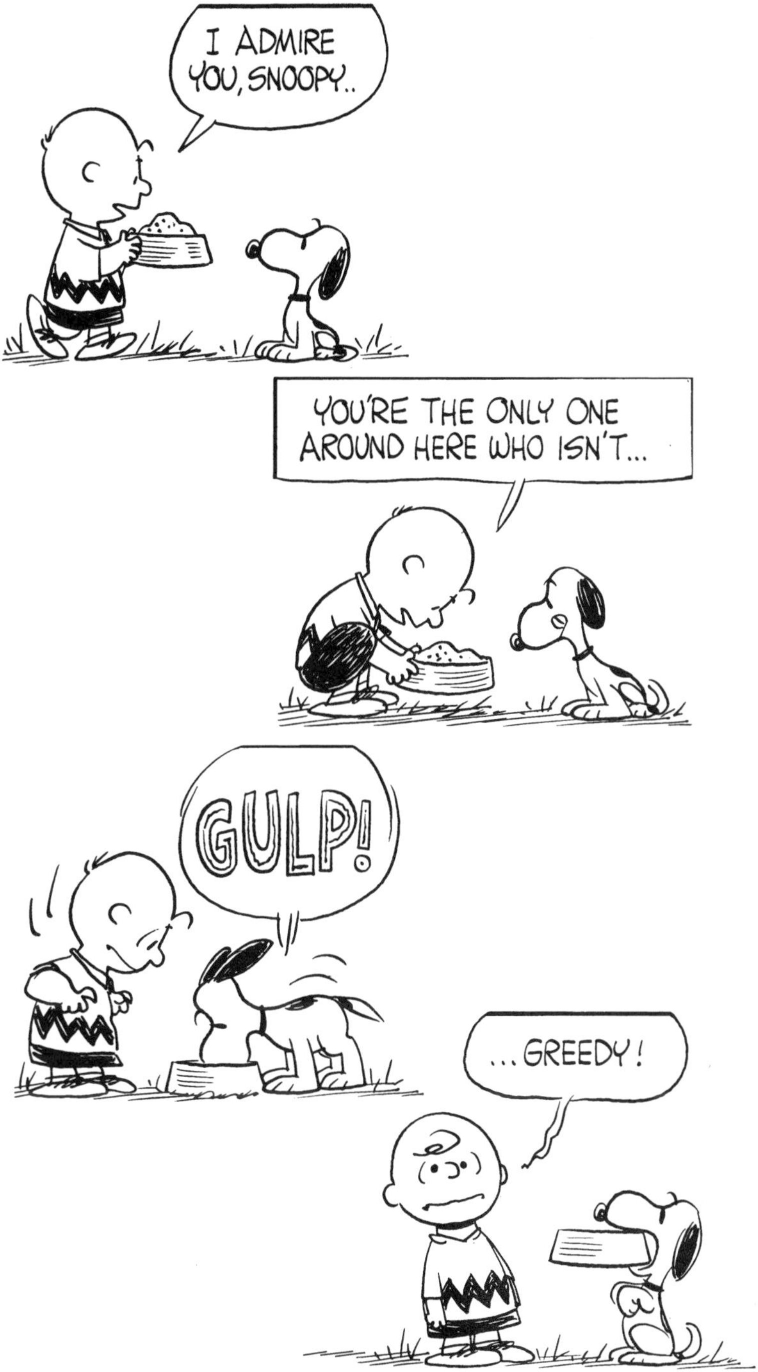
I ADMIRE YOU, SNOOPY..
YOU'RE THE ONLY ONE AROUND HERE WHO ISN'T...
GULP!
...GREEDY!

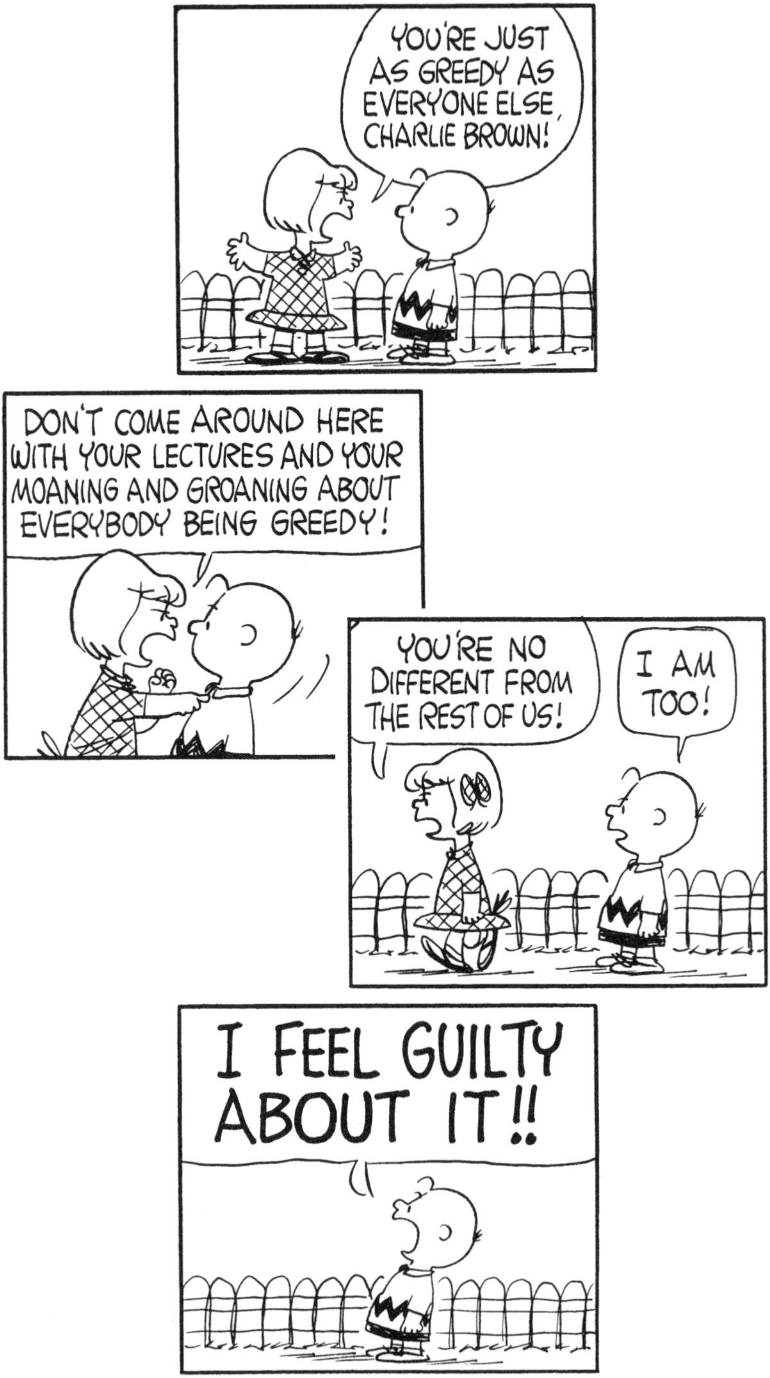

YOU'RE JUST AS GREEDY AS EVERYONE ELSE, CHARLIE BROWN!
DON'T COME AROUND HERE WITH YOUR LECTURES AND YOUR MOANING AND GROANING ABOUT EVERYBODY BEING GREEDY!
YOU'RE NO DIFFERENT FROM THE REST OF US!
I AM TOO!
I FEEL GUILTY ABOUT IT!!

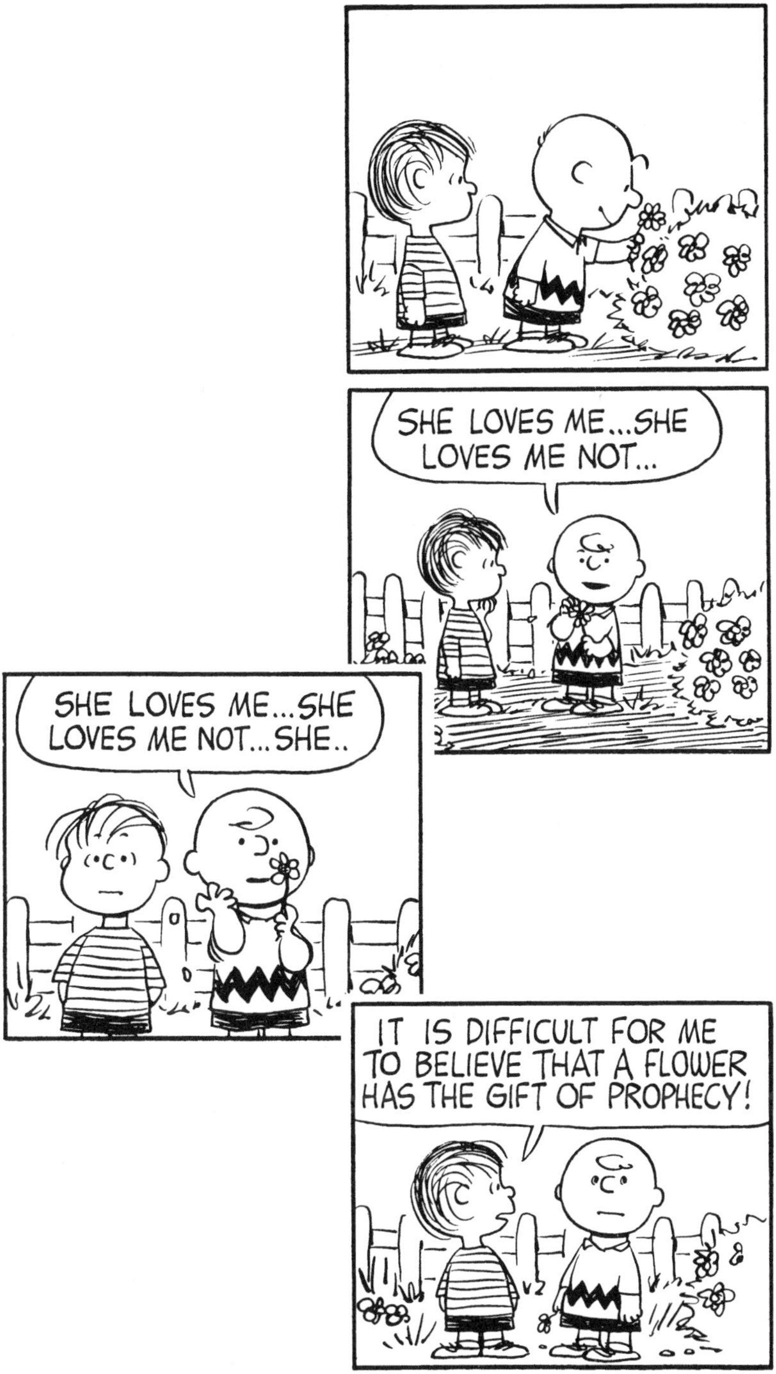
SHE LOVES ME...SHE LOVES ME NOT...
SHE LOVES ME...SHE LOVES ME NOT...SHE..
IT IS DIFFICULT FOR ME TO BELIEVE THAT A FLOWER HAS THE GIFT OF PROPHECY!

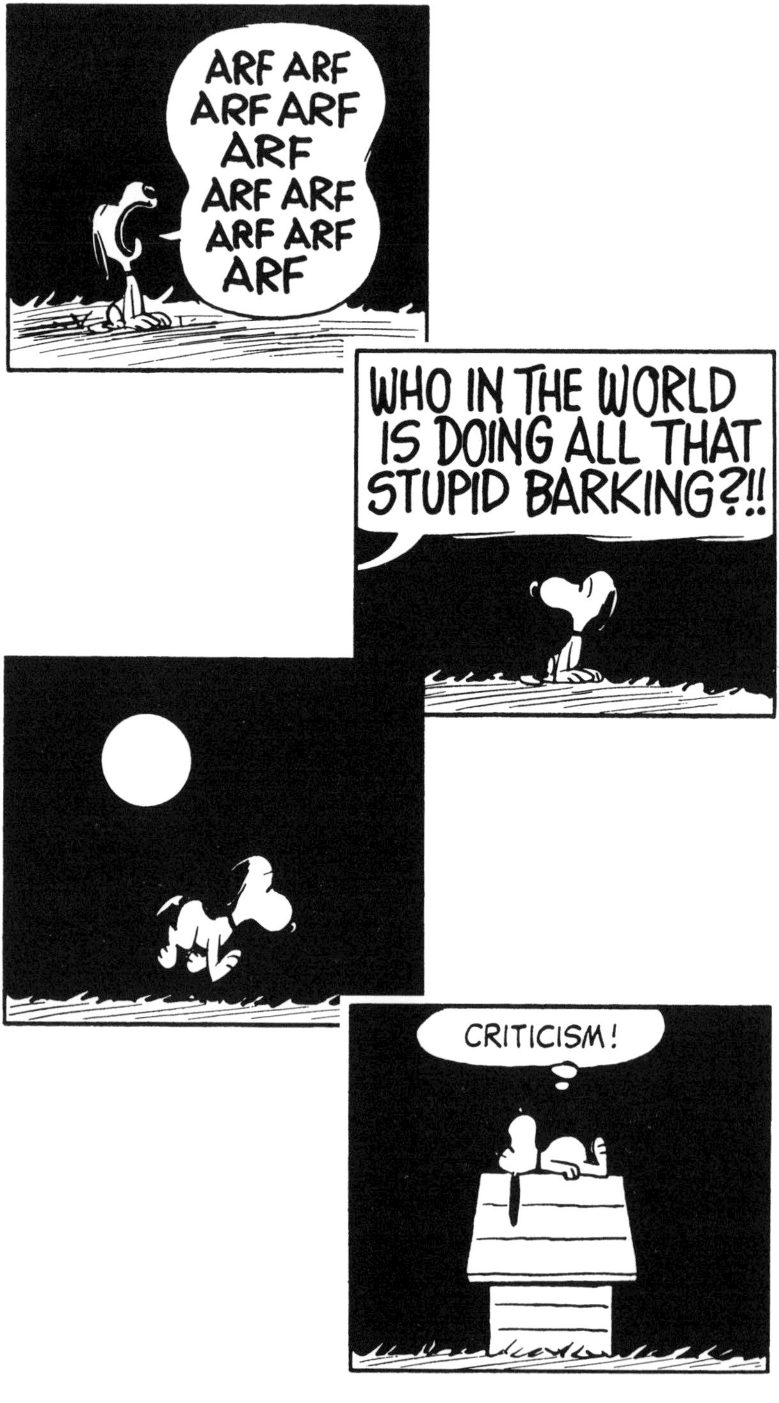
ARF ARF ARF ARF ARF ARF ARF ARF ARF ARF
WHO IN THE WORLD IS DOING ALL THAT STUPID BARKING?!!
CRITICISM!

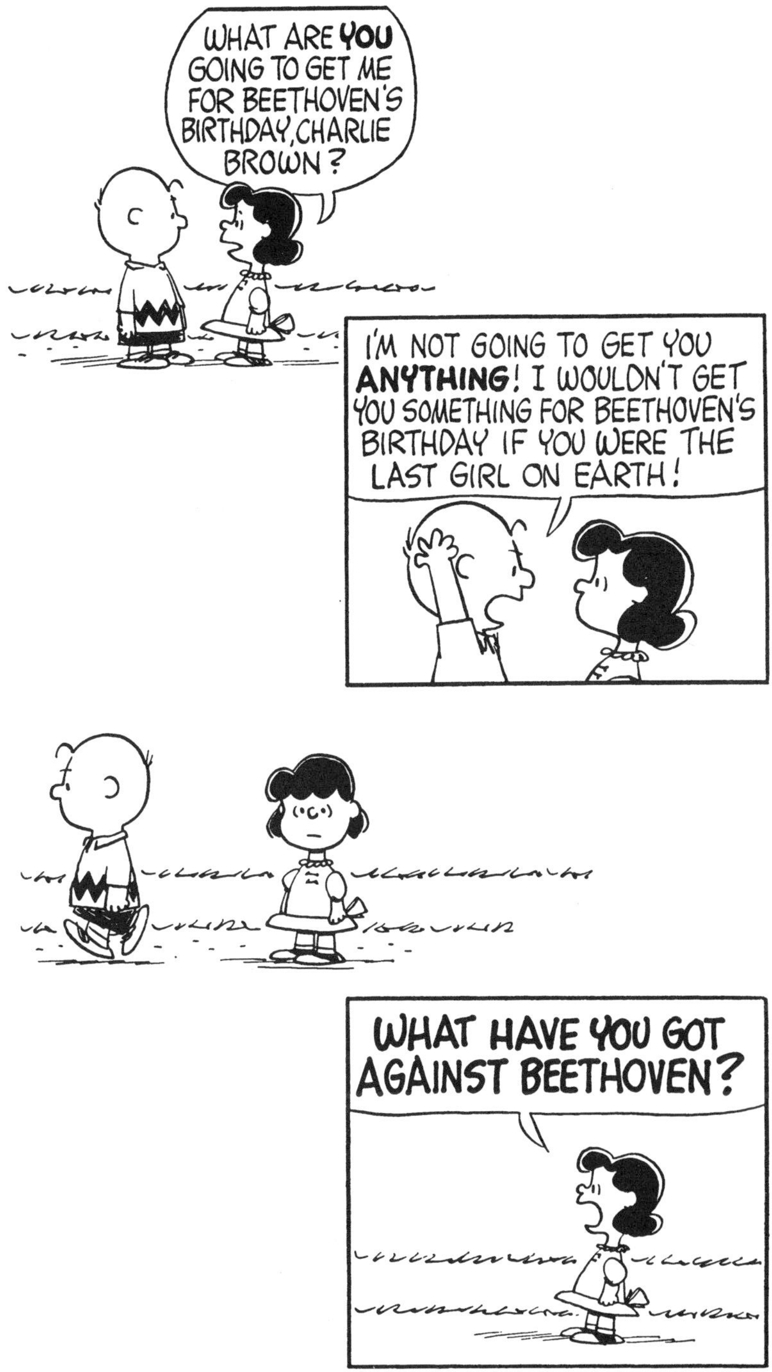
WHAT ARE **YOU** GOING TO GET ME FOR BEETHOVEN'S BIRTHDAY, CHARLIE BROWN?
I'M NOT GOING TO GET YOU **ANYTHING**! I WOULDN'T GET YOU SOMETHING FOR BEETHOVEN'S BIRTHDAY IF YOU WERE THE LAST GIRL ON EARTH!
WHAT HAVE YOU GOT AGAINST BEETHOVEN?

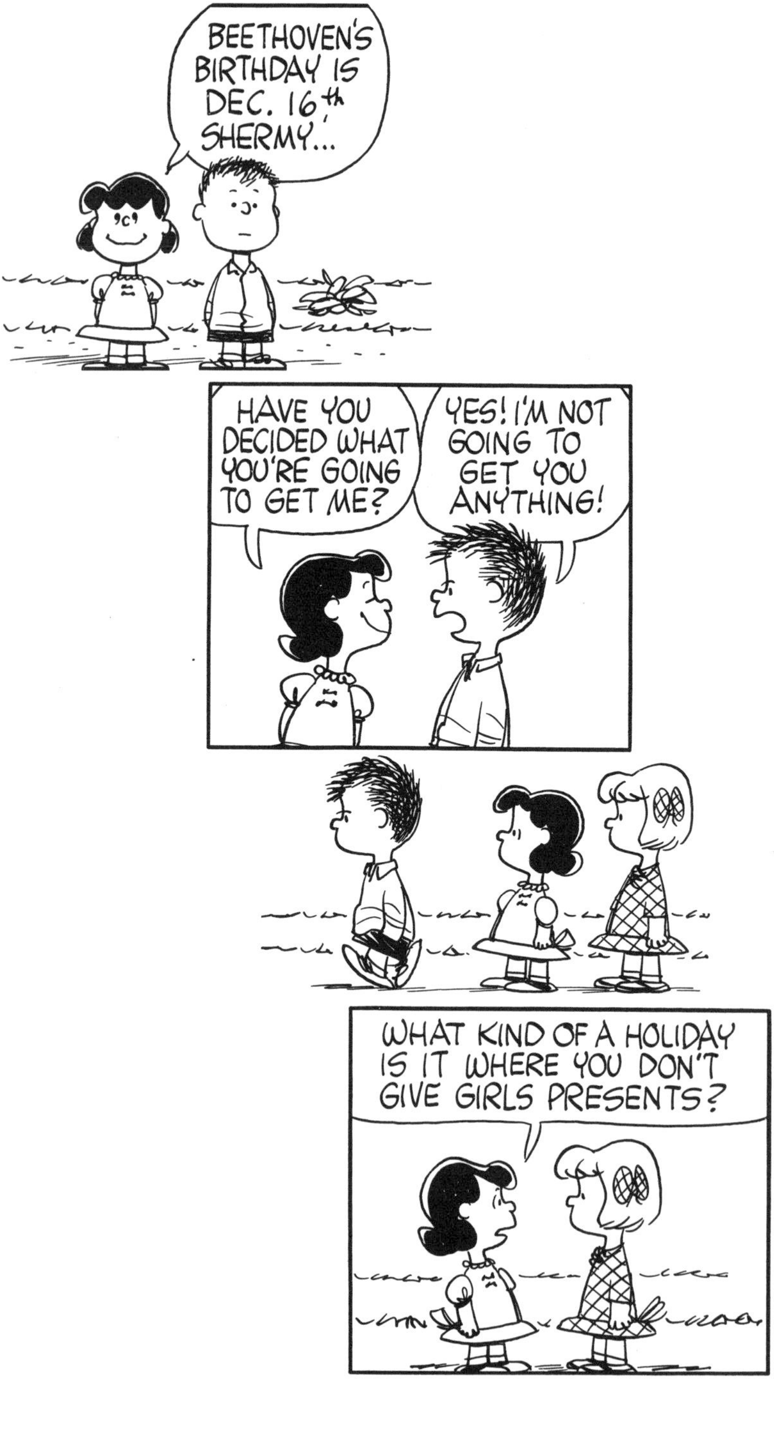
BEETHOVEN'S BIRTHDAY IS DEC. 16th, SHERMY...
HAVE YOU DECIDED WHAT YOU'RE GOING TO GET ME?
YES! I'M NOT GOING TO GET YOU ANYTHING!
WHAT KIND OF A HOLIDAY IS IT WHERE YOU DON'T GIVE GIRLS PRESENTS?

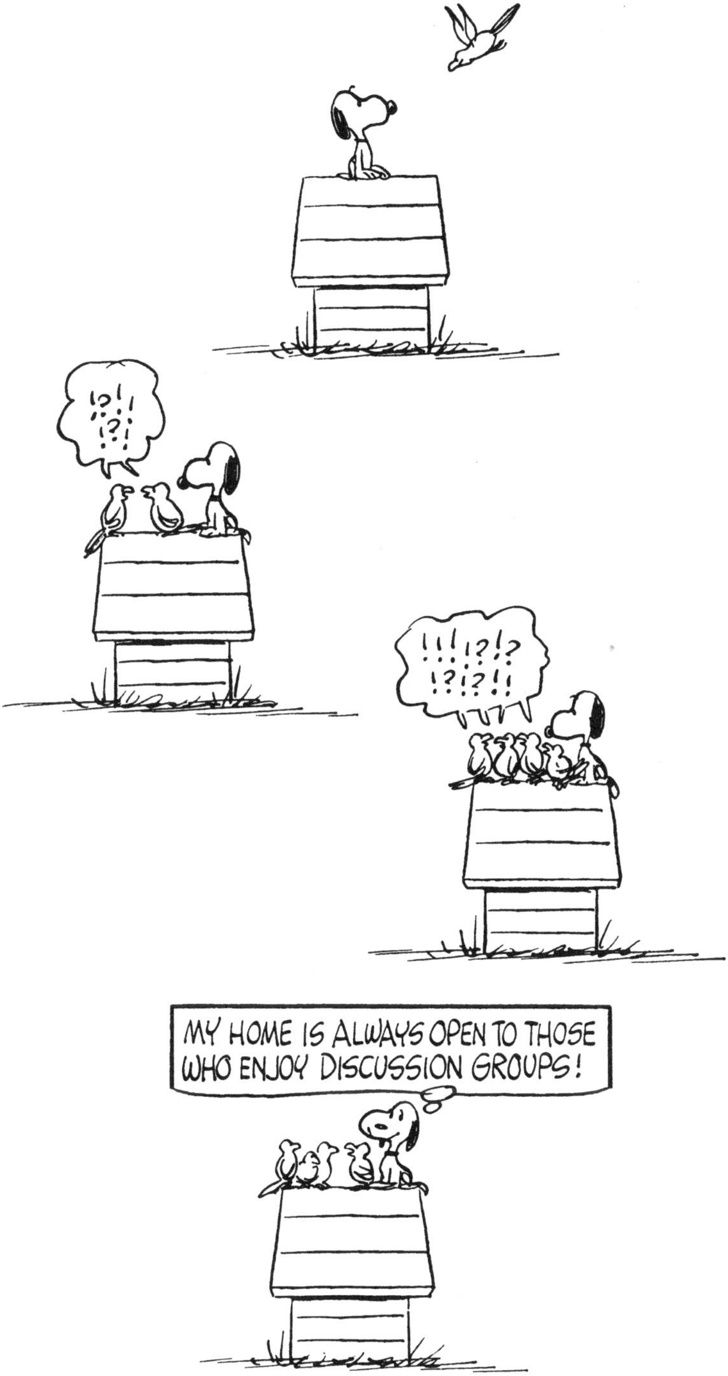
MY HOME IS ALWAYS OPEN TO THOSE WHO ENJOY DISCUSSION GROUPS!

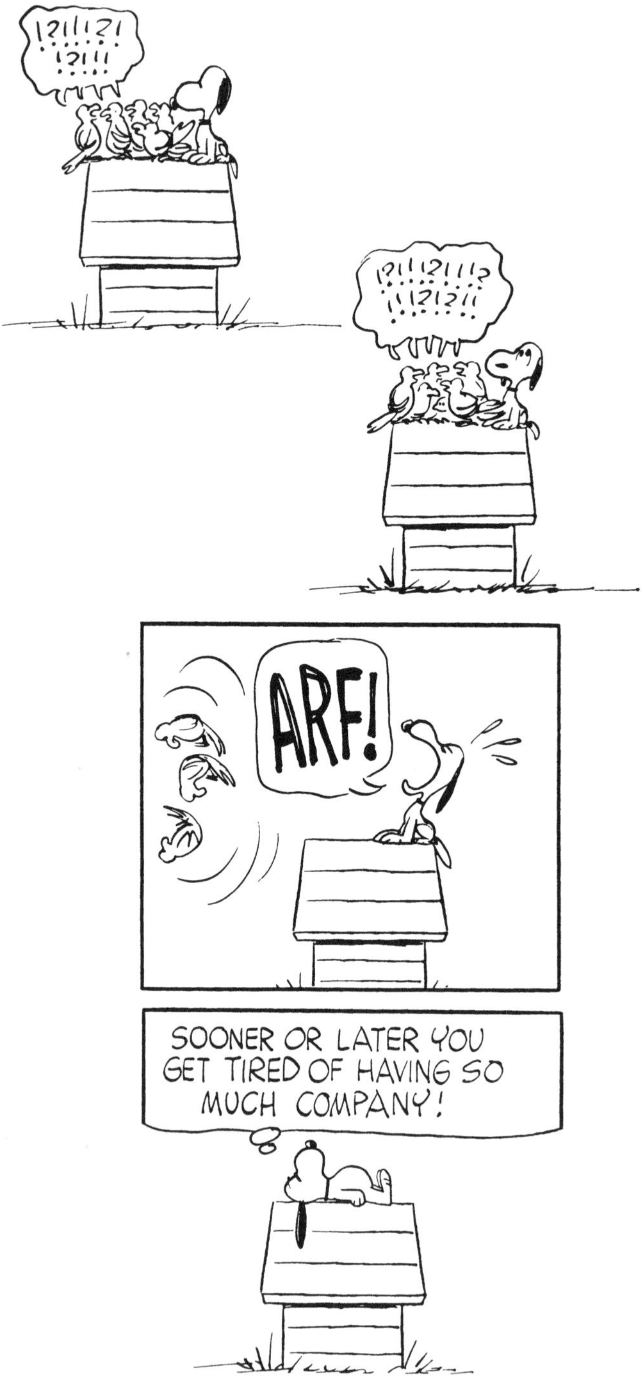
ARF!
SOONER OR LATER YOU GET TIRED OF HAVING SO MUCH COMPANY!

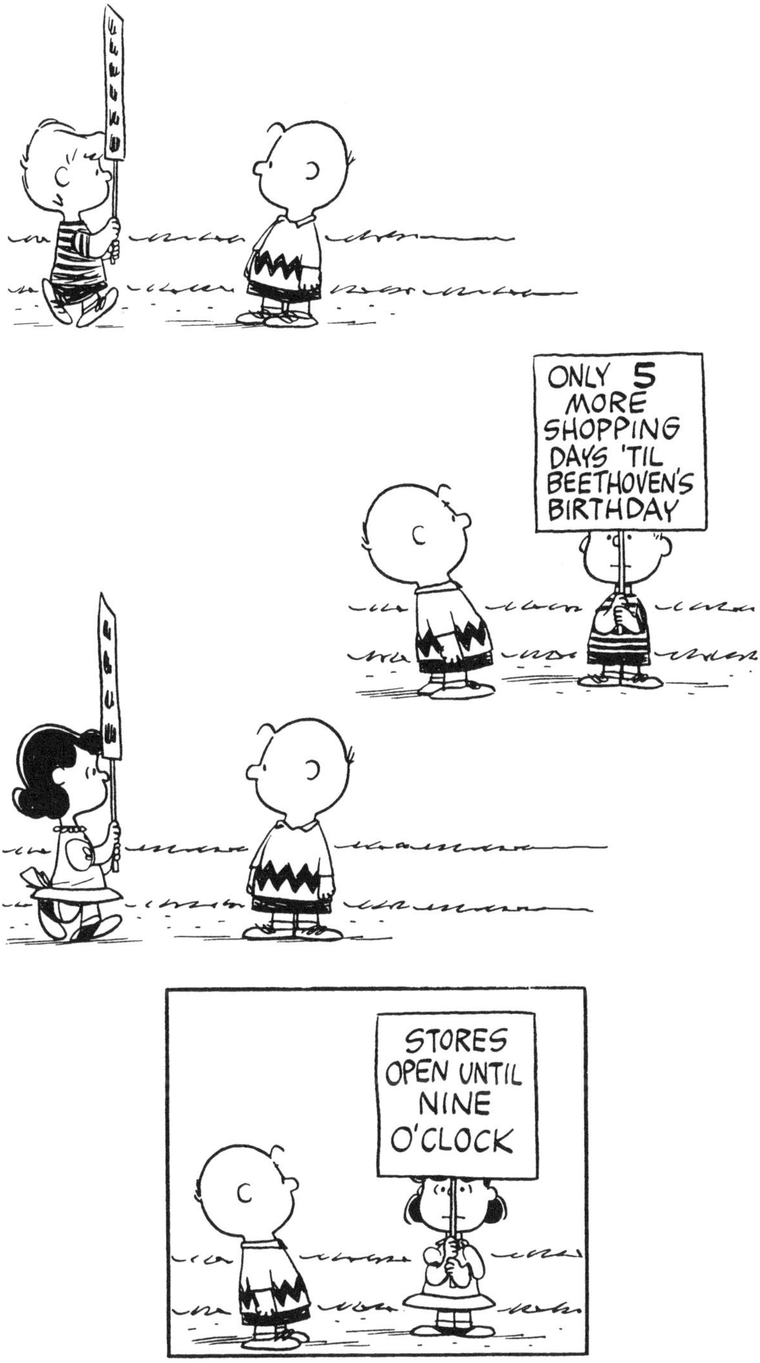
ONLY 5 MORE SHOPPING DAYS 'TIL BEETHOVEN'S BIRTHDAY
STORES OPEN UNTIL NINE O'CLOCK

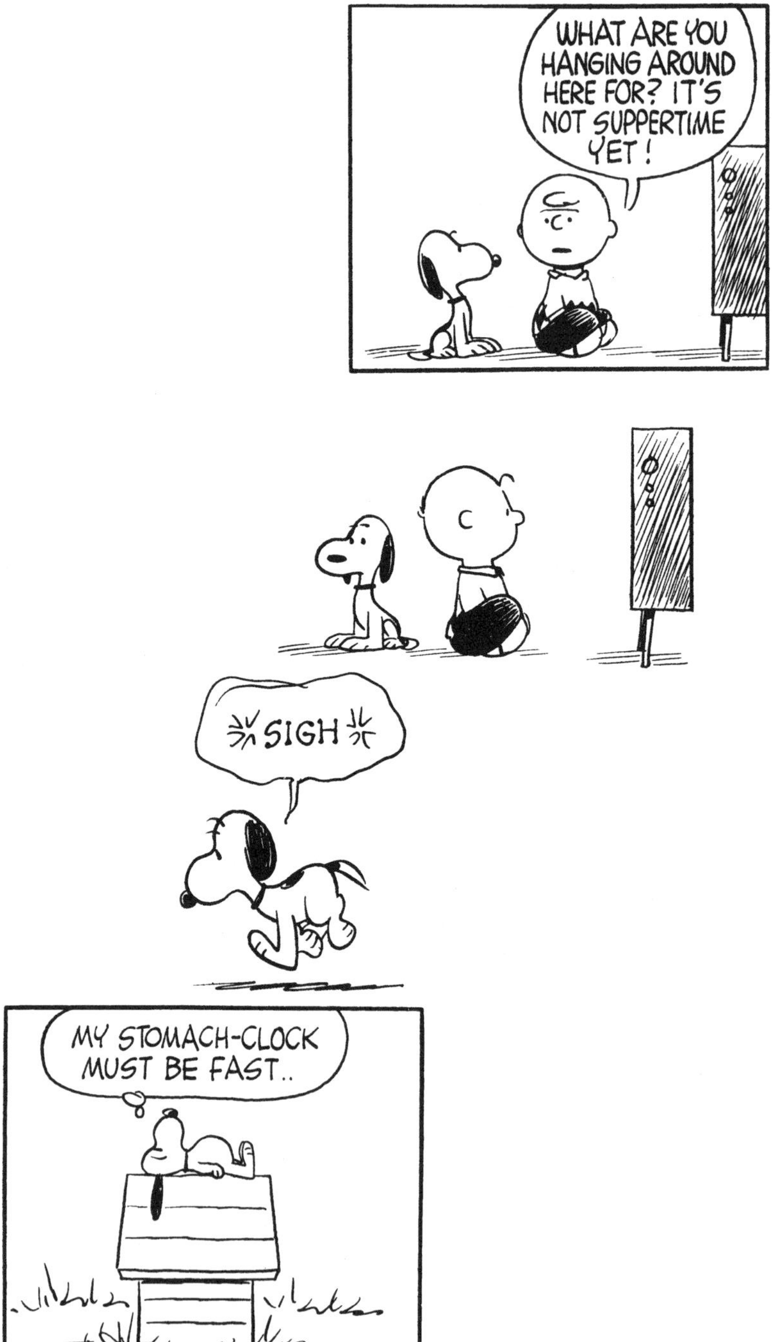
WHAT ARE YOU HANGING AROUND HERE FOR? IT'S NOT SUPPERTIME YET!
SIGH
MY STOMACH-CLOCK MUST BE FAST..

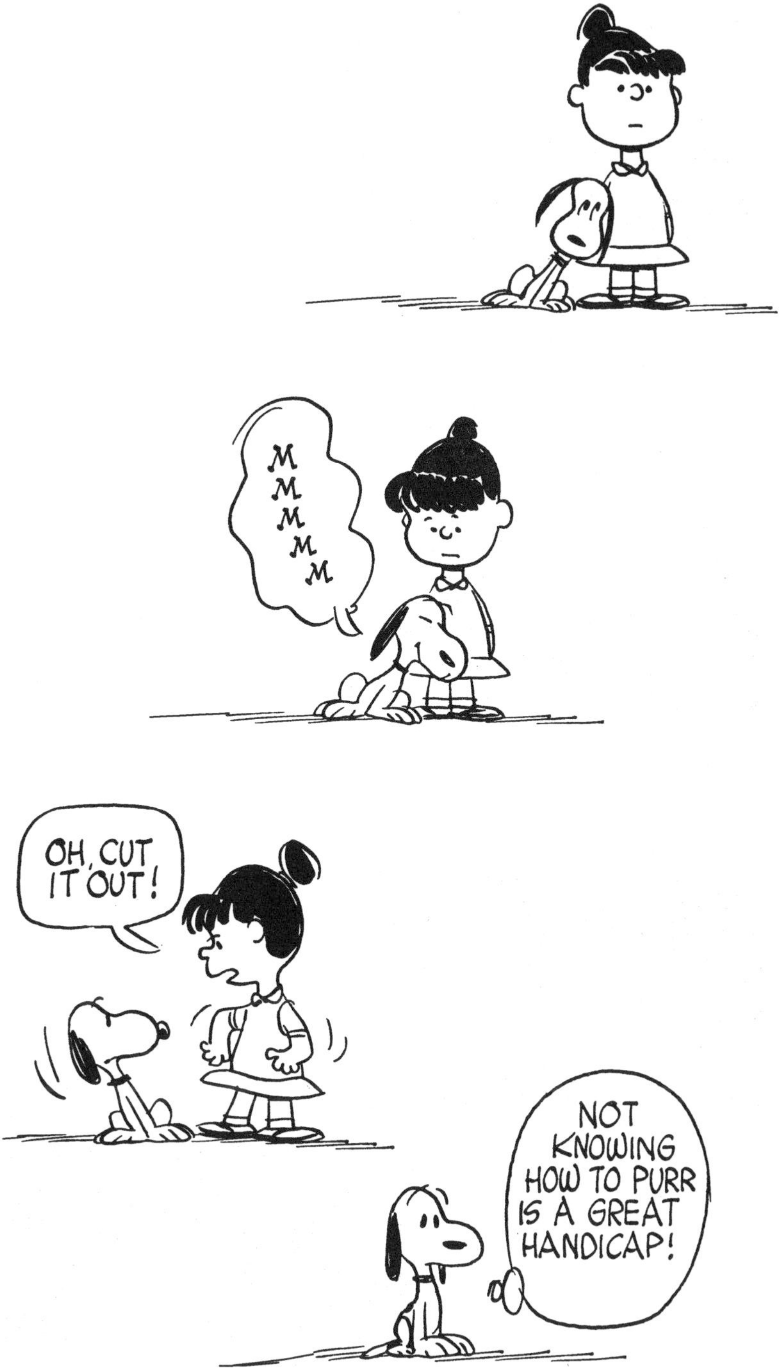
MMMMM
OH, CUT IT OUT!
NOT KNOWING HOW TO PURR IS A GREAT HANDICAP!

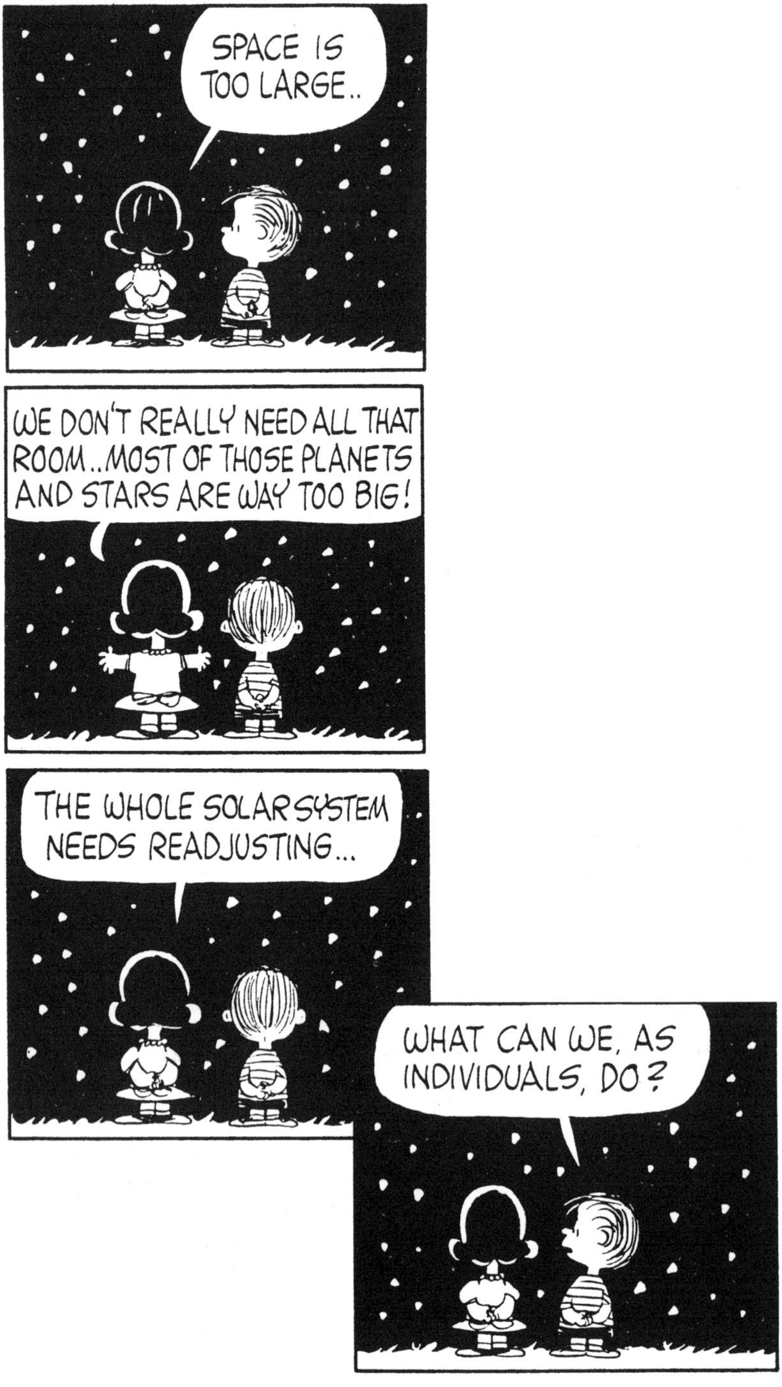
SPACE IS TOO LARGE..
WE DON'T REALLY NEED ALL THAT ROOM..MOST OF THOSE PLANETS AND STARS ARE WAY TOO BIG!
THE WHOLE SOLAR SYSTEM NEEDS READJUSTING...
WHAT CAN WE, AS INDIVIDUALS, DO?

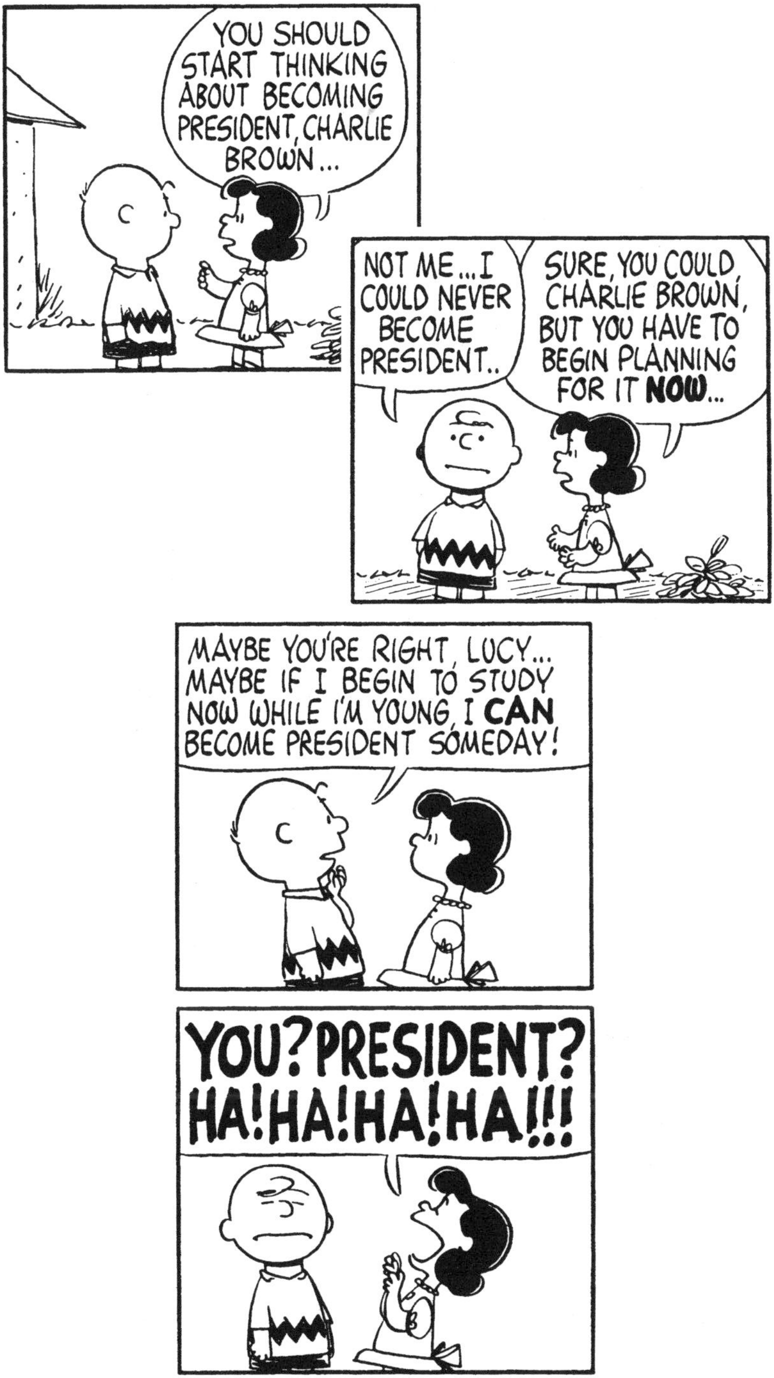
YOU SHOULD START THINKING ABOUT BECOMING PRESIDENT, CHARLIE BROWN...
NOT ME...I COULD NEVER BECOME PRESIDENT..
SURE, YOU COULD, CHARLIE BROWN, BUT YOU HAVE TO BEGIN PLANNING FOR IT **NOW**...
MAYBE YOU'RE RIGHT, LUCY... MAYBE IF I BEGIN TO STUDY NOW WHILE I'M YOUNG, I **CAN** BECOME PRESIDENT SOMEDAY!
YOU? PRESIDENT? HA! HA! HA! HA!!!

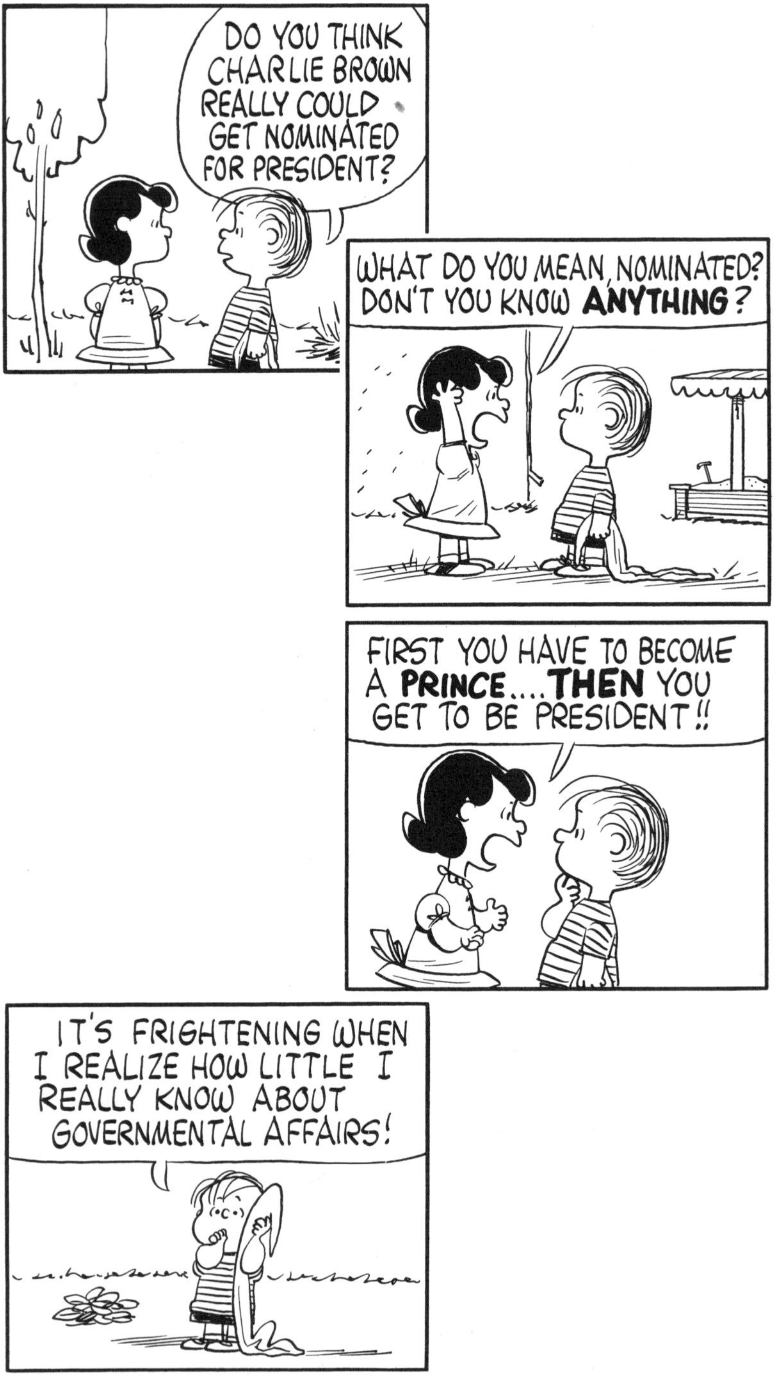
DO YOU THINK CHARLIE BROWN REALLY COULD GET NOMINATED FOR PRESIDENT?
WHAT DO YOU MEAN, NOMINATED? DON'T YOU KNOW **ANYTHING**?
FIRST YOU HAVE TO BECOME A **PRINCE**.... **THEN** YOU GET TO BE PRESIDENT!!
IT'S FRIGHTENING WHEN I REALIZE HOW LITTLE I REALLY KNOW ABOUT GOVERNMENTAL AFFAIRS!

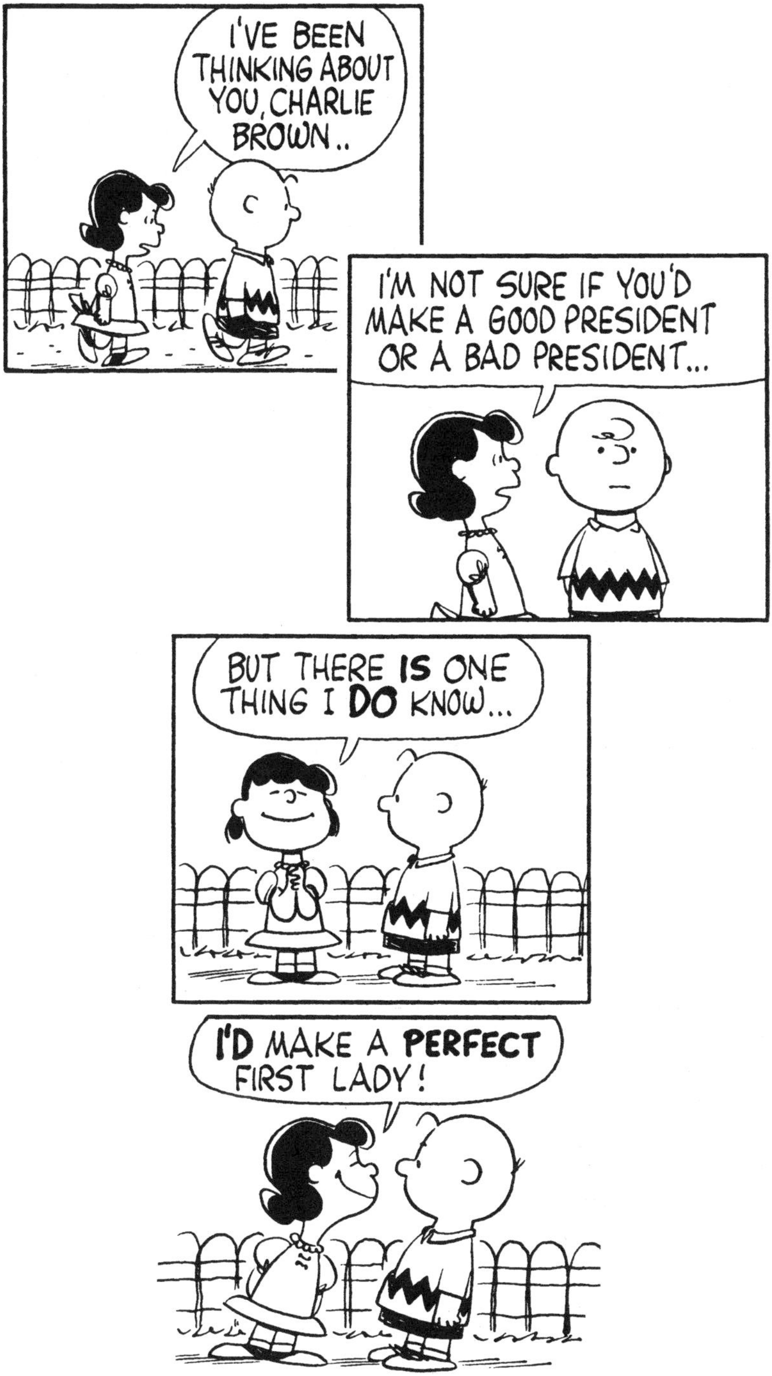
I'VE BEEN THINKING ABOUT YOU, CHARLIE BROWN..
I'M NOT SURE IF YOU'D MAKE A GOOD PRESIDENT OR A BAD PRESIDENT...
BUT THERE **IS** ONE THING I **DO** KNOW...
I'D MAKE A **PERFECT** FIRST LADY!

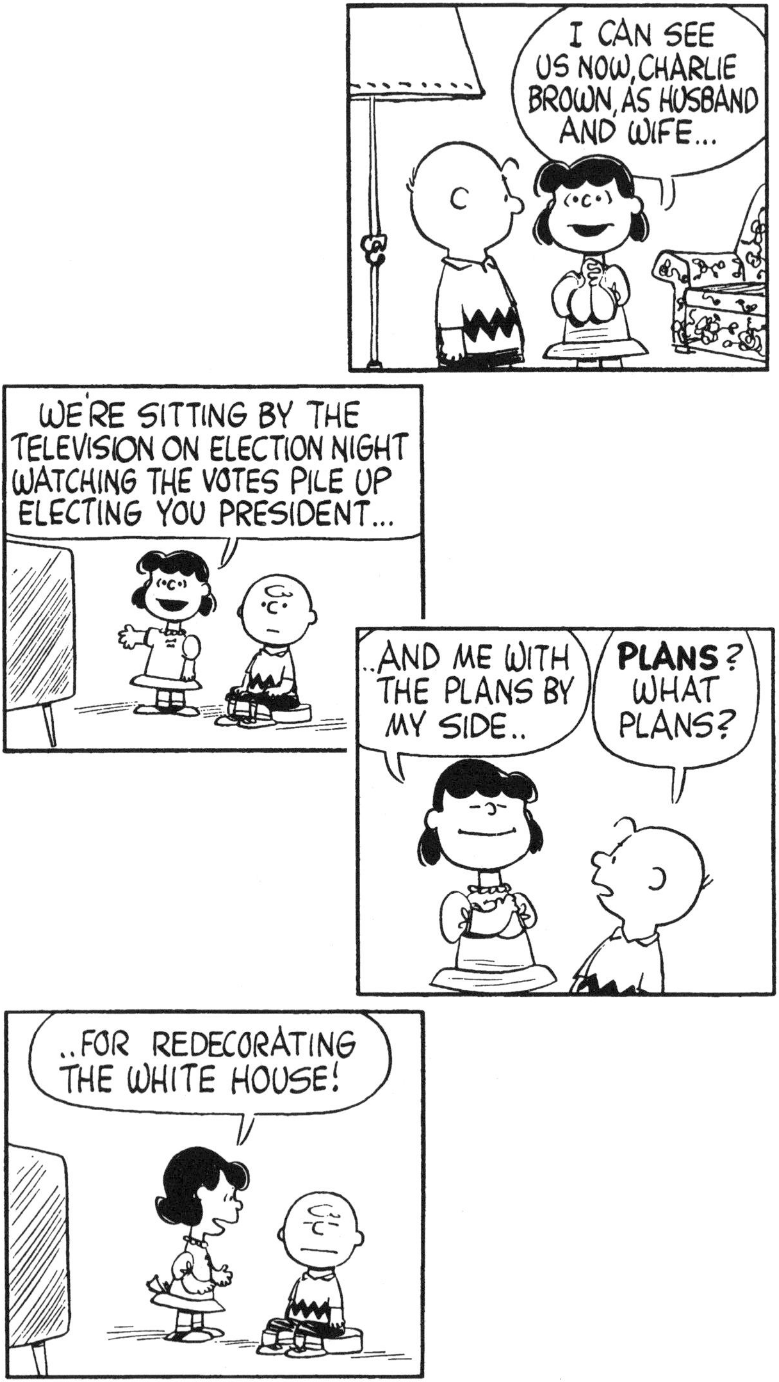
I CAN SEE US NOW, CHARLIE BROWN, AS HUSBAND AND WIFE...
WE'RE SITTING BY THE TELEVISION ON ELECTION NIGHT WATCHING THE VOTES PILE UP ELECTING YOU PRESIDENT...
..AND ME WITH THE PLANS BY MY SIDE..
PLANS? WHAT PLANS?
..FOR REDECORATING THE WHITE HOUSE!

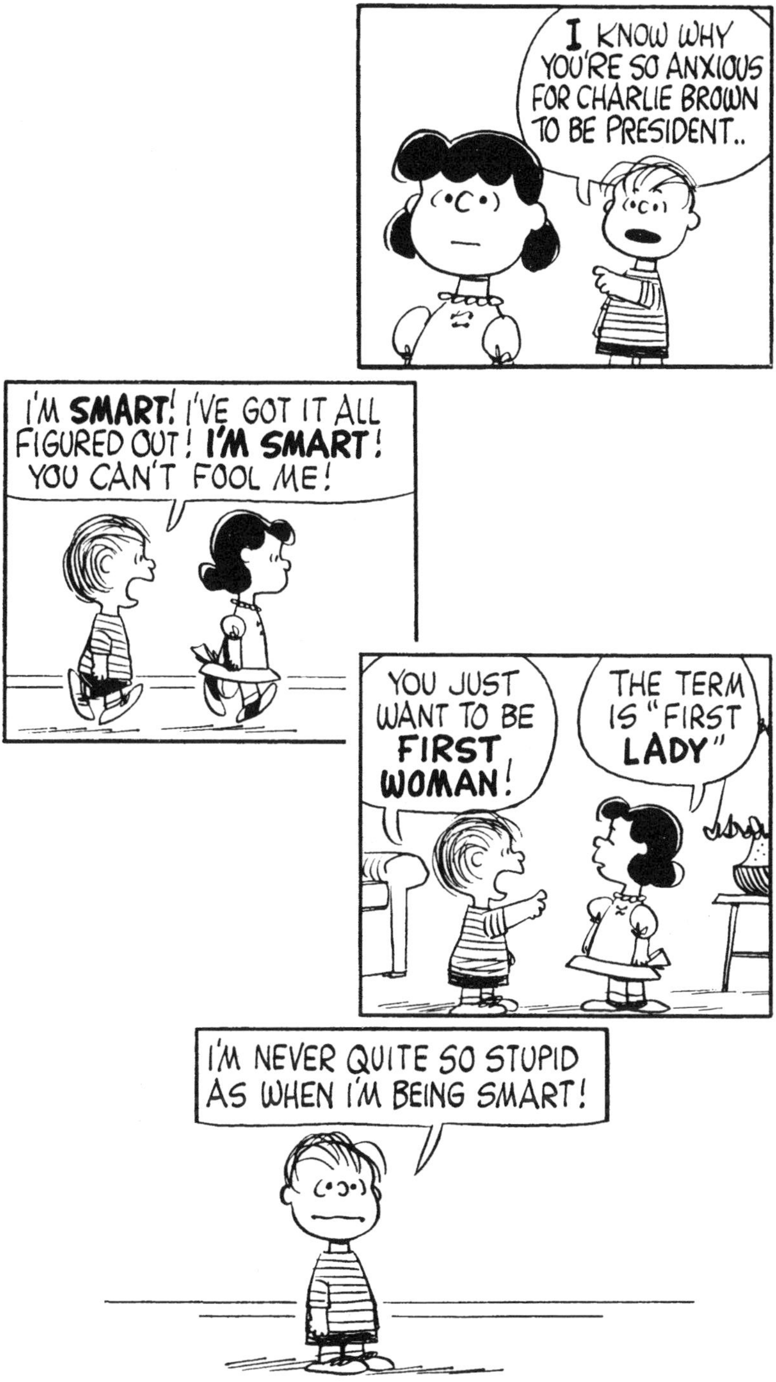
I KNOW WHY YOU'RE SO ANXIOUS FOR CHARLIE BROWN TO BE PRESIDENT..
I'M SMART! I'VE GOT IT ALL FIGURED OUT! I'M SMART! YOU CAN'T FOOL ME!
YOU JUST WANT TO BE FIRST WOMAN!
THE TERM IS "FIRST LADY"
I'M NEVER QUITE SO STUPID AS WHEN I'M BEING SMART!

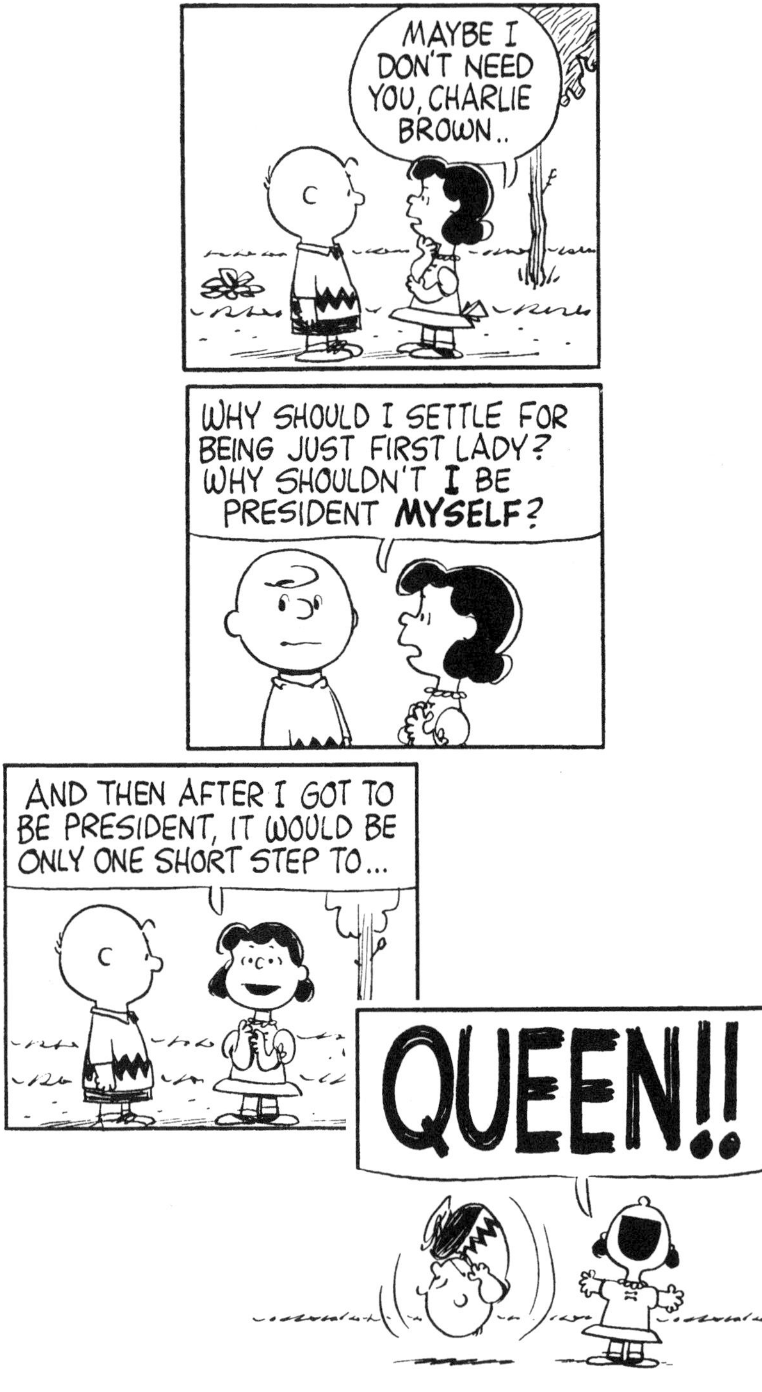
MAYBE I DON'T NEED YOU, CHARLIE BROWN..
WHY SHOULD I SETTLE FOR BEING JUST FIRST LADY? WHY SHOULDN'T I BE PRESIDENT MYSELF?
AND THEN AFTER I GOT TO BE PRESIDENT, IT WOULD BE ONLY ONE SHORT STEP TO...
QUEEN!!

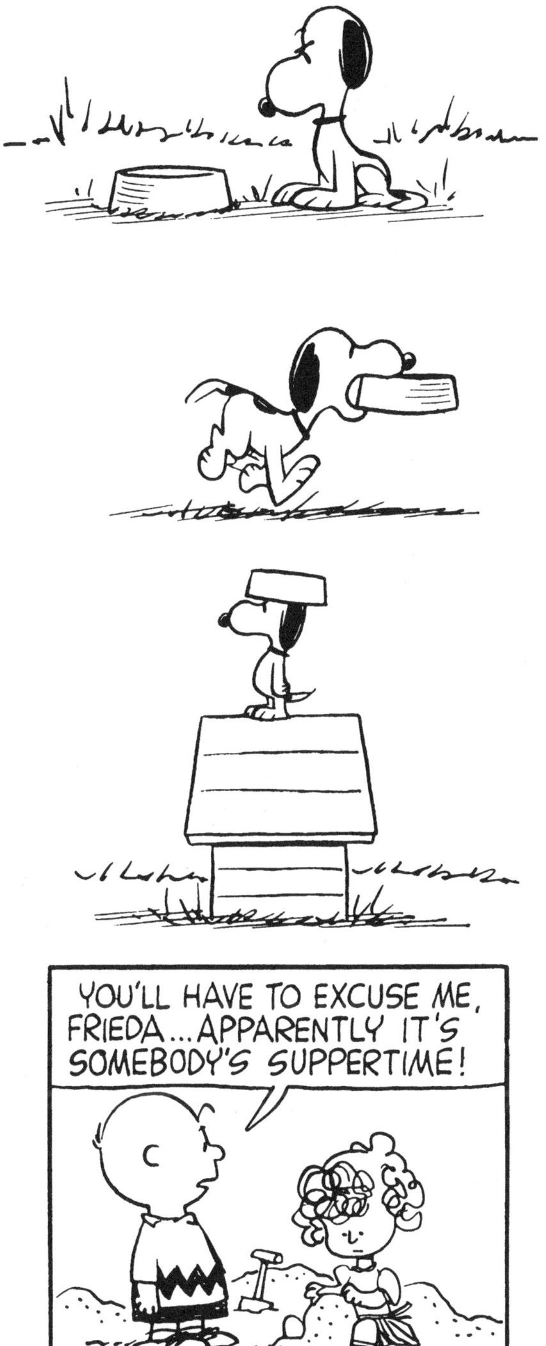
YOU'LL HAVE TO EXCUSE ME, FRIEDA...APPARENTLY IT'S SOMEBODY'S SUPPERTIME!

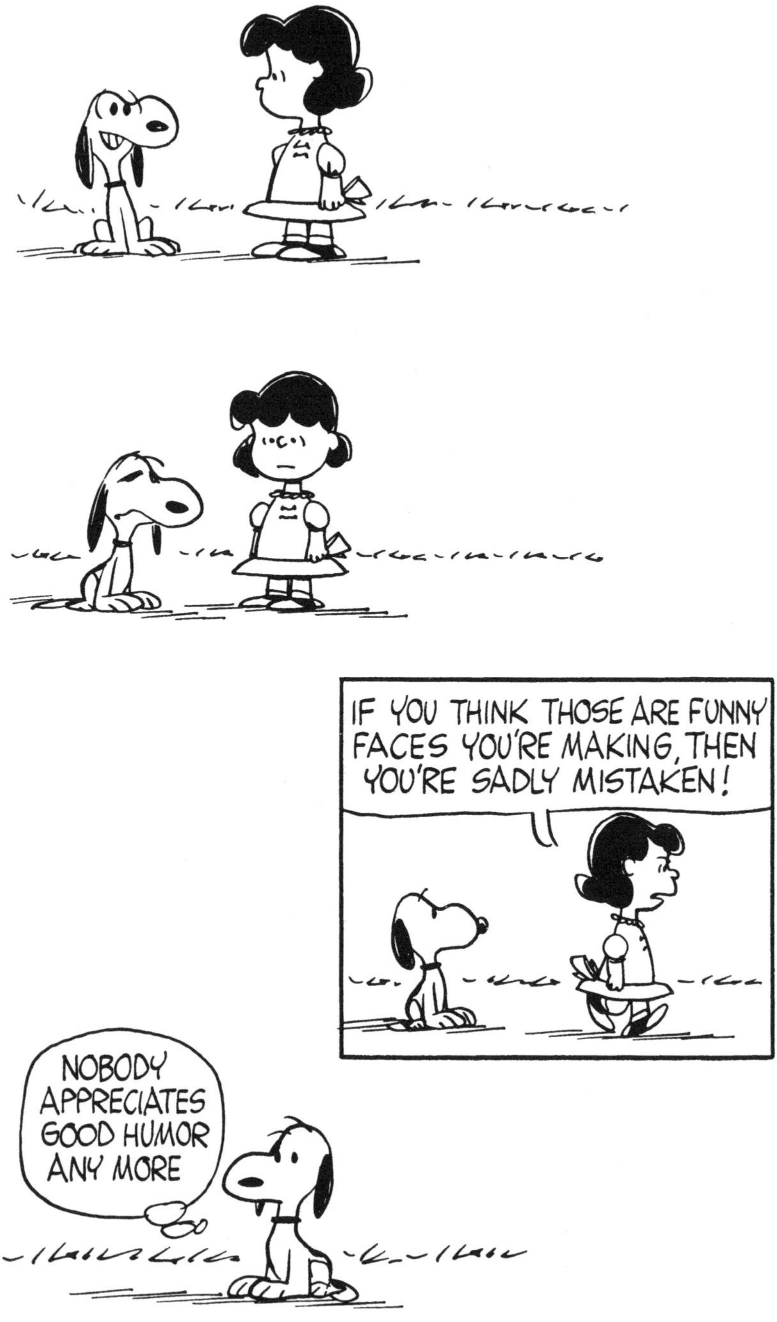
IF YOU THINK THOSE ARE FUNNY FACES YOU'RE MAKING, THEN YOU'RE SADLY MISTAKEN!
NOBODY APPRECIATES GOOD HUMOR ANY MORE

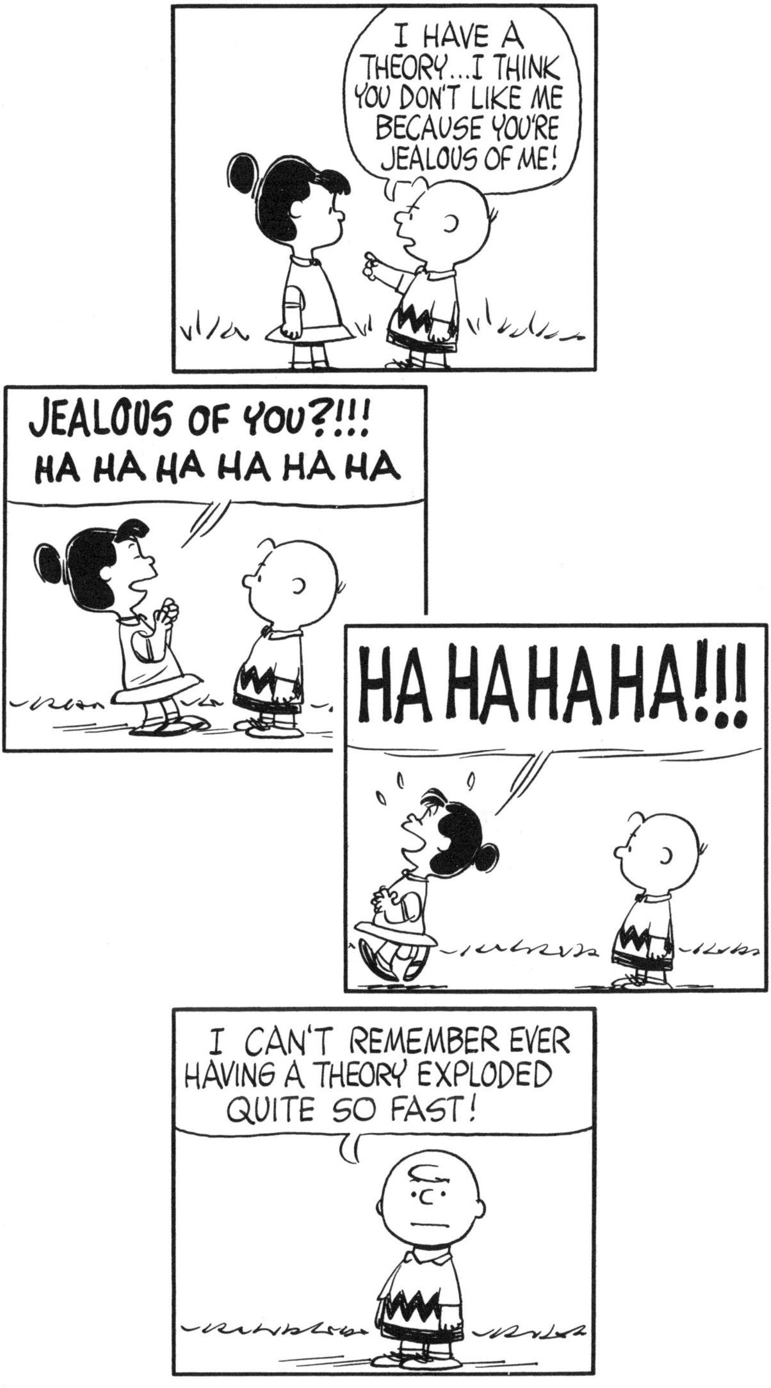
I HAVE A THEORY...I THINK YOU DON'T LIKE ME BECAUSE YOU'RE JEALOUS OF ME!
JEALOUS OF YOU?!!! HA HA HA HA HA HA
HA HA HA HA!!!
I CAN'T REMEMBER EVER HAVING A THEORY EXPLODED QUITE SO FAST!

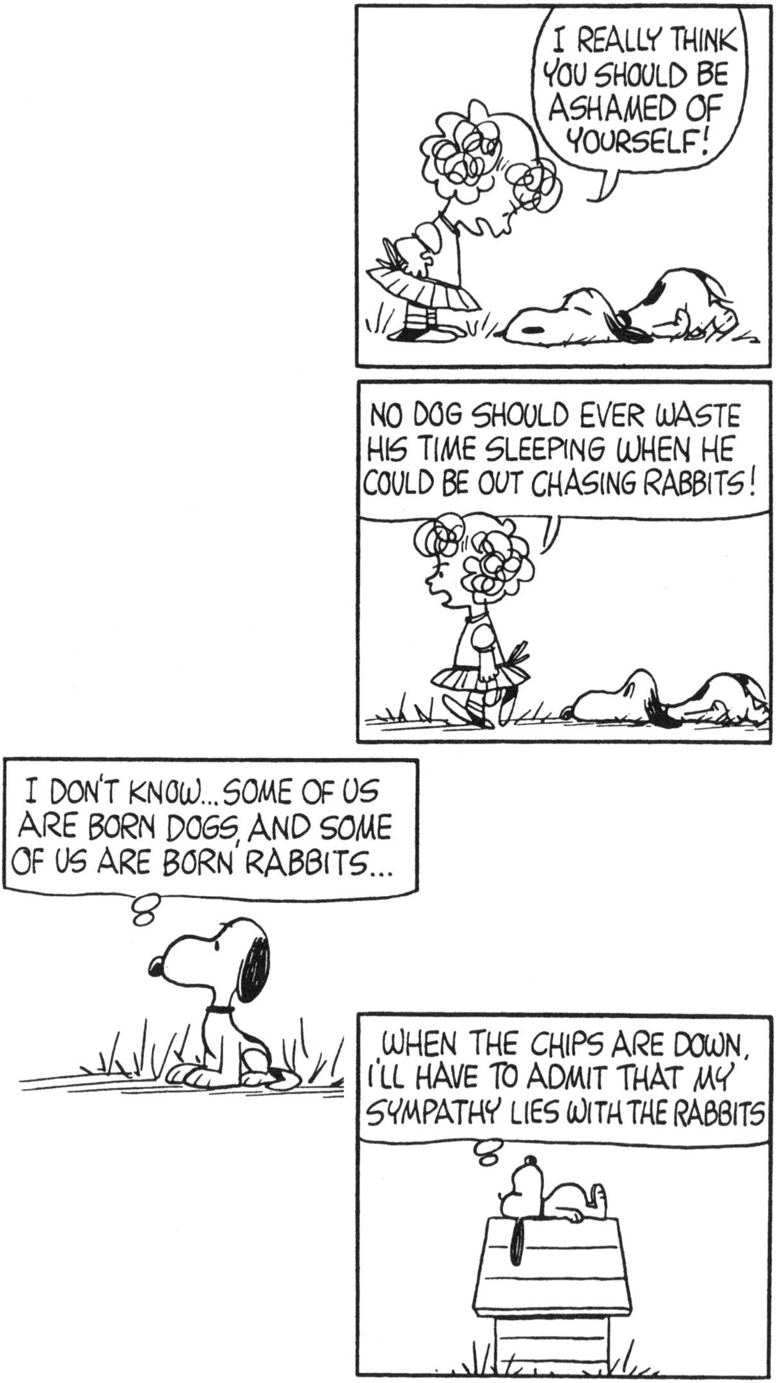
I REALLY THINK YOU SHOULD BE ASHAMED OF YOURSELF!
NO DOG SHOULD EVER WASTE HIS TIME SLEEPING WHEN HE COULD BE OUT CHASING RABBITS!
I DON'T KNOW...SOME OF US ARE BORN DOGS, AND SOME OF US ARE BORN RABBITS...
WHEN THE CHIPS ARE DOWN, I'LL HAVE TO ADMIT THAT MY SYMPATHY LIES WITH THE RABBITS

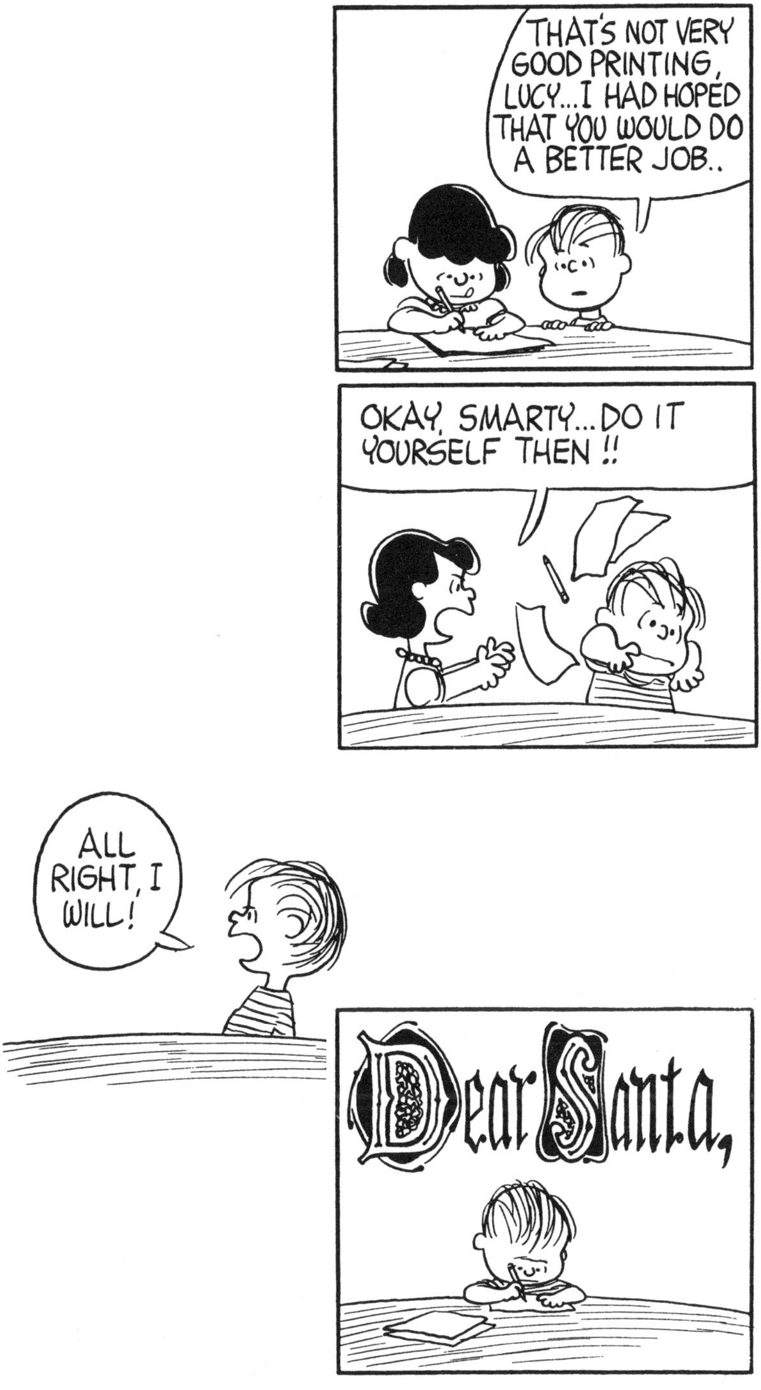
THAT'S NOT VERY GOOD PRINTING, LUCY...I HAD HOPED THAT YOU WOULD DO A BETTER JOB..
OKAY, SMARTY...DO IT YOURSELF THEN !!
ALL RIGHT, I WILL!
Dear Santa,

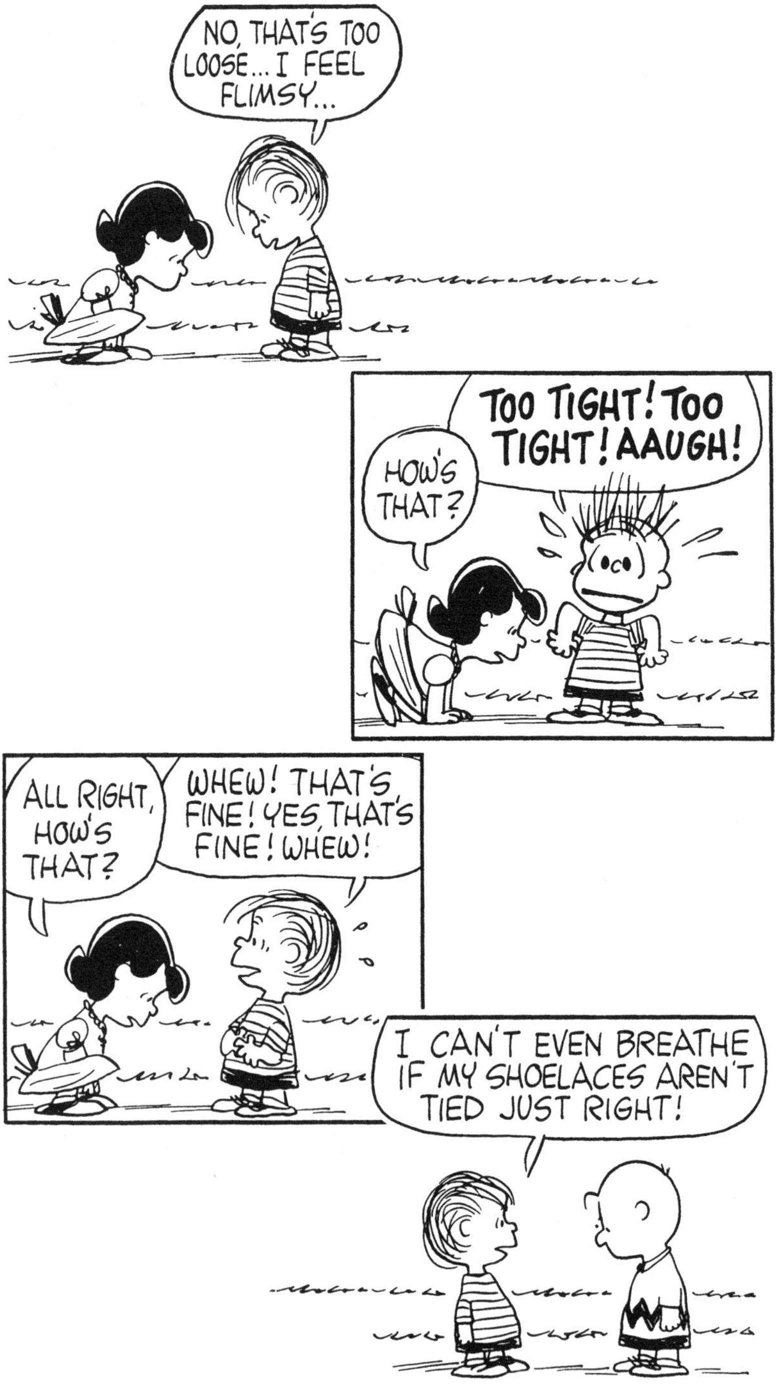
NO, THAT'S TOO LOOSE... I FEEL FLIMSY...
HOW'S THAT?
TOO TIGHT! TOO TIGHT! AAUGH!
ALL RIGHT, HOW'S THAT?
WHEW! THAT'S FINE! YES, THAT'S FINE! WHEW!
I CAN'T EVEN BREATHE IF MY SHOELACES AREN'T TIED JUST RIGHT!

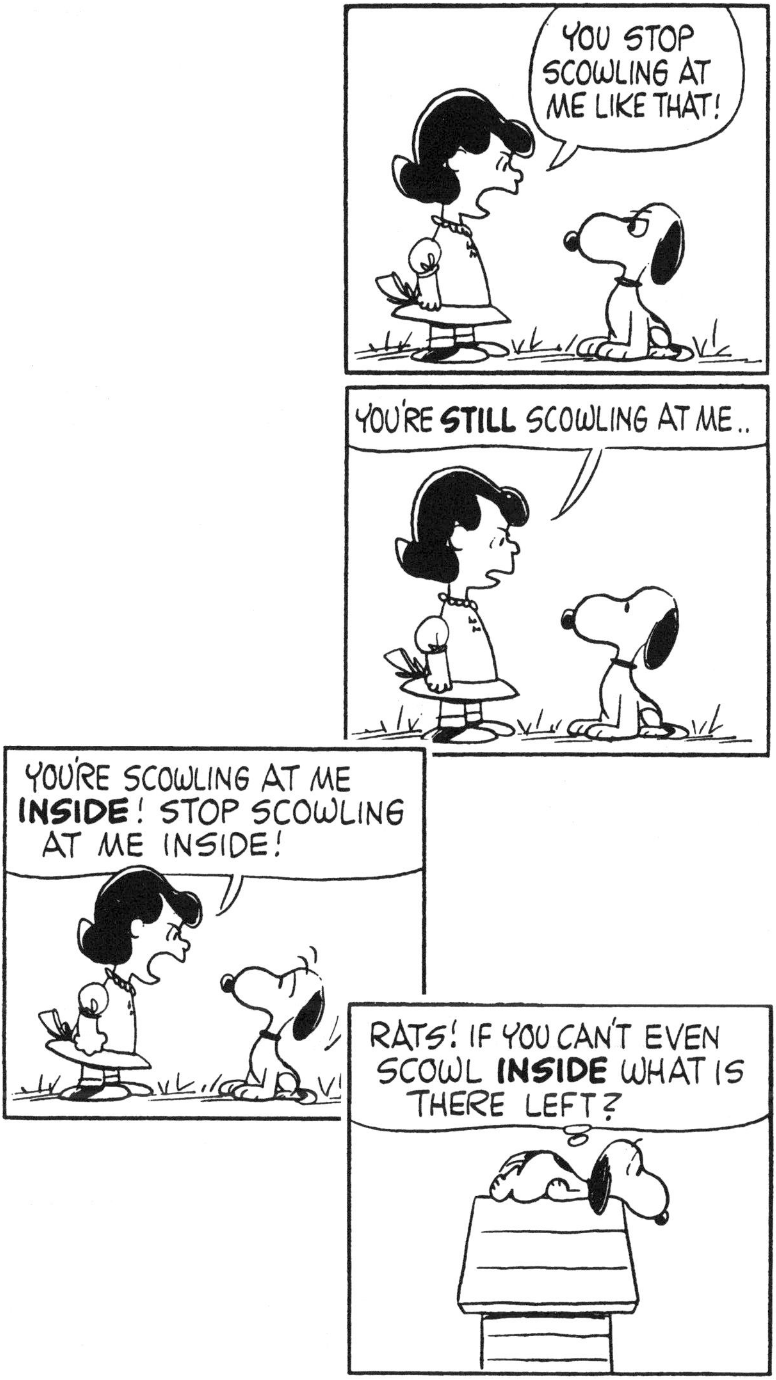
YOU STOP SCOWLING AT ME LIKE THAT!
YOU'RE **STILL** SCOWLING AT ME..
YOU'RE SCOWLING AT ME **INSIDE**! STOP SCOWLING AT ME INSIDE!
RATS! IF YOU CAN'T EVEN SCOWL **INSIDE** WHAT IS THERE LEFT?

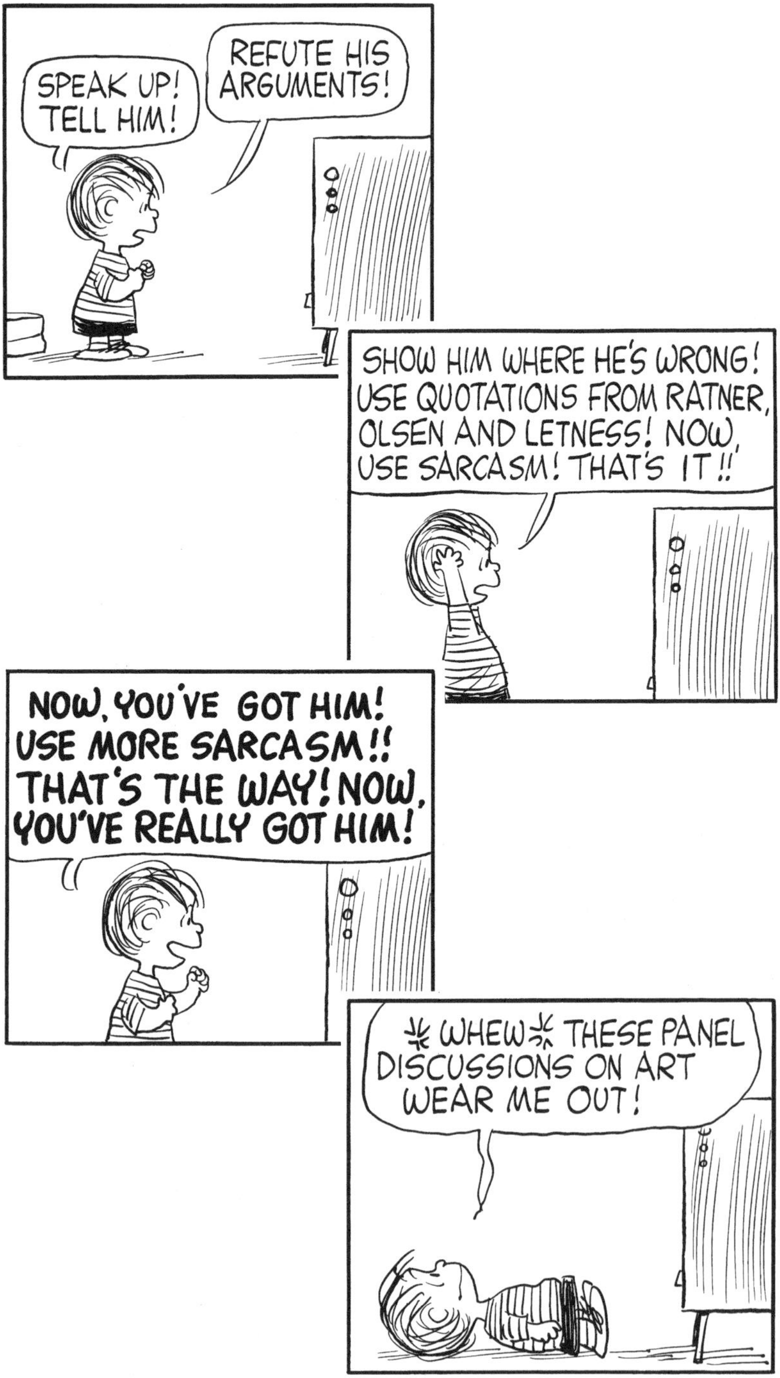
SPEAK UP! TELL HIM!
REFUTE HIS ARGUMENTS!
SHOW HIM WHERE HE'S WRONG! USE QUOTATIONS FROM RATNER, OLSEN AND LETNESS! NOW, USE SARCASM! THAT'S IT!!
NOW, YOU'VE GOT HIM! USE MORE SARCASM!! THAT'S THE WAY! NOW, YOU'VE REALLY GOT HIM!
WHEW THESE PANEL DISCUSSIONS ON ART WEAR ME OUT!

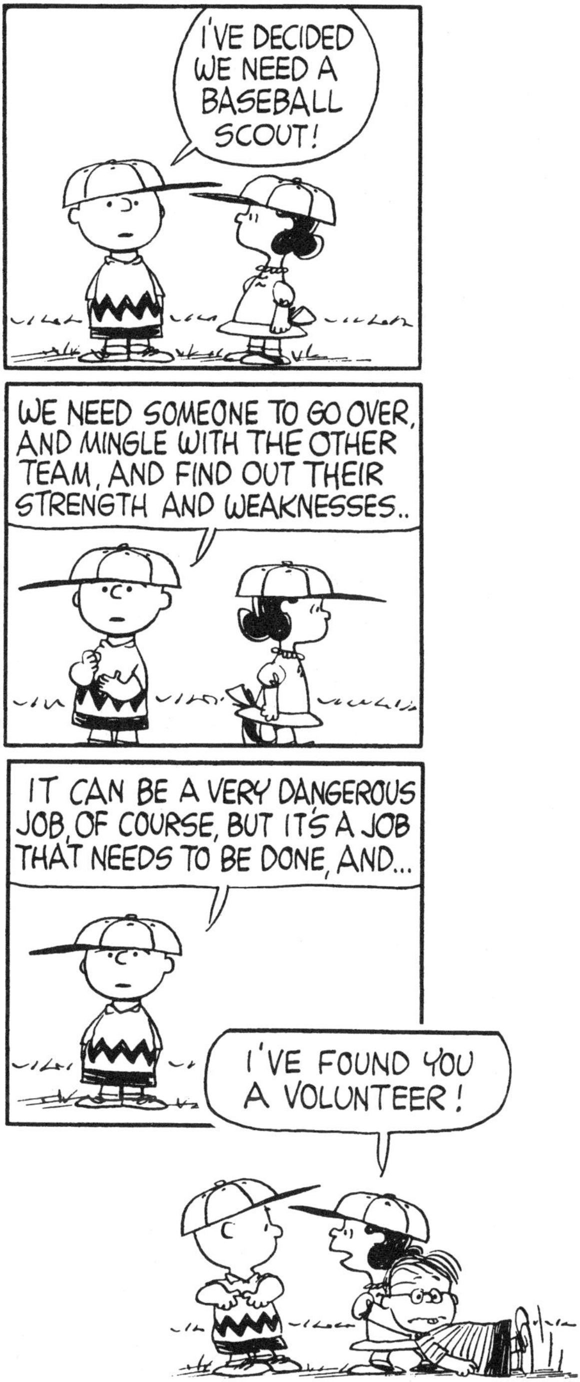

I'VE DECIDED WE NEED A BASEBALL SCOUT!
WE NEED SOMEONE TO GO OVER, AND MINGLE WITH THE OTHER TEAM, AND FIND OUT THEIR STRENGTH AND WEAKNESSES..
IT CAN BE A VERY DANGEROUS JOB, OF COURSE, BUT IT'S A JOB THAT NEEDS TO BE DONE, AND...
I'VE FOUND YOU A VOLUNTEER!

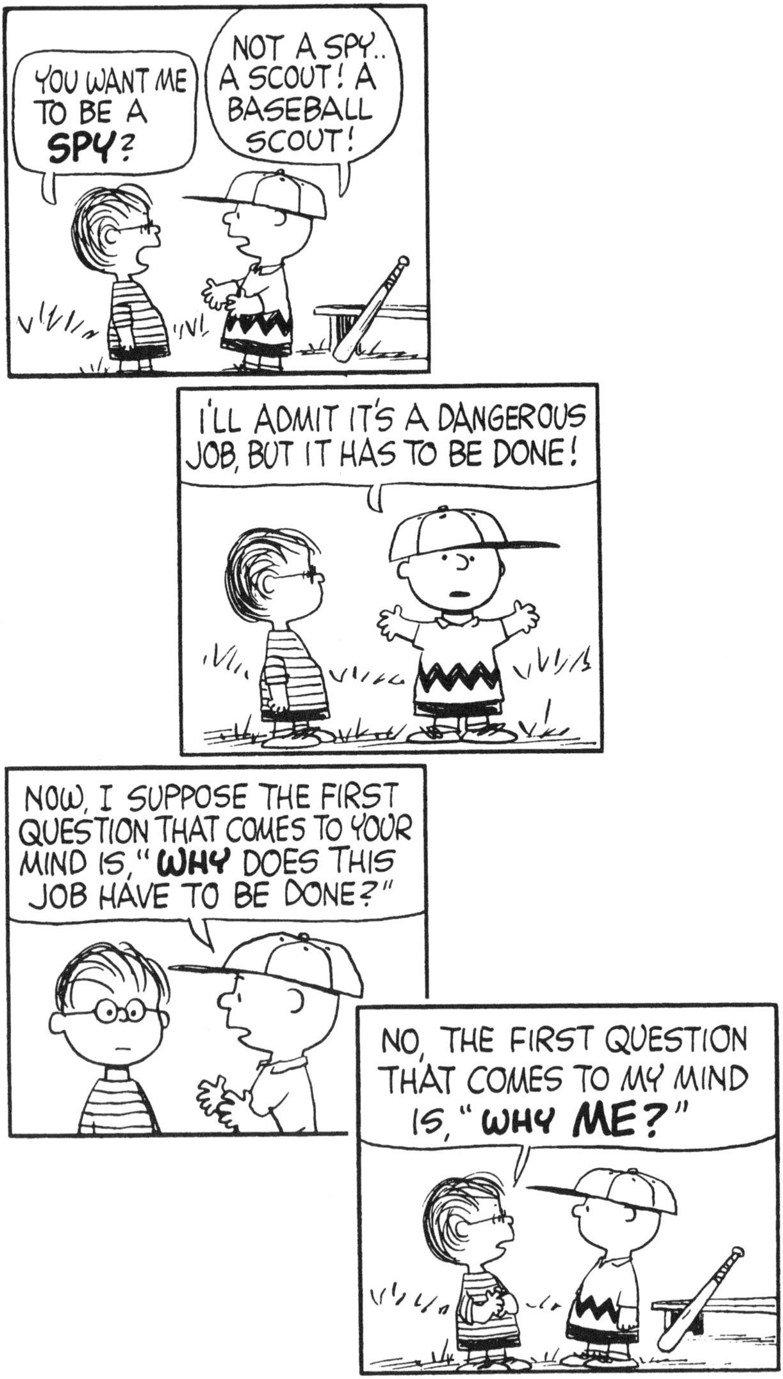
YOU WANT ME TO BE A SPY?
NOT A SPY.. A SCOUT! A BASEBALL SCOUT!
I'LL ADMIT IT'S A DANGEROUS JOB, BUT IT HAS TO BE DONE!
NOW, I SUPPOSE THE FIRST QUESTION THAT COMES TO YOUR MIND IS, "WHY DOES THIS JOB HAVE TO BE DONE?"
NO, THE FIRST QUESTION THAT COMES TO MY MIND IS, "WHY ME?"

ALL RIGHT, SO I'M A BASEBALL SCOUT...WHAT DO I DO?

YOU GO, AND FIND OUT ALL YOU CAN ABOUT THEIR PITCHERS AND HITTERS..

WRITE EVERYTHING YOU FIND OUT ON THIS SQUARE OF BUBBLE GUM..IF THEY SUSPECT THAT YOU'RE SCOUTING THEM, YOU CAN JUST CHEW UP THE EVIDENCE...

WELL, GOOD LUCK, OL' BUDDY...

THANK YOU, CHARLIE BROWN..

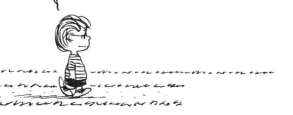

SOMEHOW I HAVE THE FEELING OF IMPENDING DOOM!

MAYBE I SHOULDN'T HAVE SENT LINUS OUT AS A BASEBALL SCOUT...

MAYBE HE'LL GET LOST..MAYBE THE OTHER TEAM WILL SEE WHAT HE'S DOING, AND BEAT HIM UP...

HEY, MANAGER, DO YOU THINK MY HAIR LOOKS ALL RIGHT THIS WAY, OR SHOULD I CHANGE IT?

NO, IT LOOKS FINE JUST THE WAY IT IS...

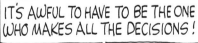

IT'S AWFUL TO HAVE TO BE THE ONE WHO MAKES ALL THE DECISIONS!

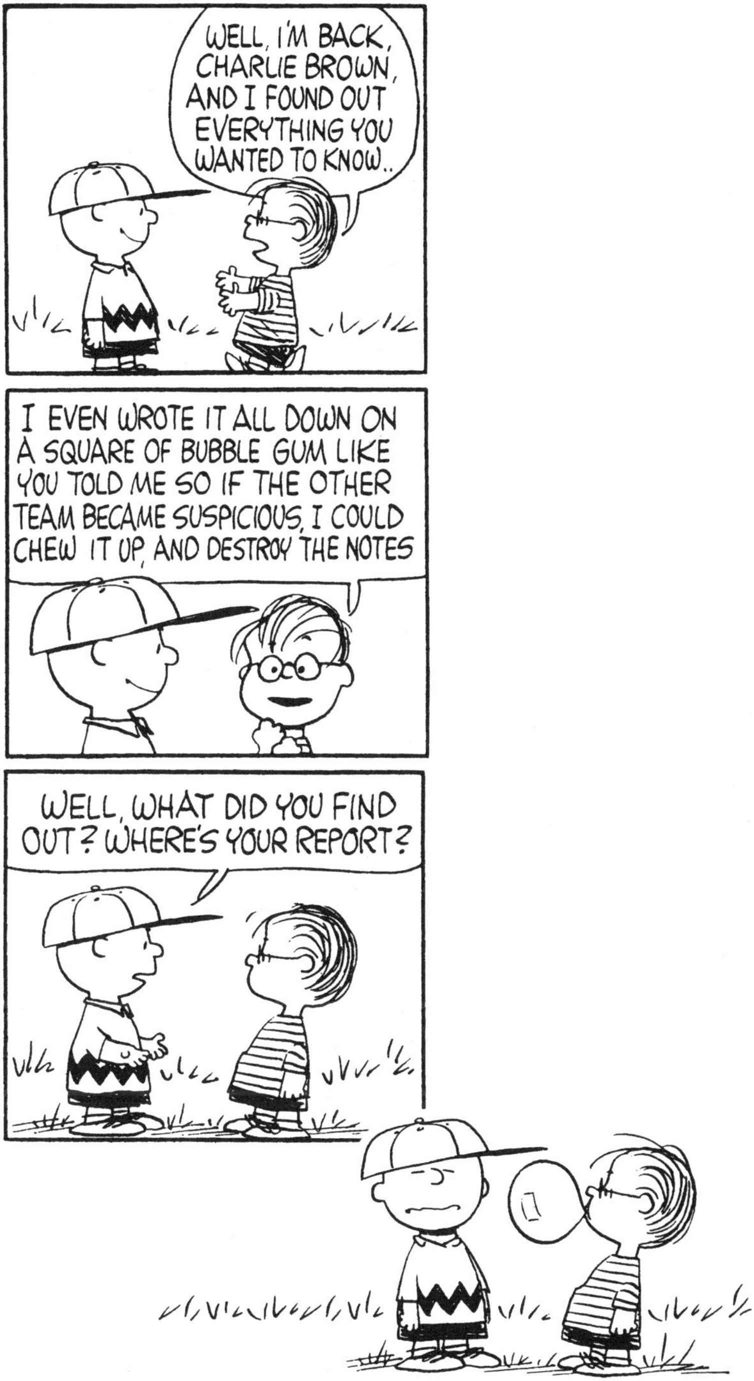
WELL, I'M BACK, CHARLIE BROWN, AND I FOUND OUT EVERYTHING YOU WANTED TO KNOW..
I EVEN WROTE IT ALL DOWN ON A SQUARE OF BUBBLE GUM LIKE YOU TOLD ME SO IF THE OTHER TEAM BECAME SUSPICIOUS, I COULD CHEW IT UP, AND DESTROY THE NOTES
WELL, WHAT DID YOU FIND OUT? WHERE'S YOUR REPORT?

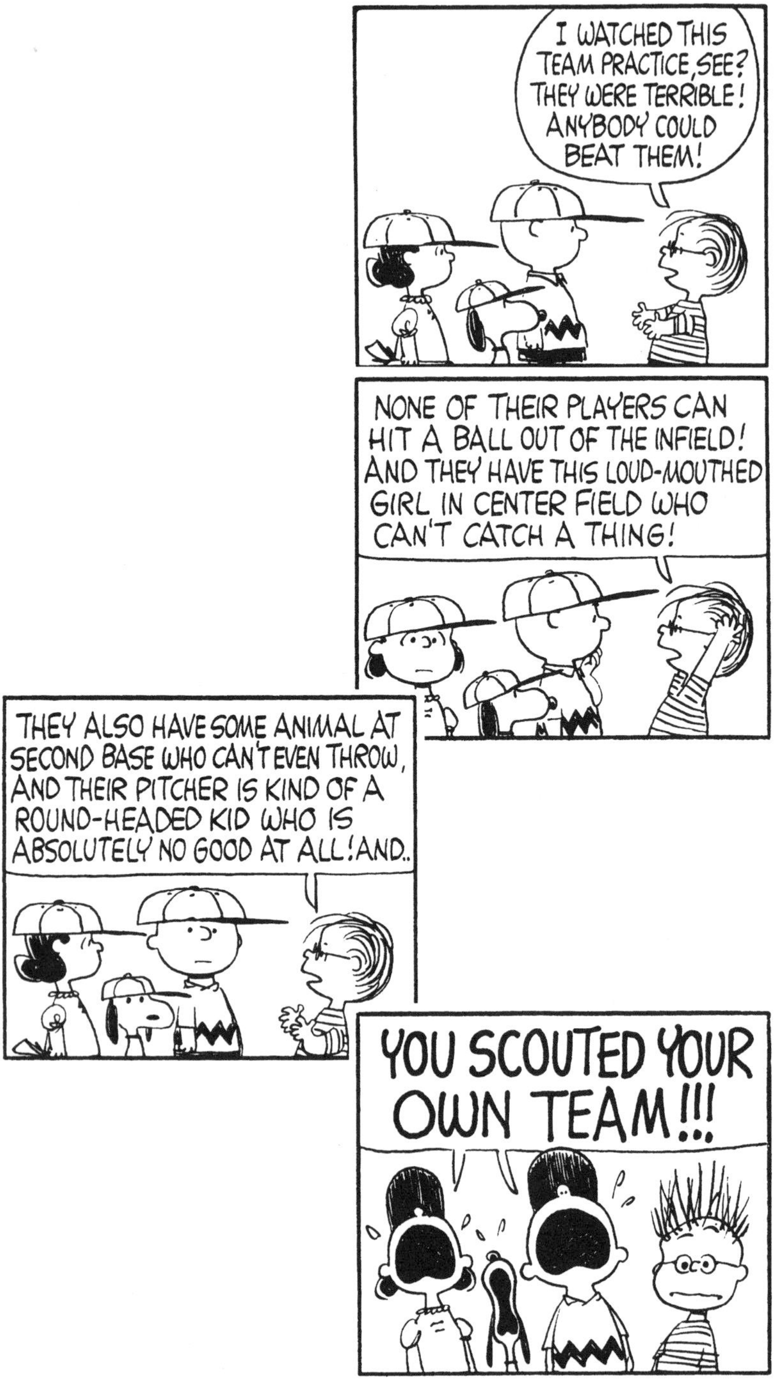
I WATCHED THIS TEAM PRACTICE, SEE? THEY WERE TERRIBLE! ANYBODY COULD BEAT THEM!
NONE OF THEIR PLAYERS CAN HIT A BALL OUT OF THE INFIELD! AND THEY HAVE THIS LOUD-MOUTHED GIRL IN CENTER FIELD WHO CAN'T CATCH A THING!
THEY ALSO HAVE SOME ANIMAL AT SECOND BASE WHO CAN'T EVEN THROW, AND THEIR PITCHER IS KIND OF A ROUND-HEADED KID WHO IS ABSOLUTELY NO GOOD AT ALL! AND..
YOU SCOUTED YOUR OWN TEAM!!!

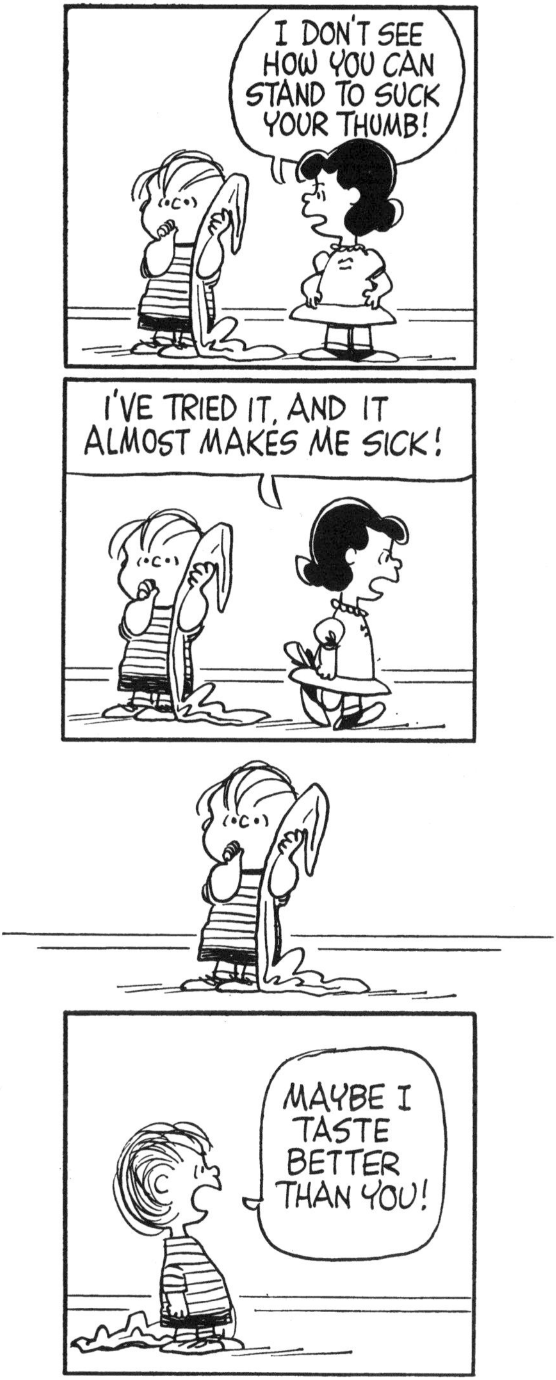
I DON'T SEE HOW YOU CAN STAND TO SUCK YOUR THUMB!
I'VE TRIED IT, AND IT ALMOST MAKES ME SICK!
MAYBE I TASTE BETTER THAN YOU!

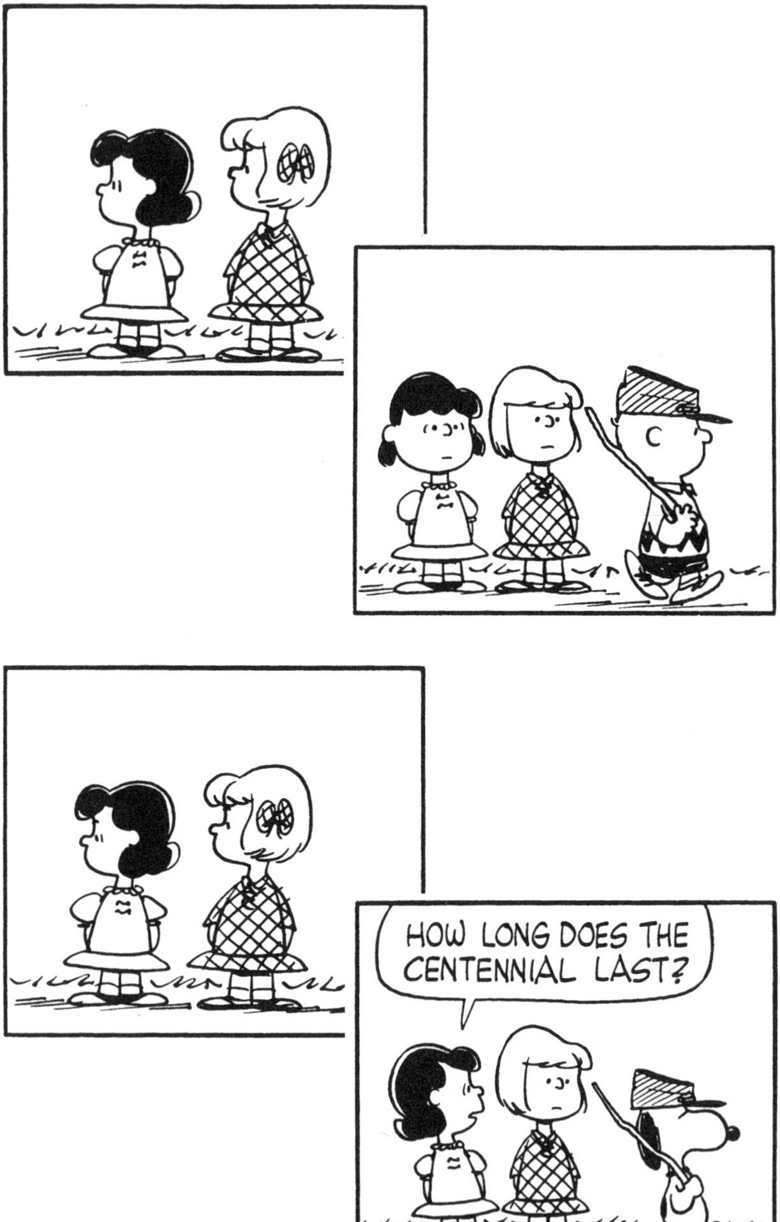
HOW LONG DOES THE CENTENNIAL LAST?

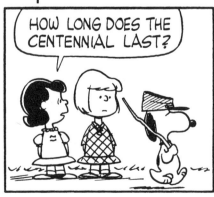

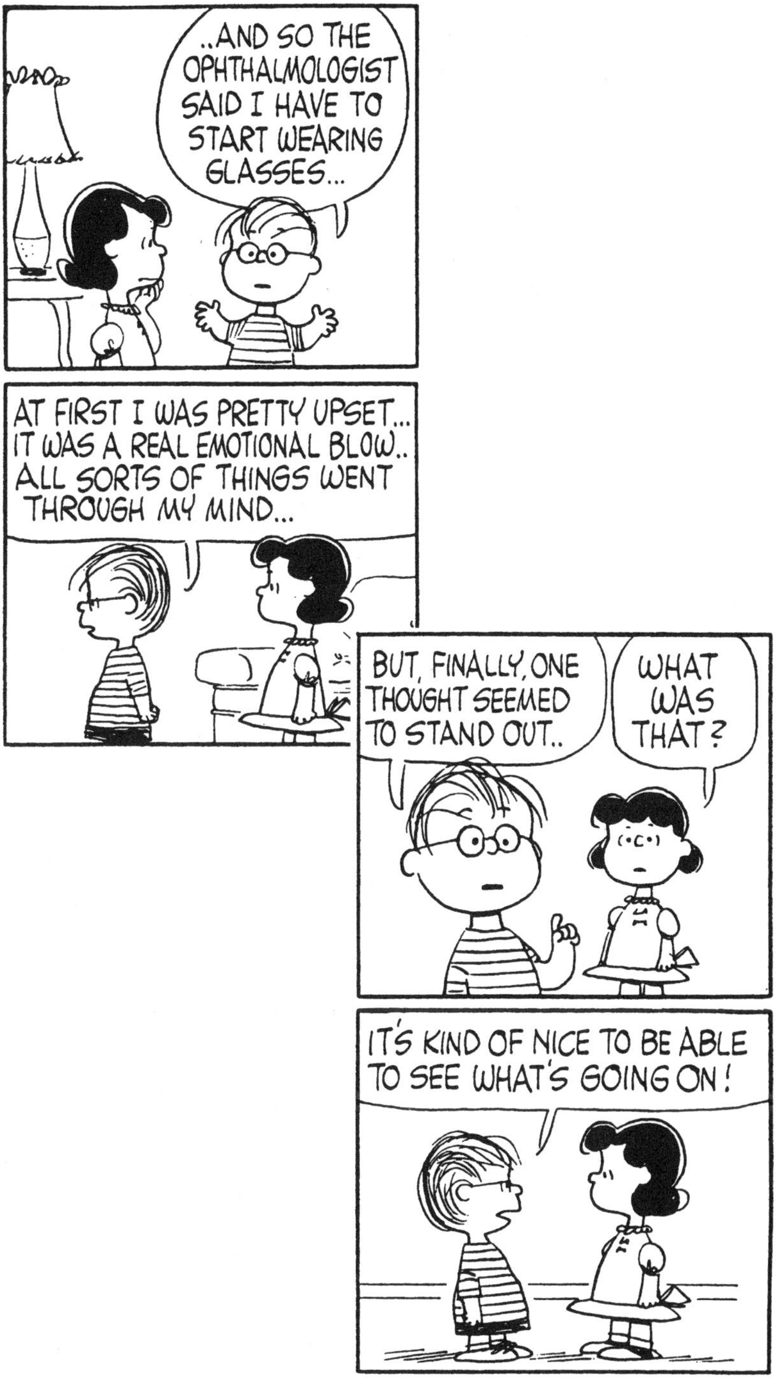
..AND SO THE OPHTHALMOLOGIST SAID I HAVE TO START WEARING GLASSES...
AT FIRST I WAS PRETTY UPSET... IT WAS A REAL EMOTIONAL BLOW.. ALL SORTS OF THINGS WENT THROUGH MY MIND...
BUT, FINALLY, ONE THOUGHT SEEMED TO STAND OUT..
WHAT WAS THAT?
IT'S KIND OF NICE TO BE ABLE TO SEE WHAT'S GOING ON!

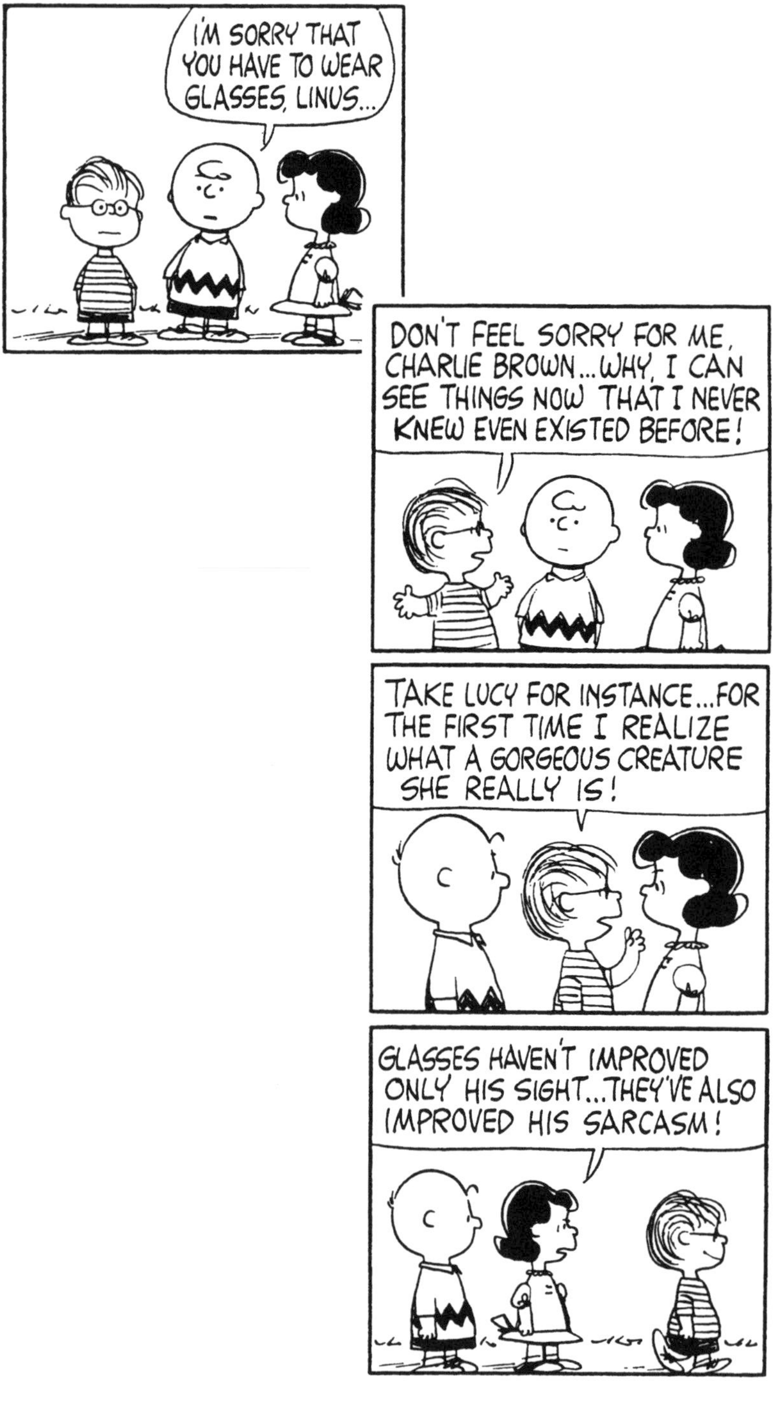
I'M SORRY THAT YOU HAVE TO WEAR GLASSES, LINUS...
DON'T FEEL SORRY FOR ME, CHARLIE BROWN...WHY, I CAN SEE THINGS NOW THAT I NEVER KNEW EVEN EXISTED BEFORE!
TAKE LUCY FOR INSTANCE...FOR THE FIRST TIME I REALIZE WHAT A GORGEOUS CREATURE SHE REALLY IS!
GLASSES HAVEN'T IMPROVED ONLY HIS SIGHT...THEY'VE ALSO IMPROVED HIS SARCASM!

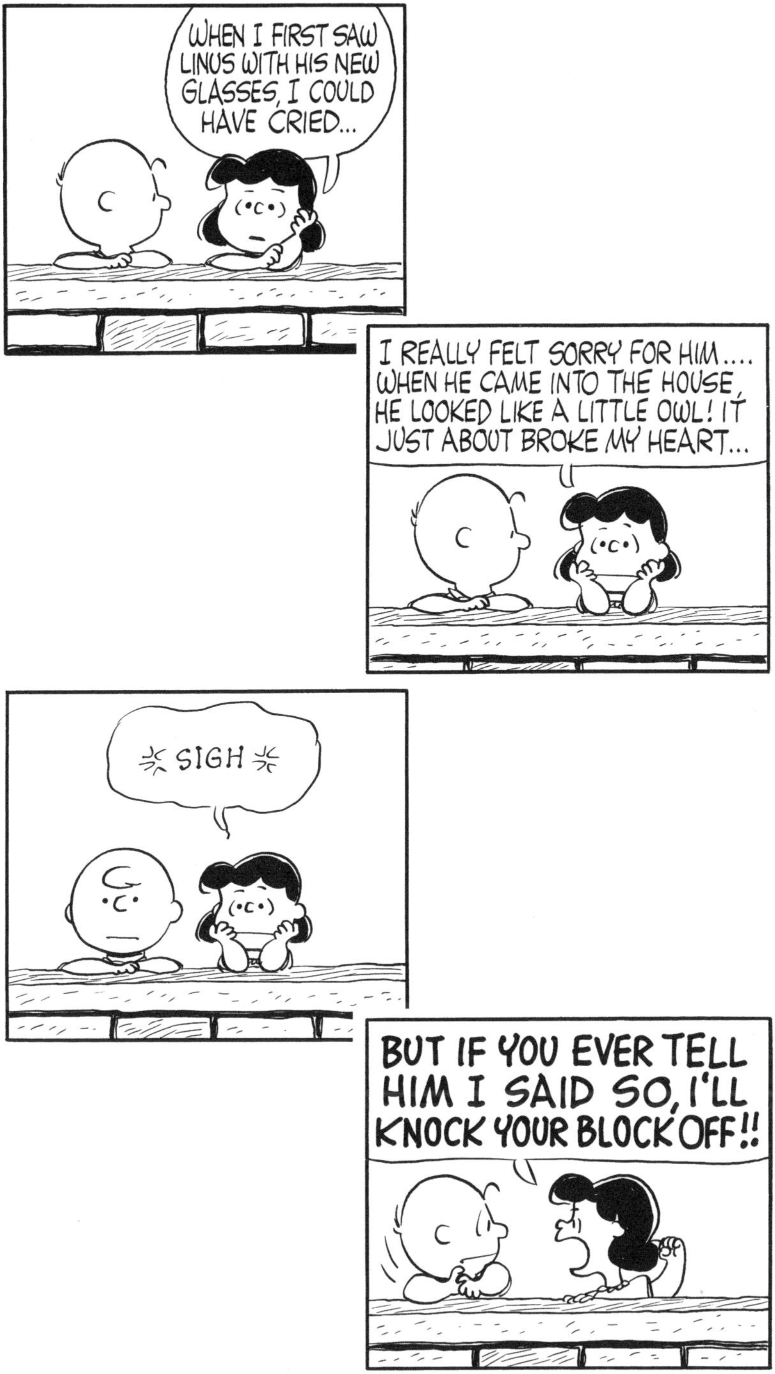
WHEN I FIRST SAW LINUS WITH HIS NEW GLASSES, I COULD HAVE CRIED...
I REALLY FELT SORRY FOR HIM.... WHEN HE CAME INTO THE HOUSE, HE LOOKED LIKE A LITTLE OWL! IT JUST ABOUT BROKE MY HEART...
SIGH
BUT IF YOU EVER TELL HIM I SAID SO, I'LL KNOCK YOUR BLOCK OFF!!

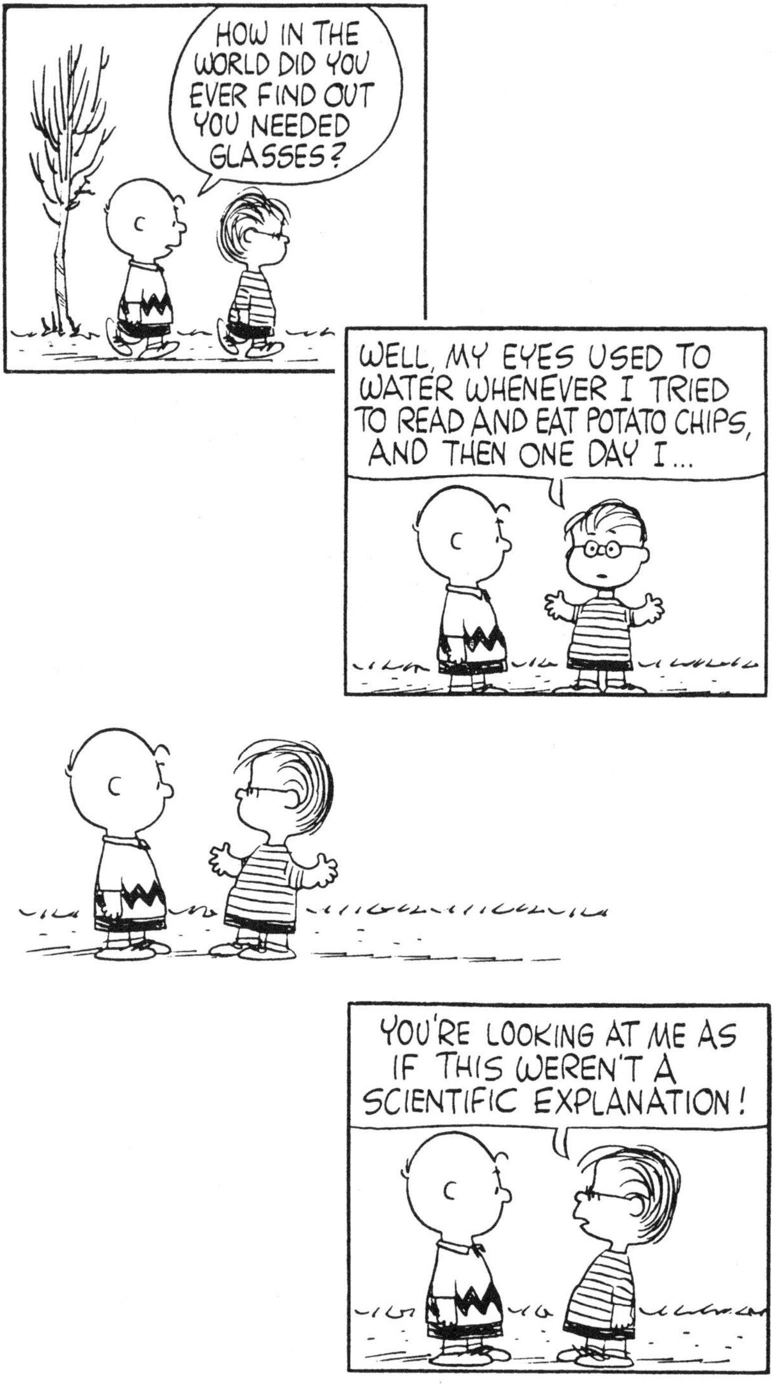
HOW IN THE WORLD DID YOU EVER FIND OUT YOU NEEDED GLASSES?
WELL, MY EYES USED TO WATER WHENEVER I TRIED TO READ AND EAT POTATO CHIPS, AND THEN ONE DAY I...
YOU'RE LOOKING AT ME AS IF THIS WEREN'T A SCIENTIFIC EXPLANATION!

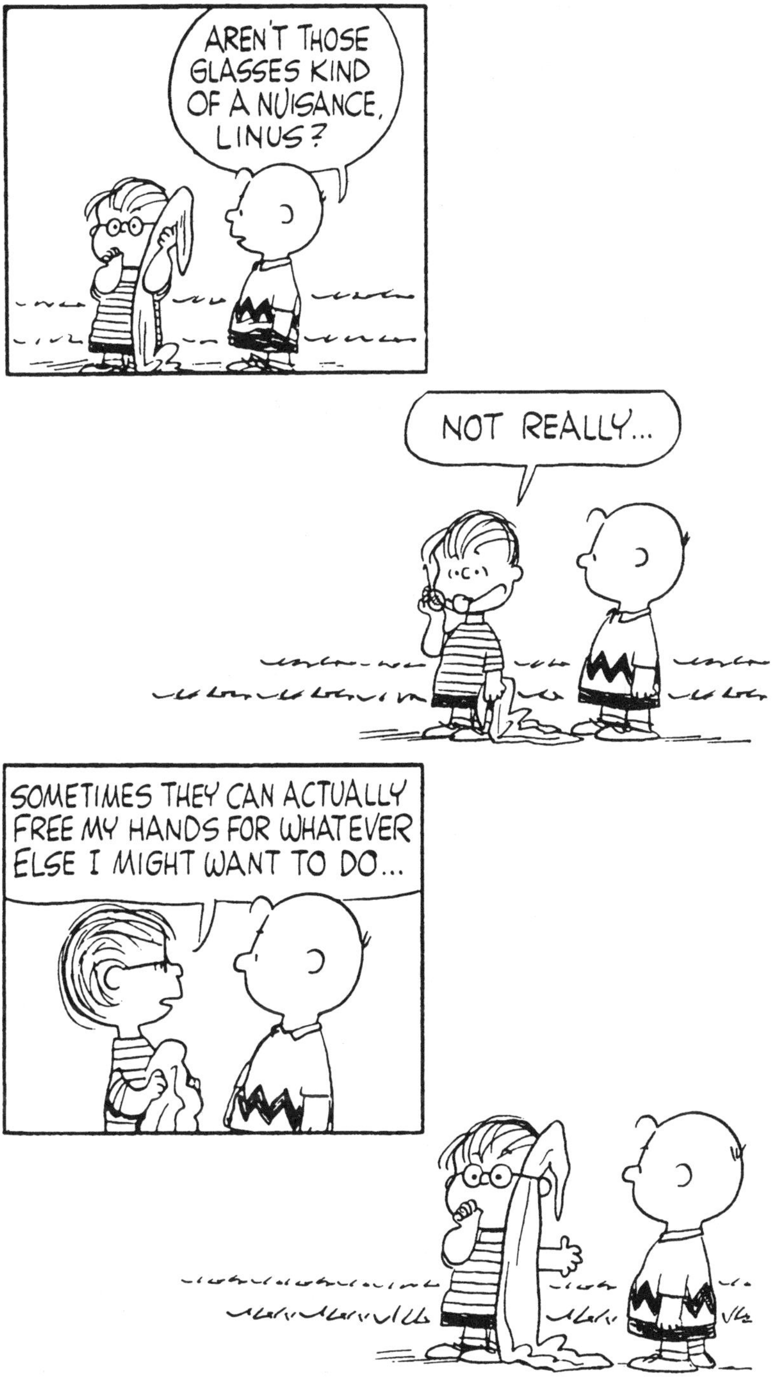
AREN'T THOSE GLASSES KIND OF A NUISANCE, LINUS?
NOT REALLY...
SOMETIMES THEY CAN ACTUALLY FREE MY HANDS FOR WHATEVER ELSE I MIGHT WANT TO DO...

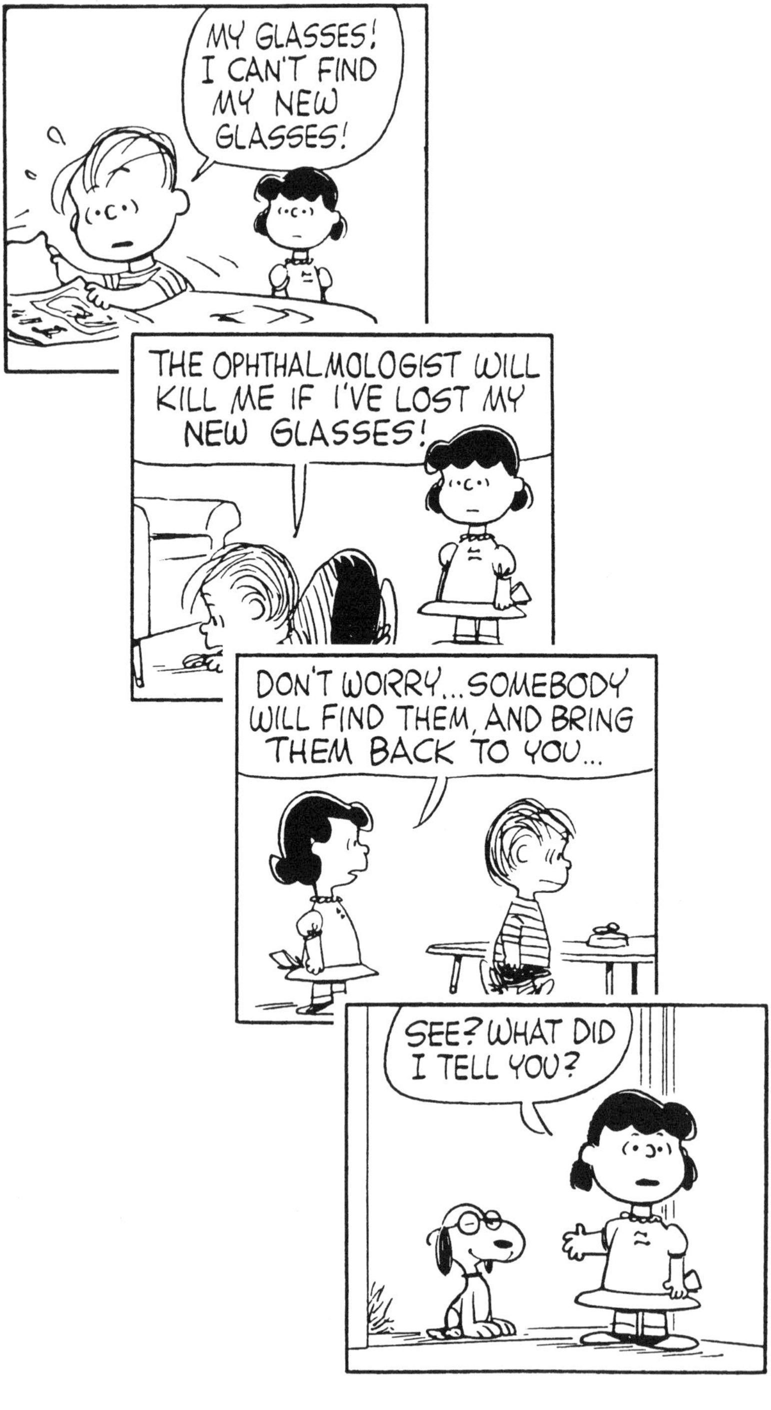
MY GLASSES! I CAN'T FIND MY NEW GLASSES!
THE OPHTHALMOLOGIST WILL KILL ME IF I'VE LOST MY NEW GLASSES!
DON'T WORRY...SOMEBODY WILL FIND THEM, AND BRING THEM BACK TO YOU...
SEE? WHAT DID I TELL YOU?

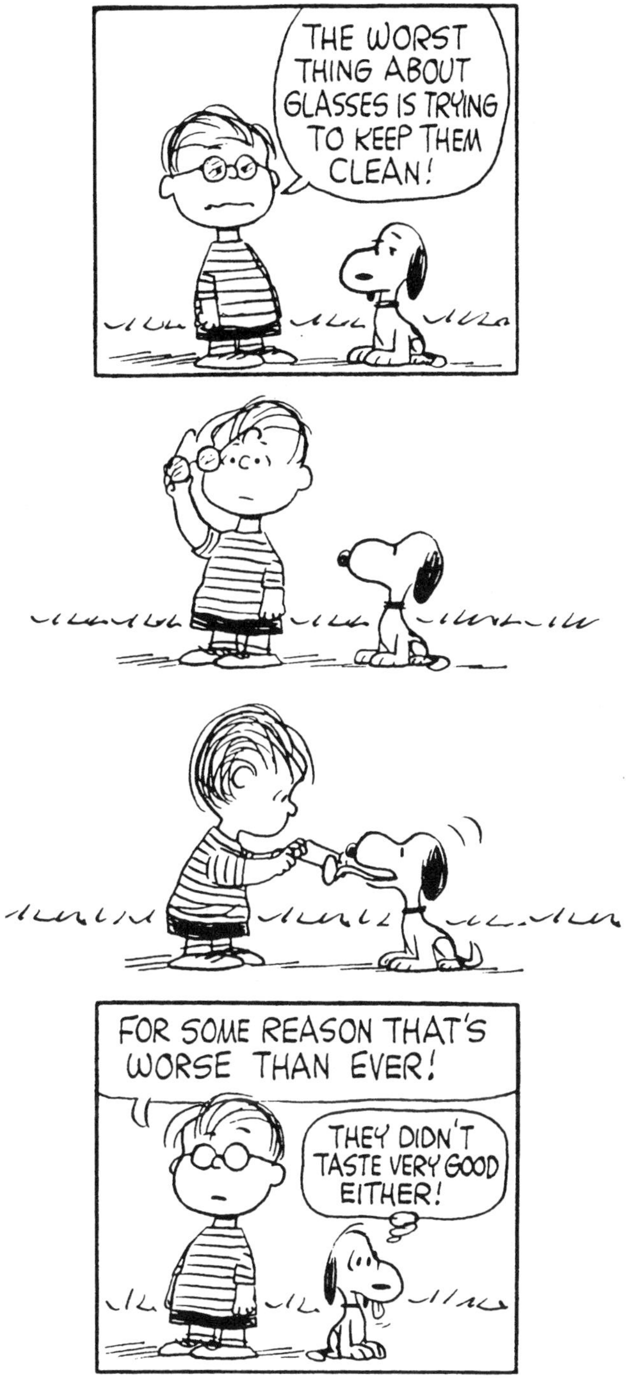
THE WORST THING ABOUT GLASSES IS TRYING TO KEEP THEM CLEAN!
FOR SOME REASON THAT'S WORSE THAN EVER!
THEY DIDN'T TASTE VERY GOOD EITHER!

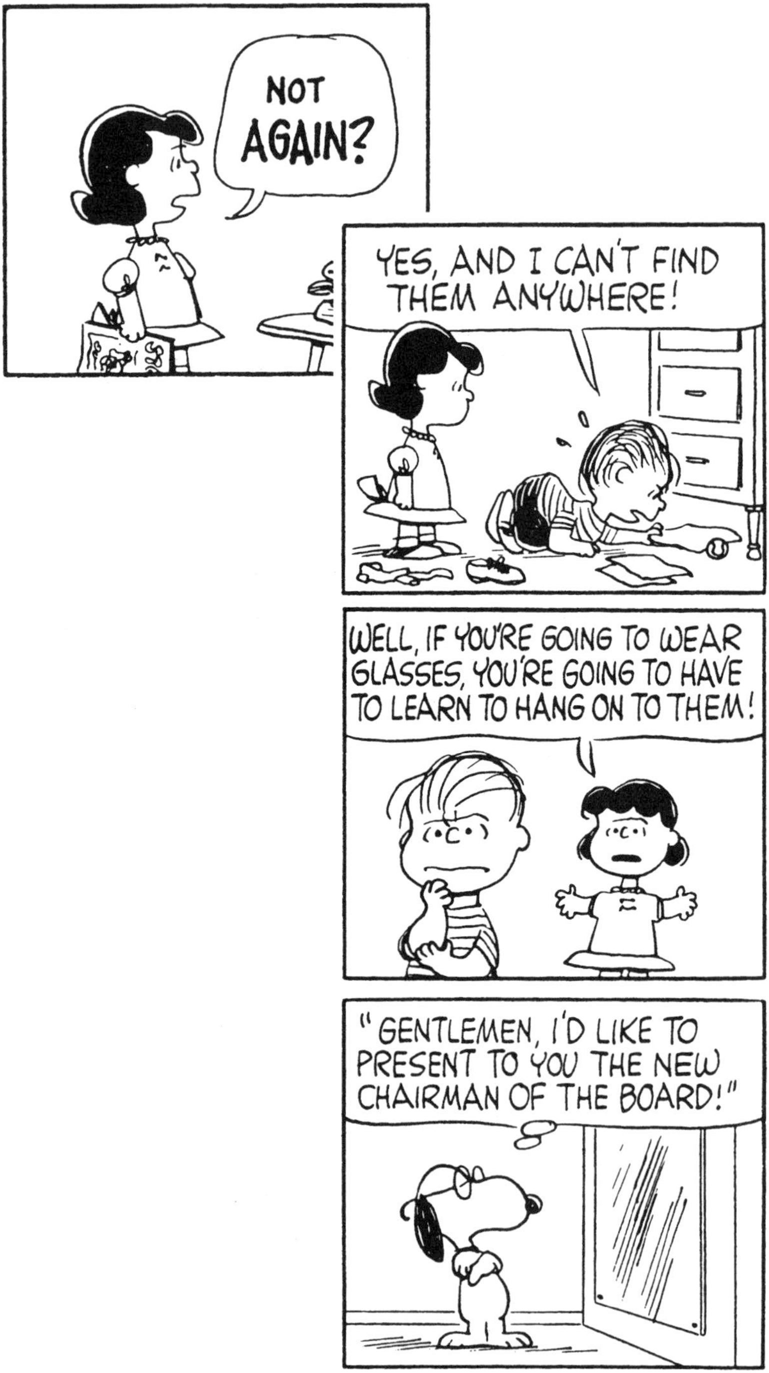
NOT AGAIN?
YES, AND I CAN'T FIND THEM ANYWHERE!
WELL, IF YOU'RE GOING TO WEAR GLASSES, YOU'RE GOING TO HAVE TO LEARN TO HANG ON TO THEM!
"GENTLEMEN, I'D LIKE TO PRESENT TO YOU THE NEW CHAIRMAN OF THE BOARD!"

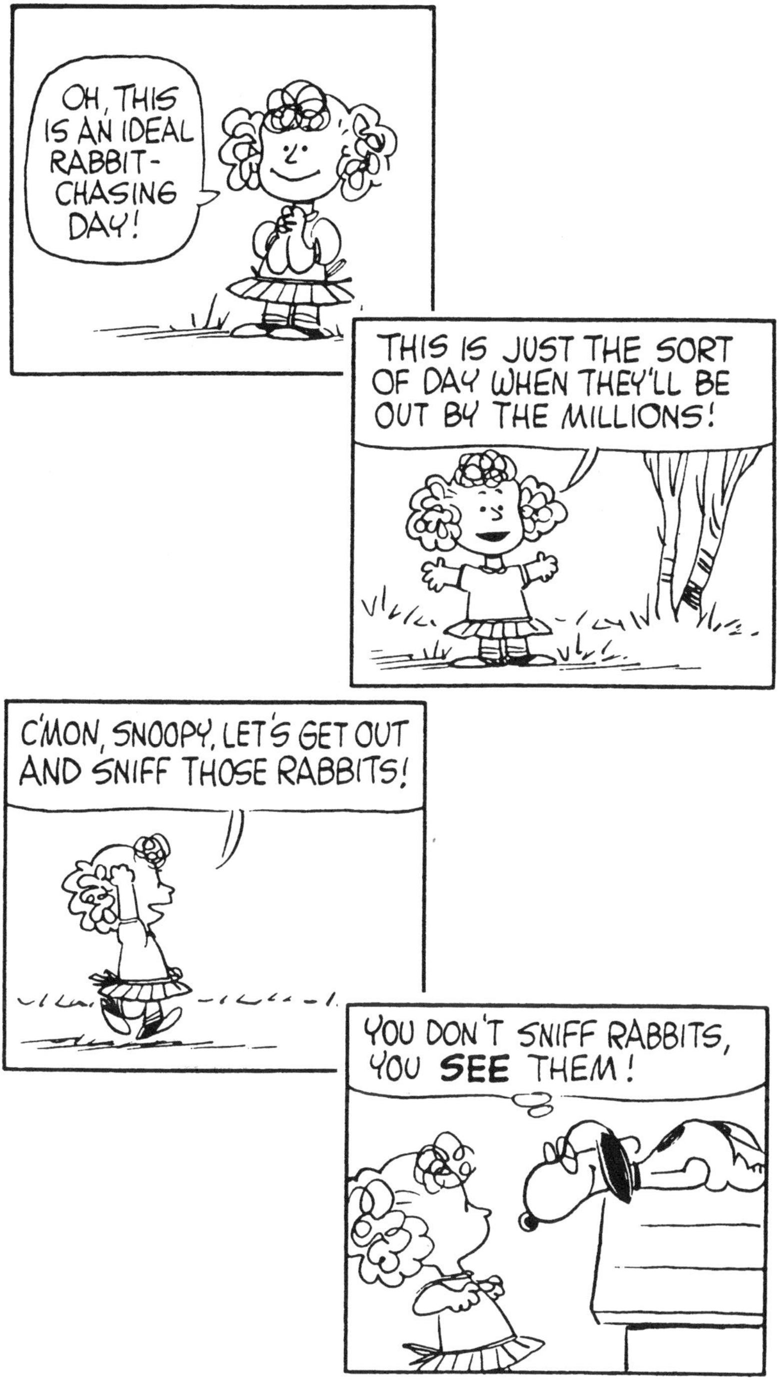
OH, THIS IS AN IDEAL RABBIT-CHASING DAY!
THIS IS JUST THE SORT OF DAY WHEN THEY'LL BE OUT BY THE MILLIONS!
C'MON, SNOOPY, LET'S GET OUT AND SNIFF THOSE RABBITS!
YOU DON'T SNIFF RABBITS, YOU **SEE** THEM!

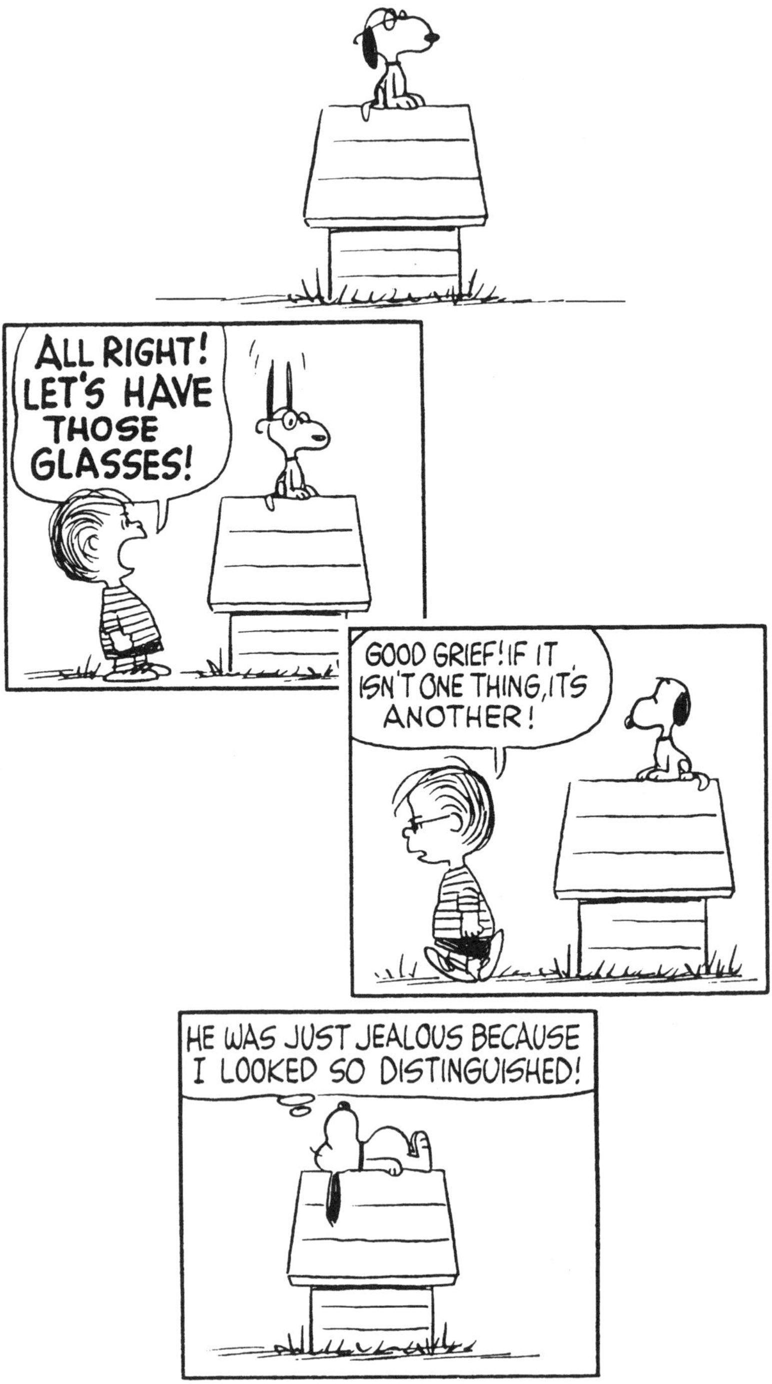
ALL RIGHT! LET'S HAVE THOSE GLASSES!
GOOD GRIEF! IF IT ISN'T ONE THING, IT'S ANOTHER!
HE WAS JUST JEALOUS BECAUSE I LOOKED SO DISTINGUISHED!

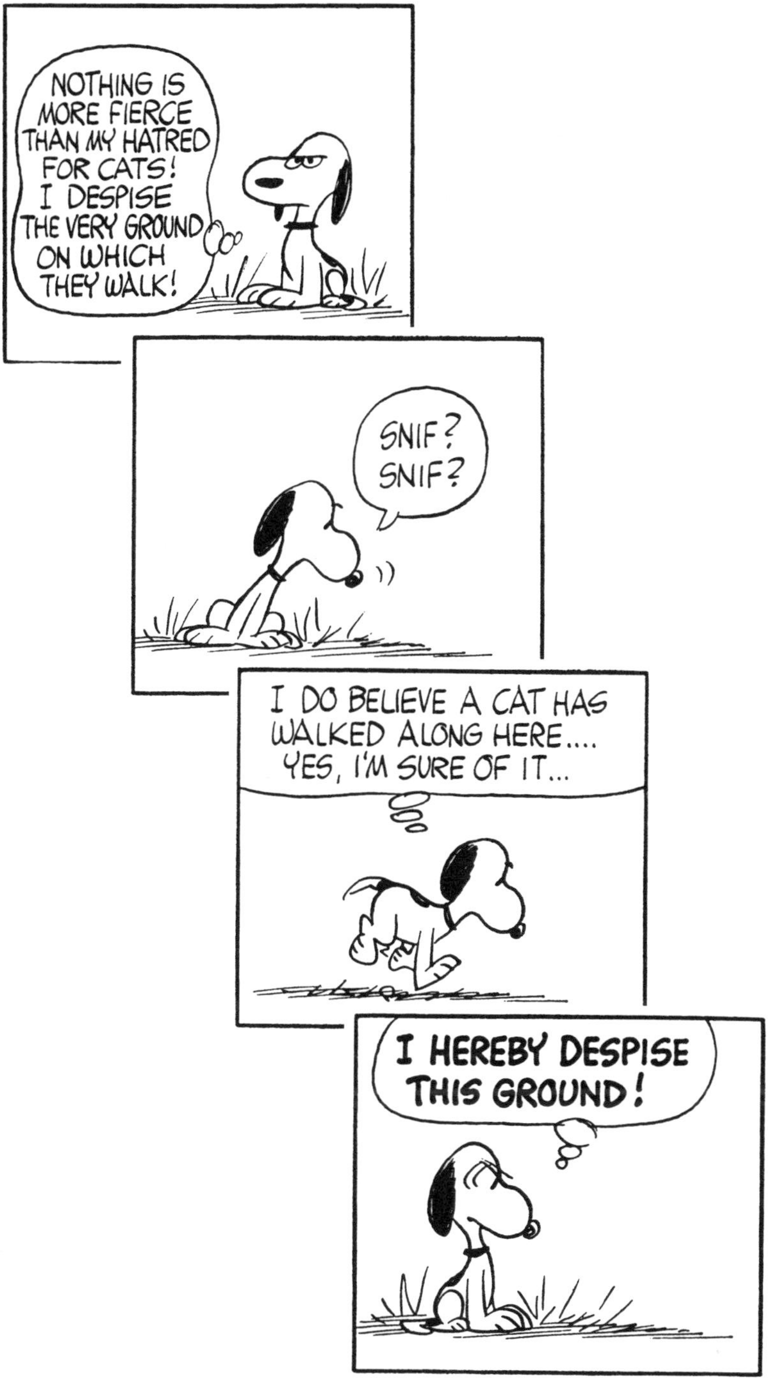
NOTHING IS MORE FIERCE THAN MY HATRED FOR CATS! I DESPISE THE VERY GROUND ON WHICH THEY WALK!
SNIF? SNIF?
I DO BELIEVE A CAT HAS WALKED ALONG HERE.... YES, I'M SURE OF IT...
I HEREBY DESPISE THIS GROUND!

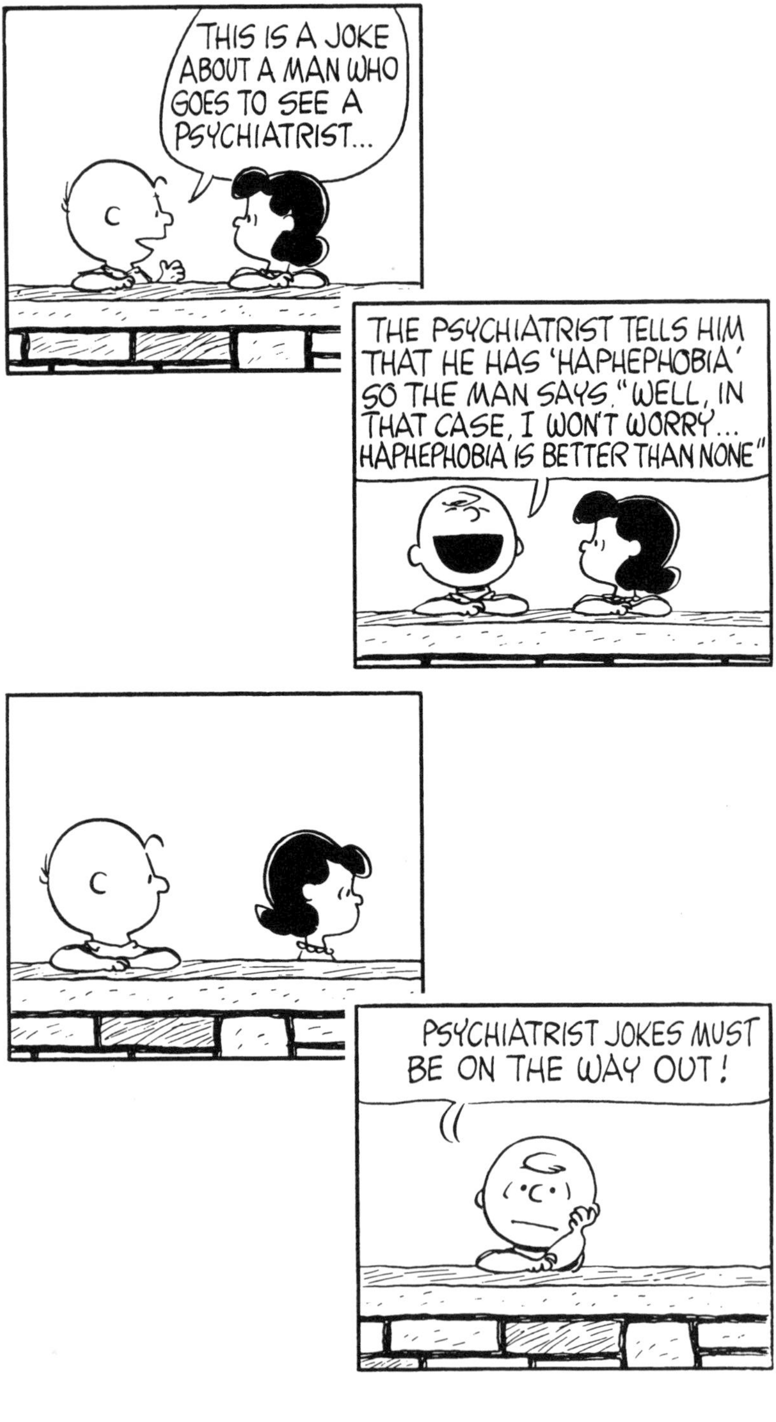
THIS IS A JOKE ABOUT A MAN WHO GOES TO SEE A PSYCHIATRIST...
THE PSYCHIATRIST TELLS HIM THAT HE HAS 'HAPHEPHOBIA' SO THE MAN SAYS, "WELL, IN THAT CASE, I WON'T WORRY... HAPHEPHOBIA IS BETTER THAN NONE"
PSYCHIATRIST JOKES MUST BE ON THE WAY OUT!

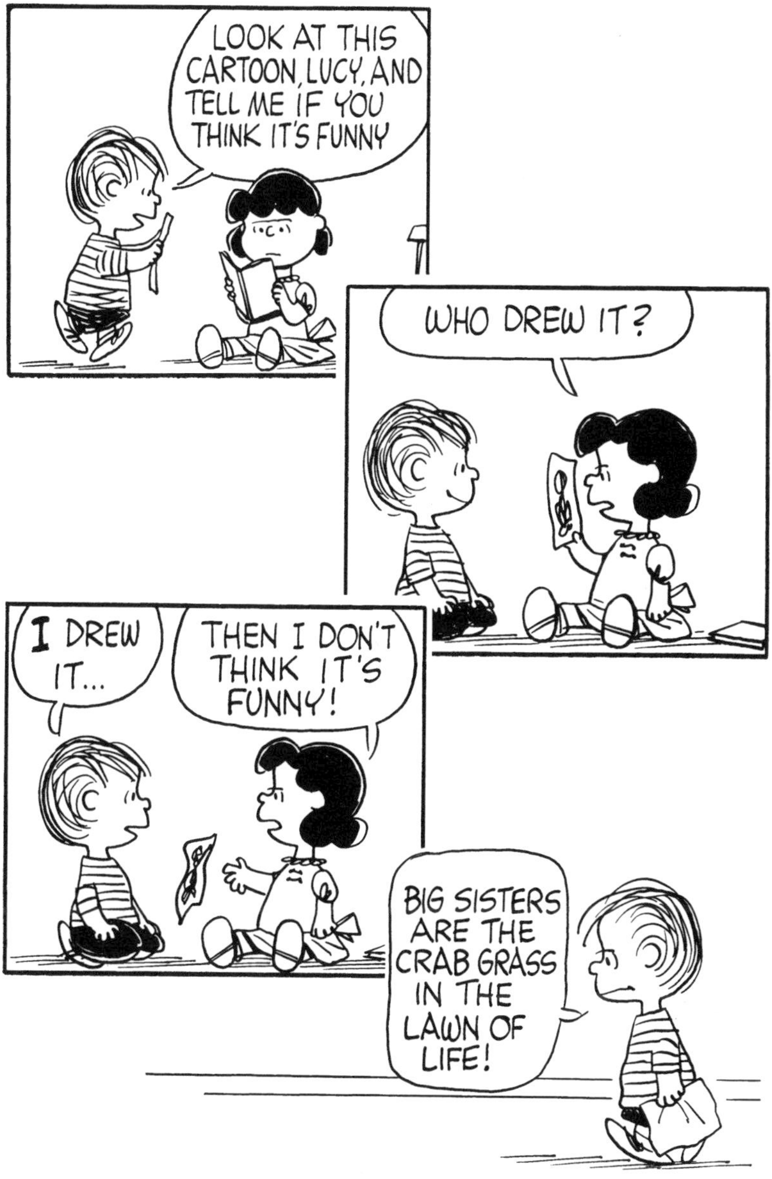
LOOK AT THIS CARTOON, LUCY, AND TELL ME IF YOU THINK IT'S FUNNY
WHO DREW IT?
I DREW IT...
THEN I DON'T THINK IT'S FUNNY!
BIG SISTERS ARE THE CRAB GRASS IN THE LAWN OF LIFE!

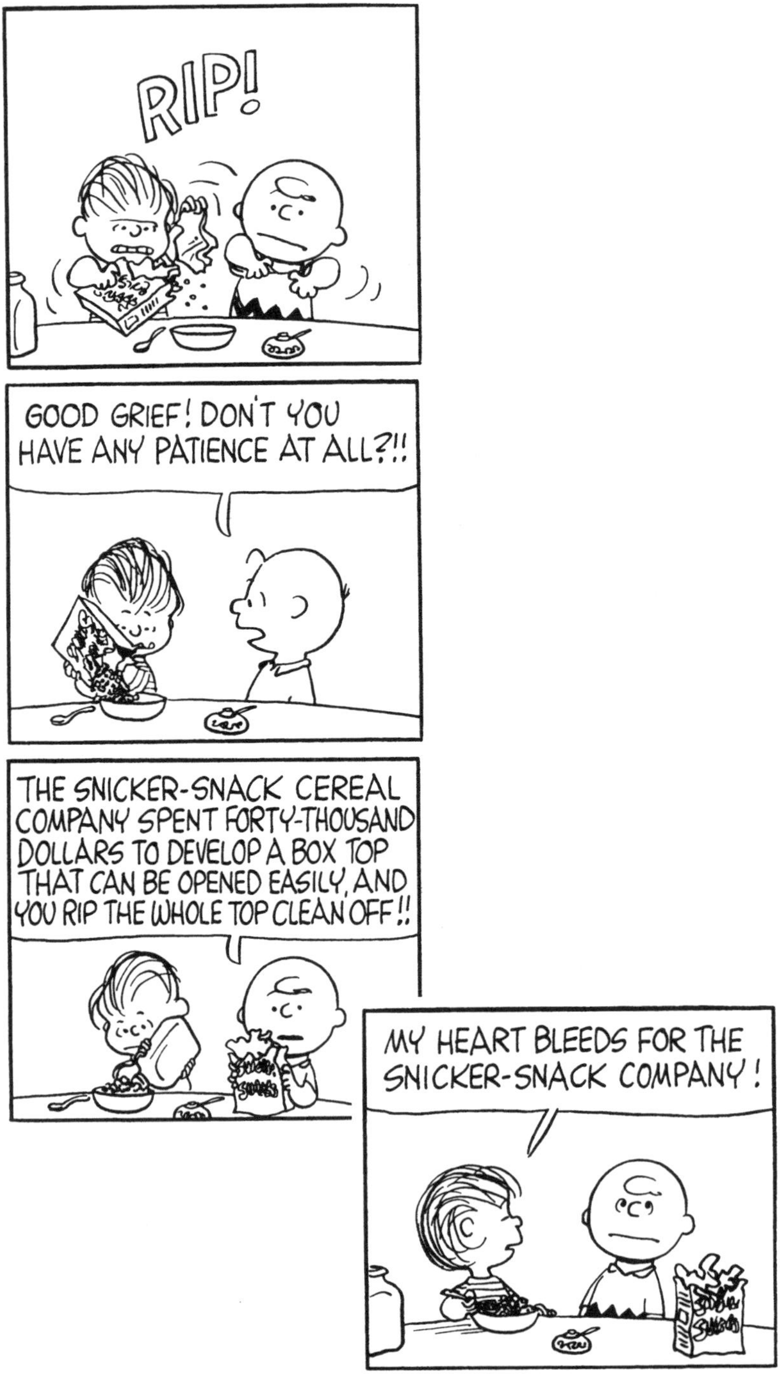
RIP!
GOOD GRIEF! DON'T YOU HAVE ANY PATIENCE AT ALL?!!
THE SNICKER-SNACK CEREAL COMPANY SPENT FORTY-THOUSAND DOLLARS TO DEVELOP A BOX TOP THAT CAN BE OPENED EASILY, AND YOU RIP THE WHOLE TOP CLEAN OFF!!
MY HEART BLEEDS FOR THE SNICKER-SNACK COMPANY!

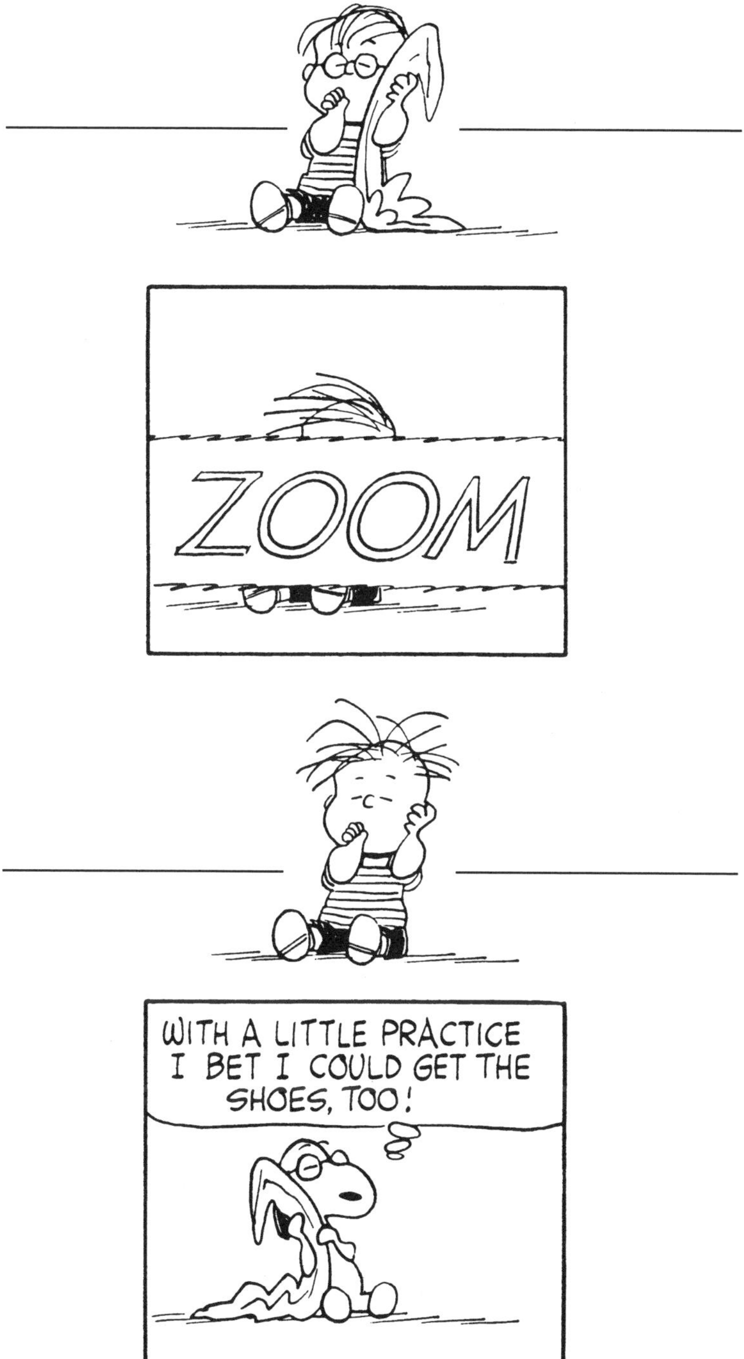
ZOOM
WITH A LITTLE PRACTICE I BET I COULD GET THE SHOES, TOO!

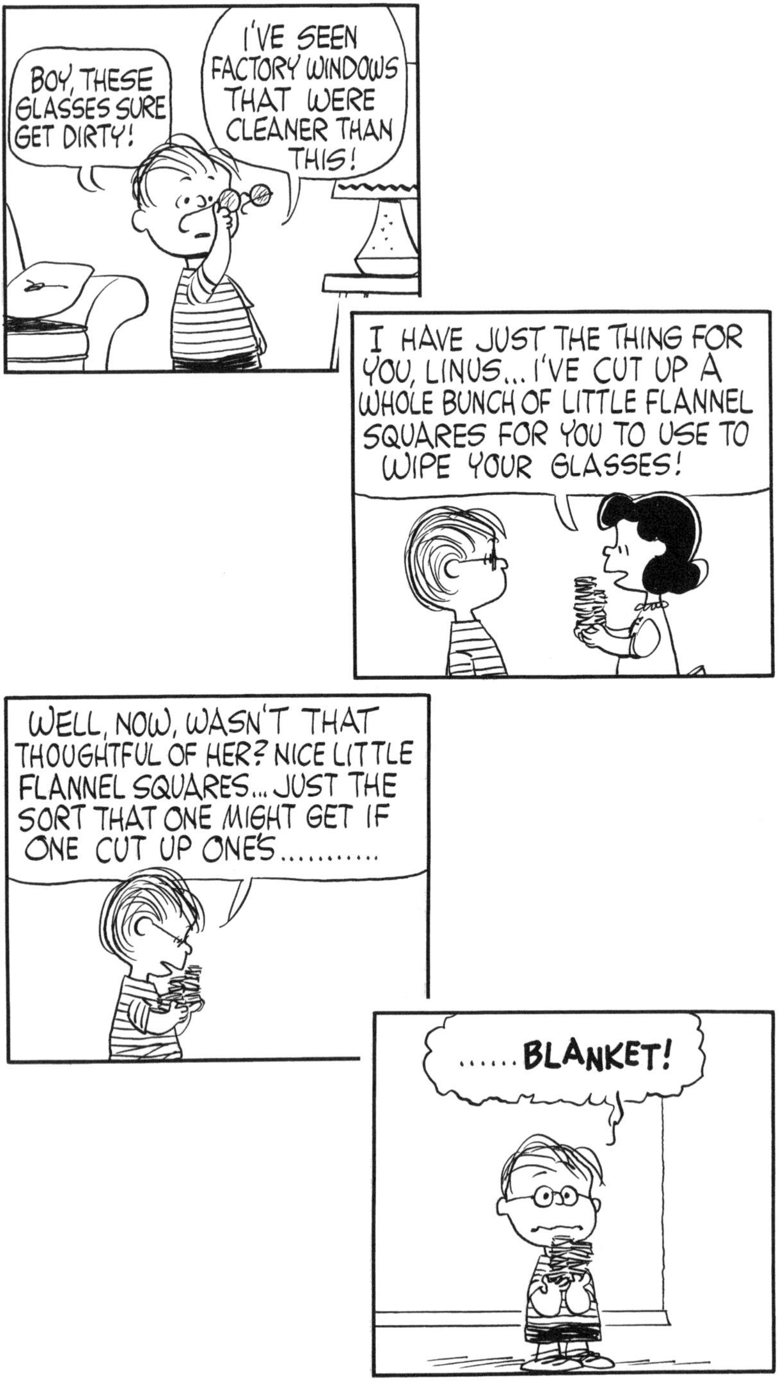
BOY, THESE GLASSES SURE GET DIRTY!
I'VE SEEN FACTORY WINDOWS THAT WERE CLEANER THAN THIS!
I HAVE JUST THE THING FOR YOU, LINUS... I'VE CUT UP A WHOLE BUNCH OF LITTLE FLANNEL SQUARES FOR YOU TO USE TO WIPE YOUR GLASSES!
WELL, NOW, WASN'T THAT THOUGHTFUL OF HER? NICE LITTLE FLANNEL SQUARES... JUST THE SORT THAT ONE MIGHT GET IF ONE CUT UP ONE'S..........
......BLANKET!

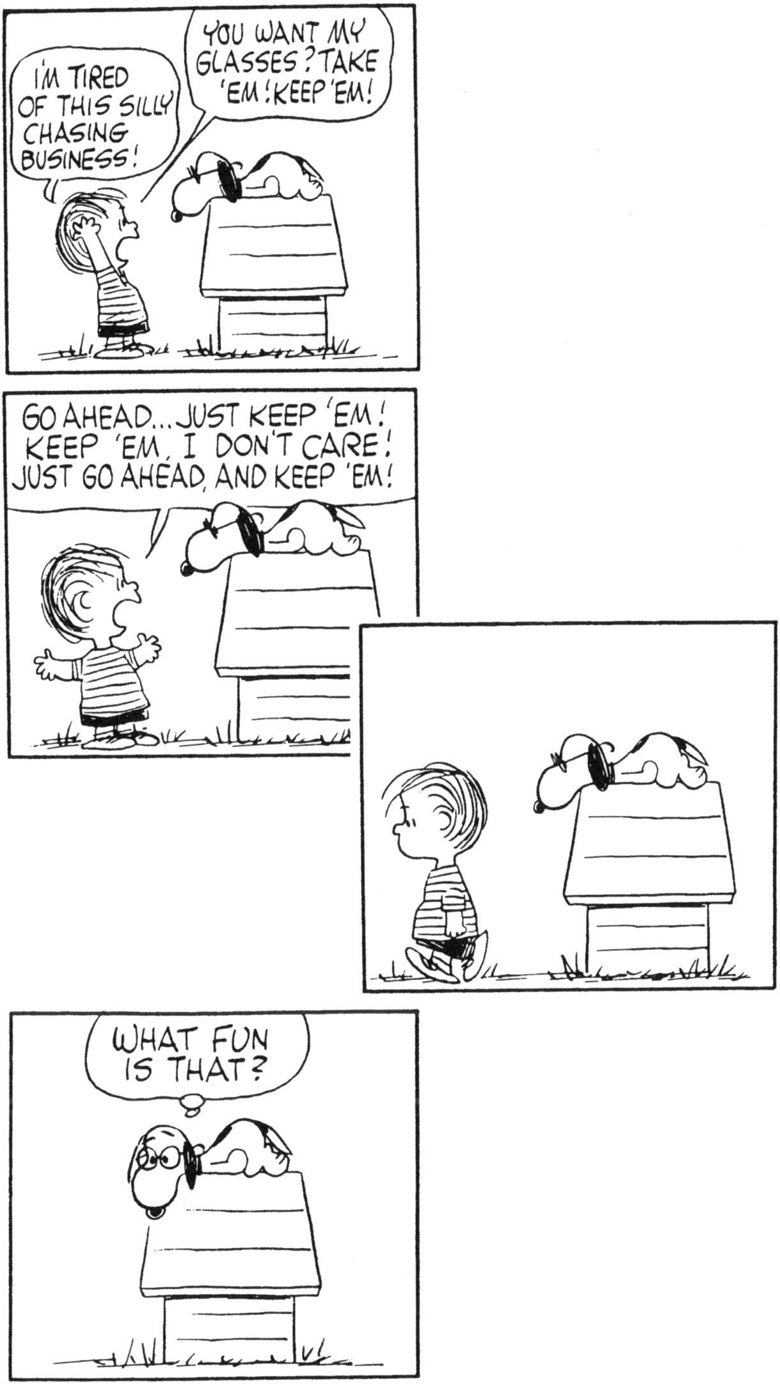
I'M TIRED OF THIS SILLY CHASING BUSINESS!
YOU WANT MY GLASSES? TAKE 'EM! KEEP 'EM!
GO AHEAD... JUST KEEP 'EM! KEEP 'EM, I DON'T CARE! JUST GO AHEAD, AND KEEP 'EM!
WHAT FUN IS THAT?

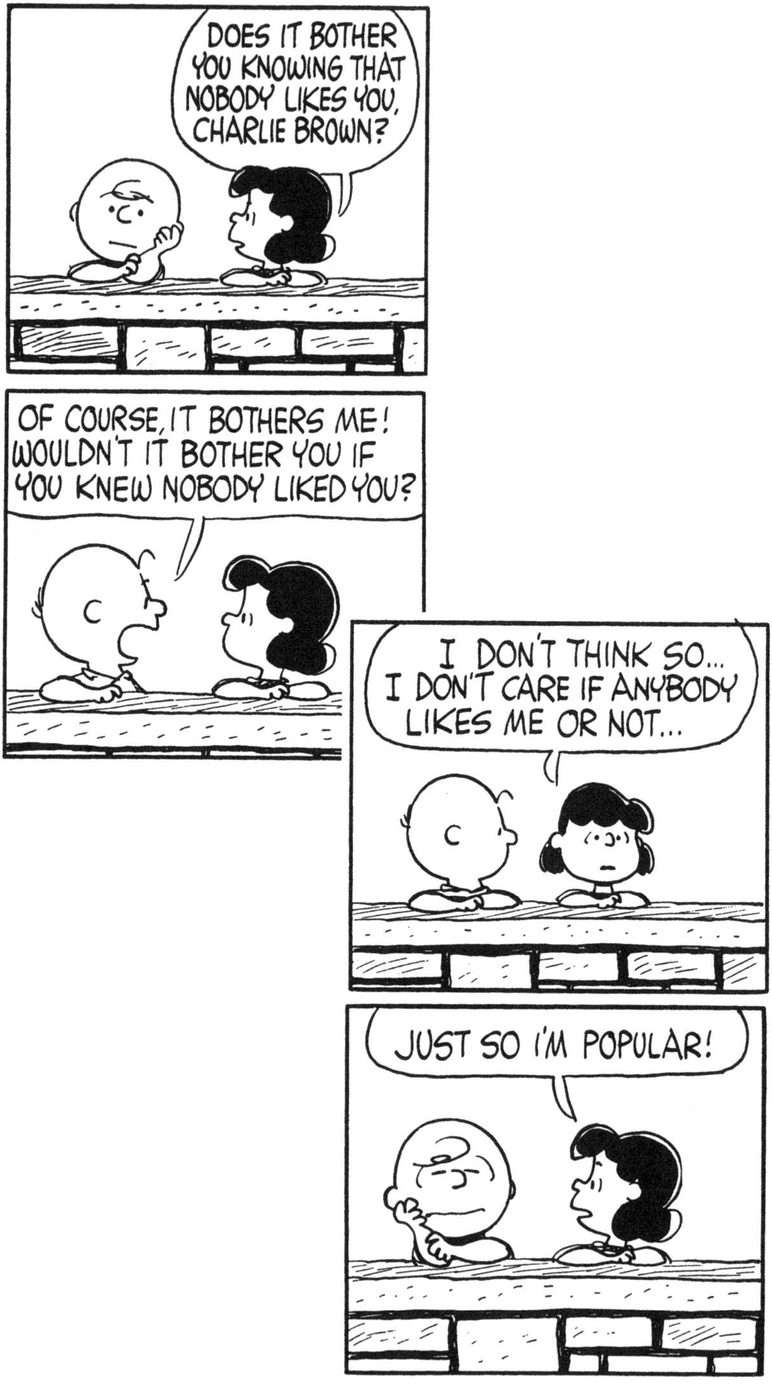
DOES IT BOTHER YOU KNOWING THAT NOBODY LIKES YOU, CHARLIE BROWN?
OF COURSE, IT BOTHERS ME! WOULDN'T IT BOTHER YOU IF YOU KNEW NOBODY LIKED YOU?
I DON'T THINK SO... I DON'T CARE IF ANYBODY LIKES ME OR NOT...
JUST SO I'M POPULAR!

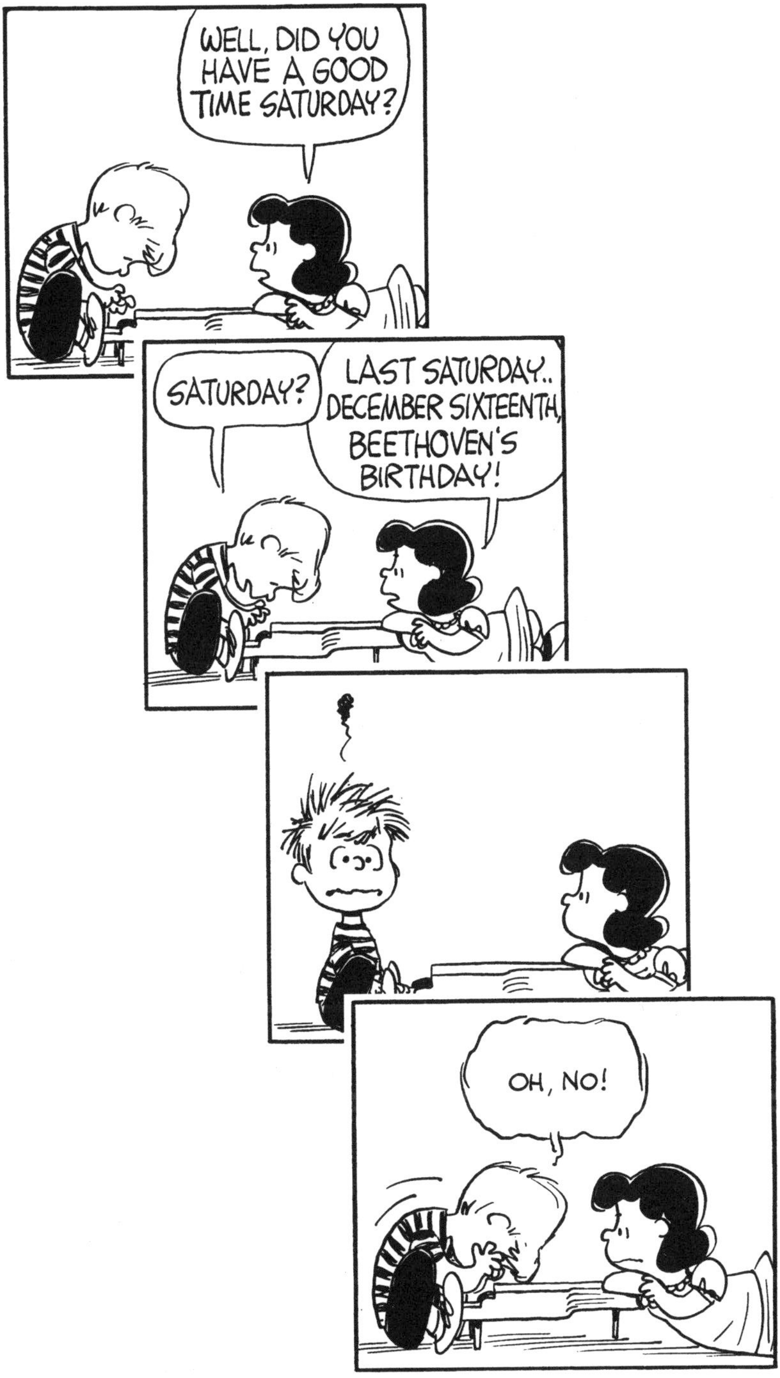

WELL, DID YOU HAVE A GOOD TIME SATURDAY?
SATURDAY?
LAST SATURDAY.. DECEMBER SIXTEENTH, BEETHOVEN'S BIRTHDAY!
OH, NO!

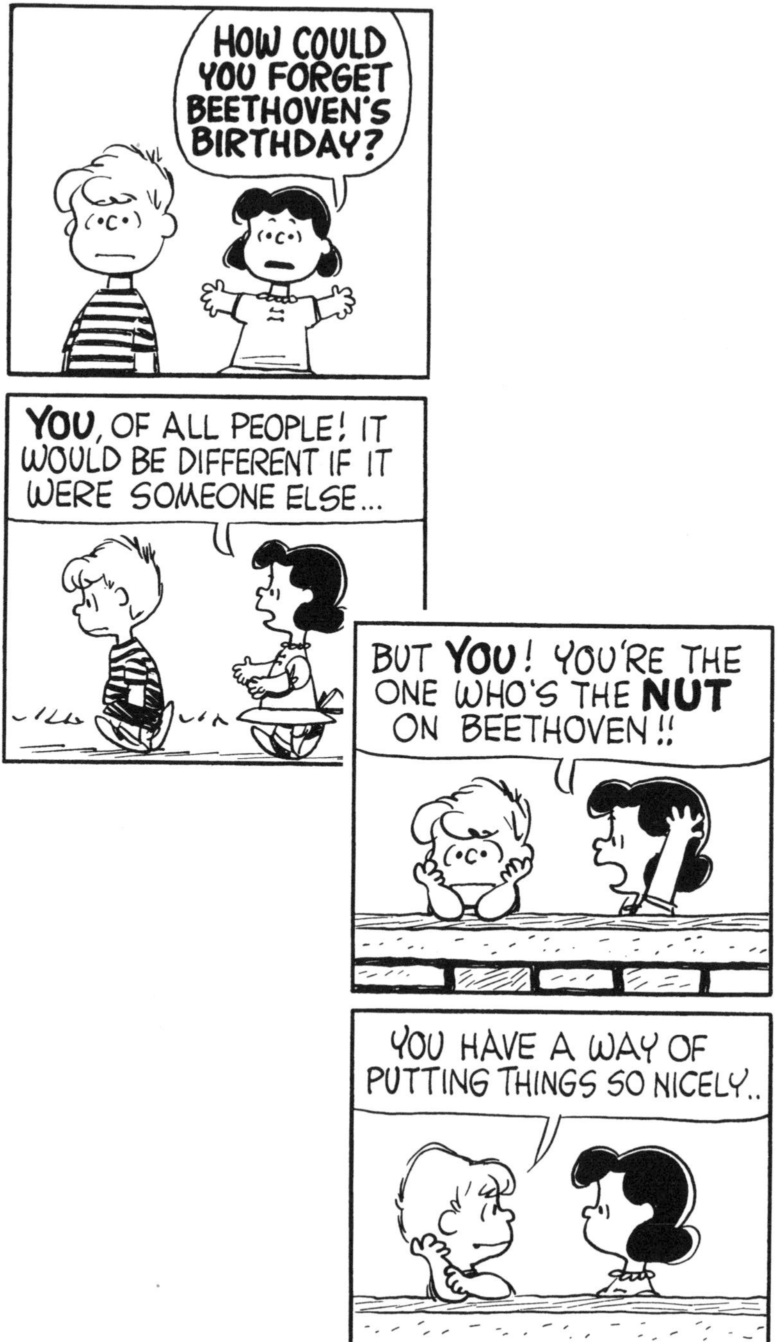
HOW COULD YOU FORGET BEETHOVEN'S BIRTHDAY?
YOU, OF ALL PEOPLE! IT WOULD BE DIFFERENT IF IT WERE SOMEONE ELSE...
BUT YOU! YOU'RE THE ONE WHO'S THE NUT ON BEETHOVEN!!
YOU HAVE A WAY OF PUTTING THINGS SO NICELY..

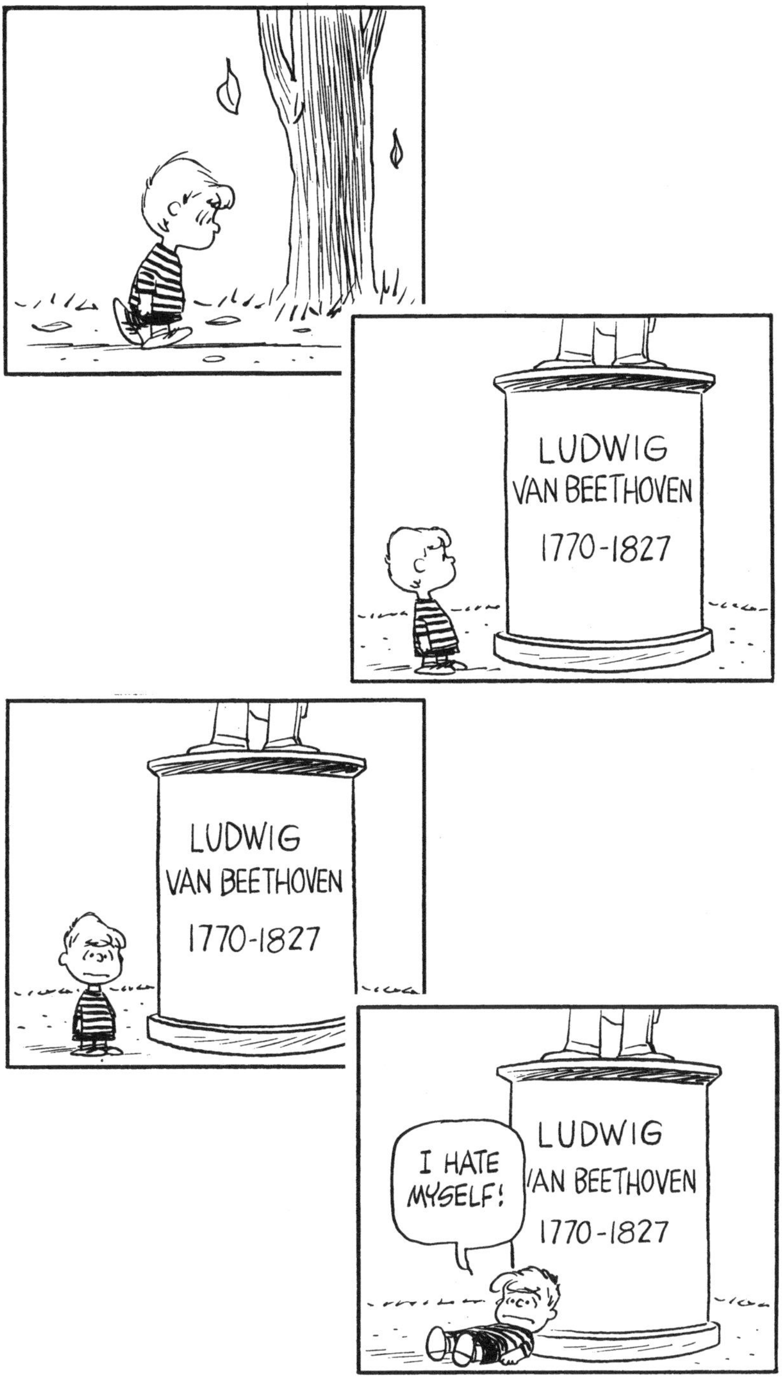

LUDWIG VAN BEETHOVEN 1770-1827
LUDWIG VAN BEETHOVEN 1770-1827
LUDWIG VAN BEETHOVEN 1770-1827
I HATE MYSELF!

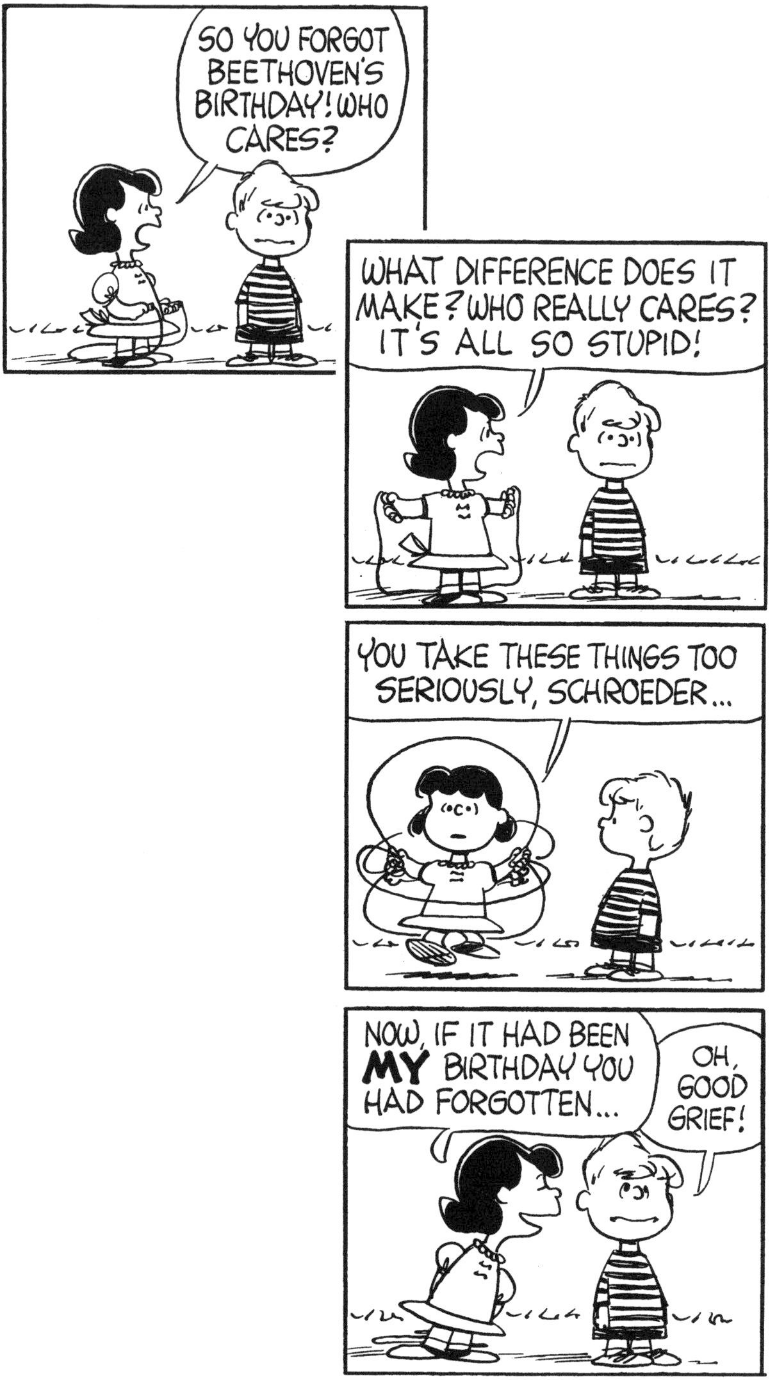
SO YOU FORGOT BEETHOVEN'S BIRTHDAY! WHO CARES?
WHAT DIFFERENCE DOES IT MAKE? WHO REALLY CARES? IT'S ALL SO STUPID!
YOU TAKE THESE THINGS TOO SERIOUSLY, SCHROEDER...
NOW, IF IT HAD BEEN MY BIRTHDAY YOU HAD FORGOTTEN...
OH, GOOD GRIEF!

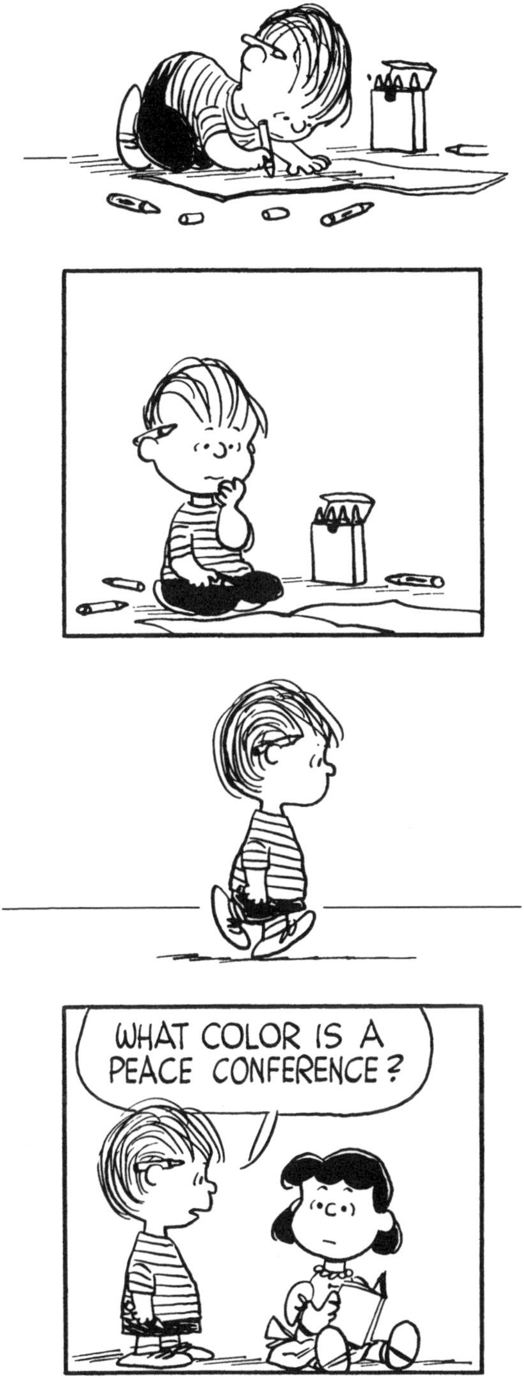
WHAT COLOR IS A PEACE CONFERENCE?

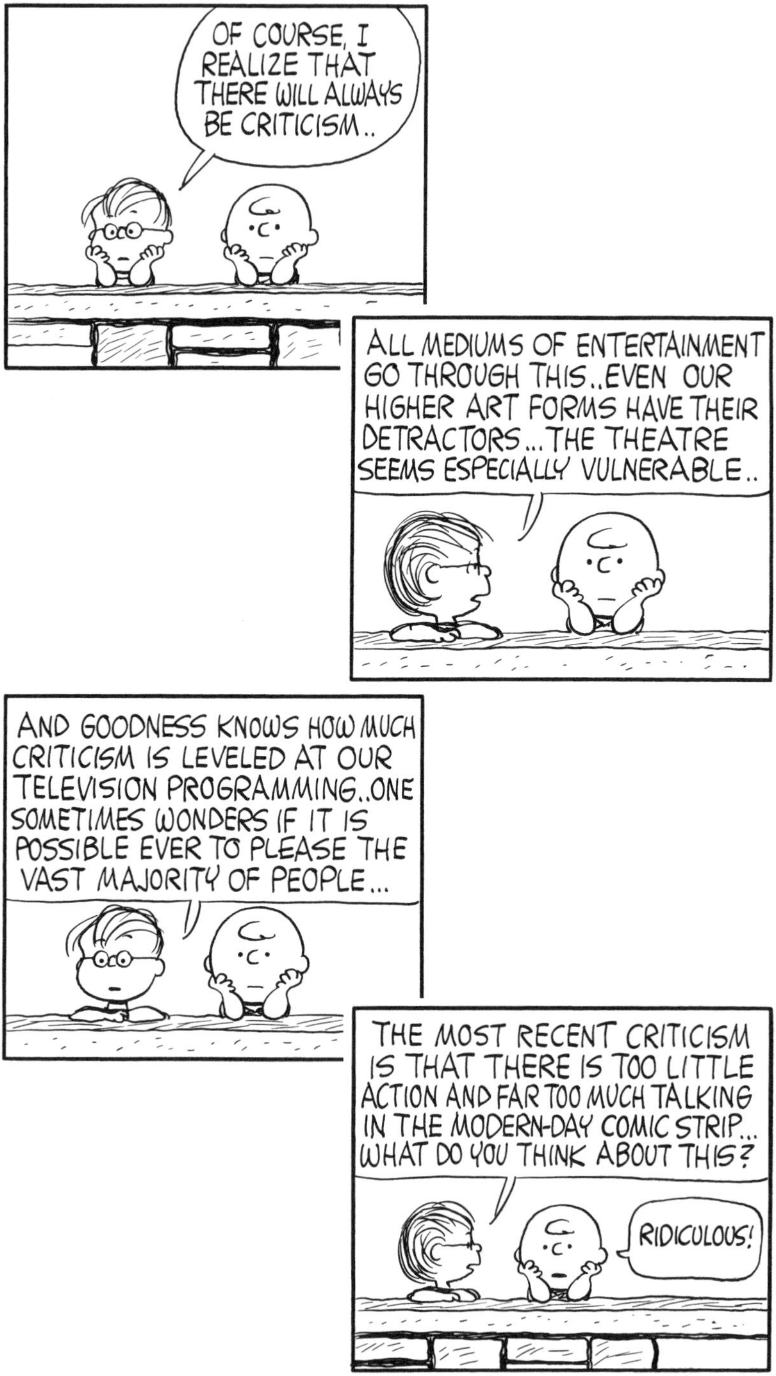
OF COURSE, I REALIZE THAT THERE WILL ALWAYS BE CRITICISM..
ALL MEDIUMS OF ENTERTAINMENT GO THROUGH THIS..EVEN OUR HIGHER ART FORMS HAVE THEIR DETRACTORS...THE THEATRE SEEMS ESPECIALLY VULNERABLE..
AND GOODNESS KNOWS HOW MUCH CRITICISM IS LEVELED AT OUR TELEVISION PROGRAMMING..ONE SOMETIMES WONDERS IF IT IS POSSIBLE EVER TO PLEASE THE VAST MAJORITY OF PEOPLE...
THE MOST RECENT CRITICISM IS THAT THERE IS TOO LITTLE ACTION AND FAR TOO MUCH TALKING IN THE MODERN-DAY COMIC STRIP... WHAT DO YOU THINK ABOUT THIS?
RIDICULOUS!

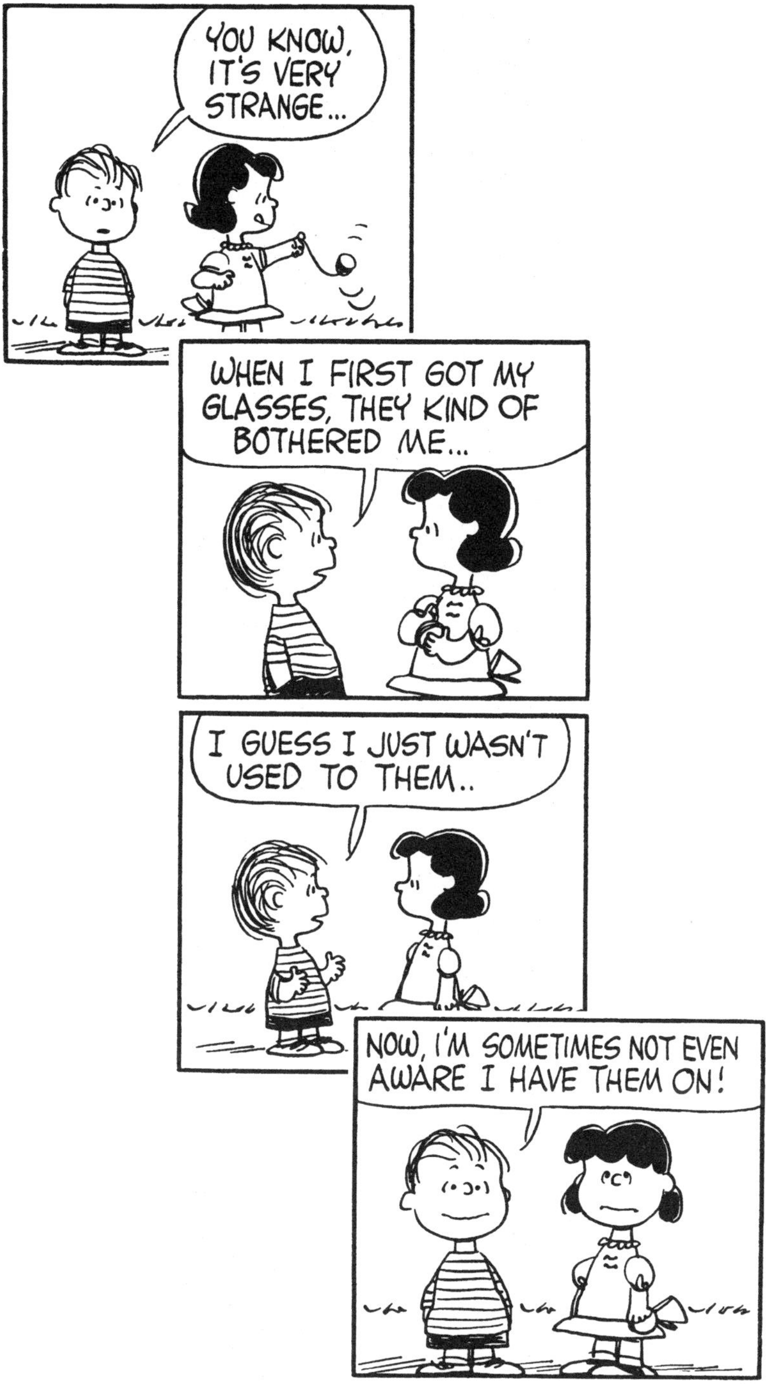
YOU KNOW, IT'S VERY STRANGE...
WHEN I FIRST GOT MY GLASSES, THEY KIND OF BOTHERED ME...
I GUESS I JUST WASN'T USED TO THEM..
NOW, I'M SOMETIMES NOT EVEN AWARE I HAVE THEM ON!

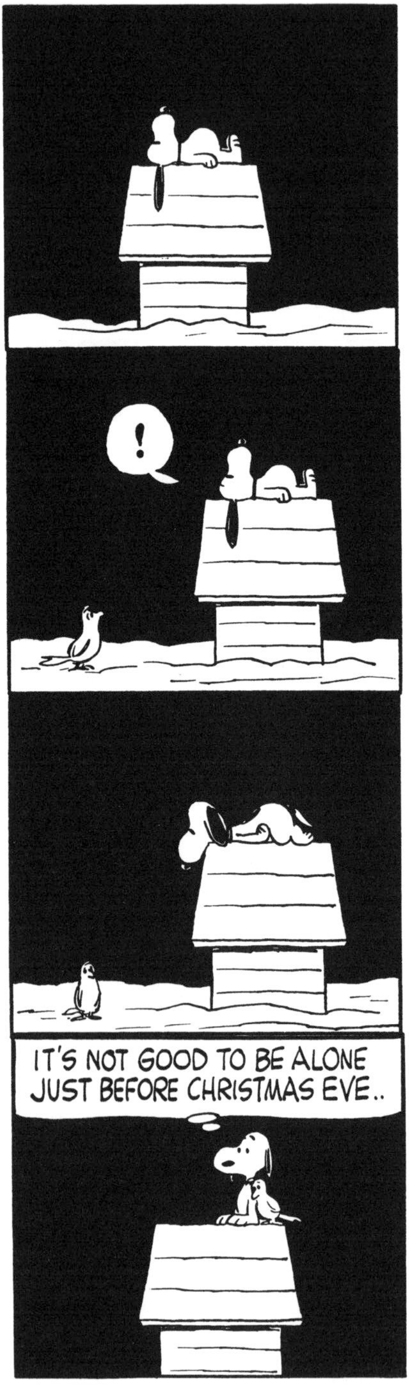
!
IT'S NOT GOOD TO BE ALONE JUST BEFORE CHRISTMAS EVE..

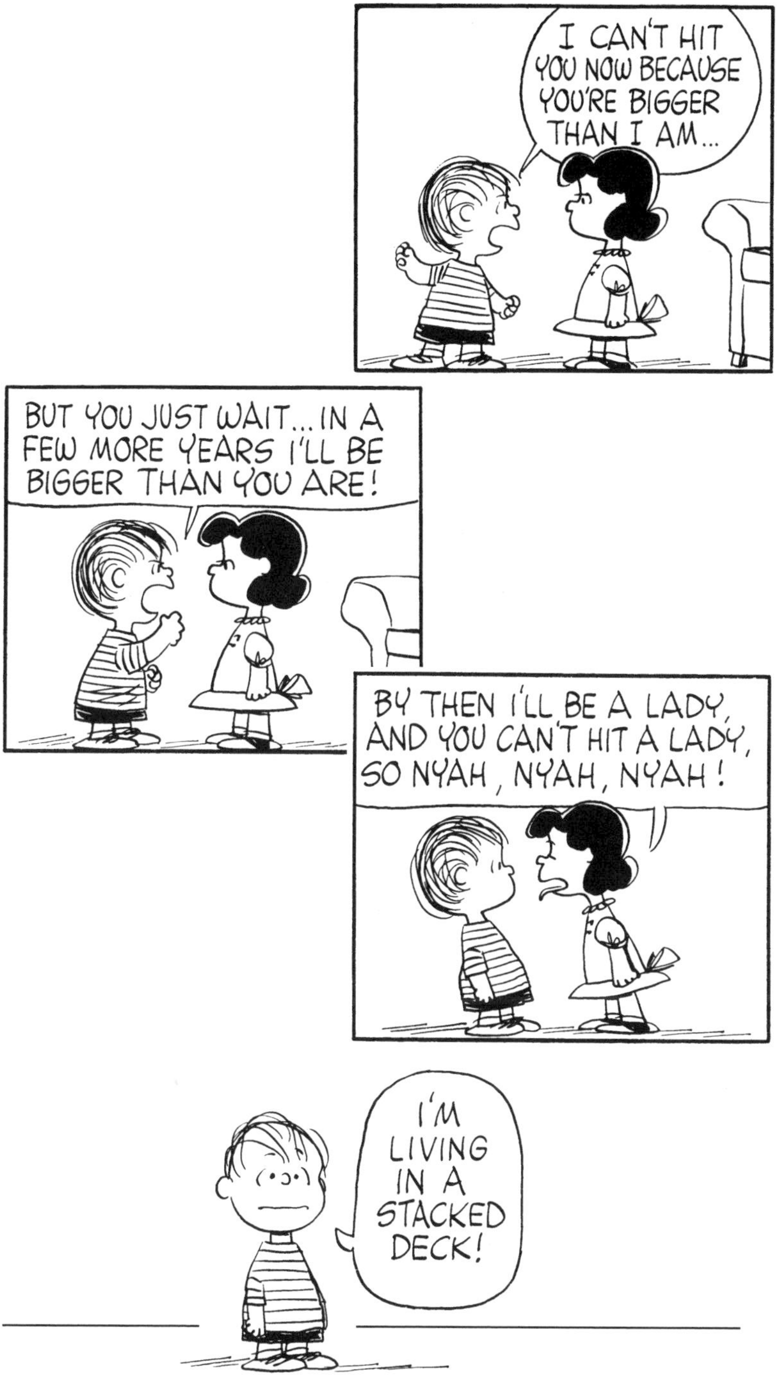
I CAN'T HIT YOU NOW BECAUSE YOU'RE BIGGER THAN I AM...
BUT YOU JUST WAIT...IN A FEW MORE YEARS I'LL BE BIGGER THAN YOU ARE!
BY THEN I'LL BE A LADY, AND YOU CAN'T HIT A LADY, SO NYAH, NYAH, NYAH!
I'M LIVING IN A STACKED DECK!

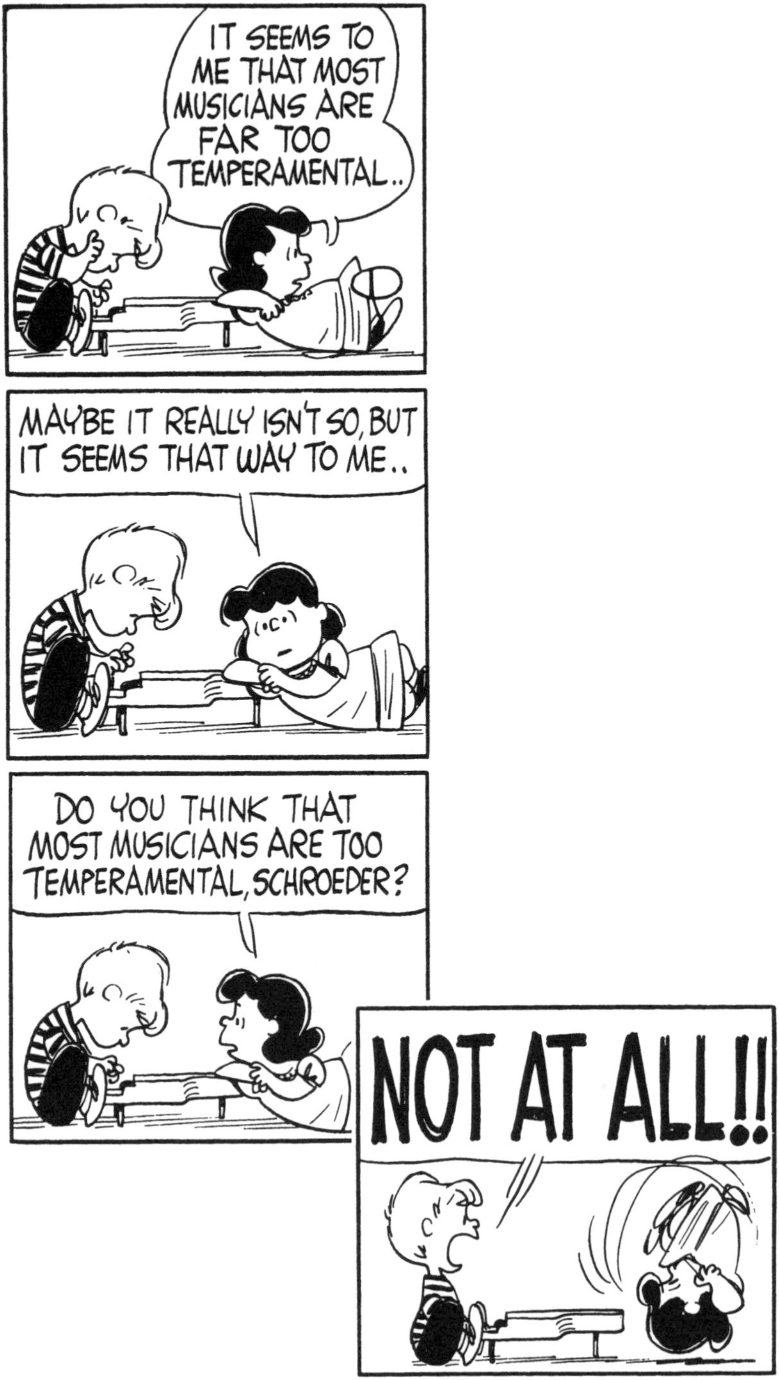
IT SEEMS TO ME THAT MOST MUSICIANS ARE FAR TOO TEMPERAMENTAL..
MAYBE IT REALLY ISN'T SO, BUT IT SEEMS THAT WAY TO ME..
DO YOU THINK THAT MOST MUSICIANS ARE TOO TEMPERAMENTAL, SCHROEDER?
NOT AT ALL!!

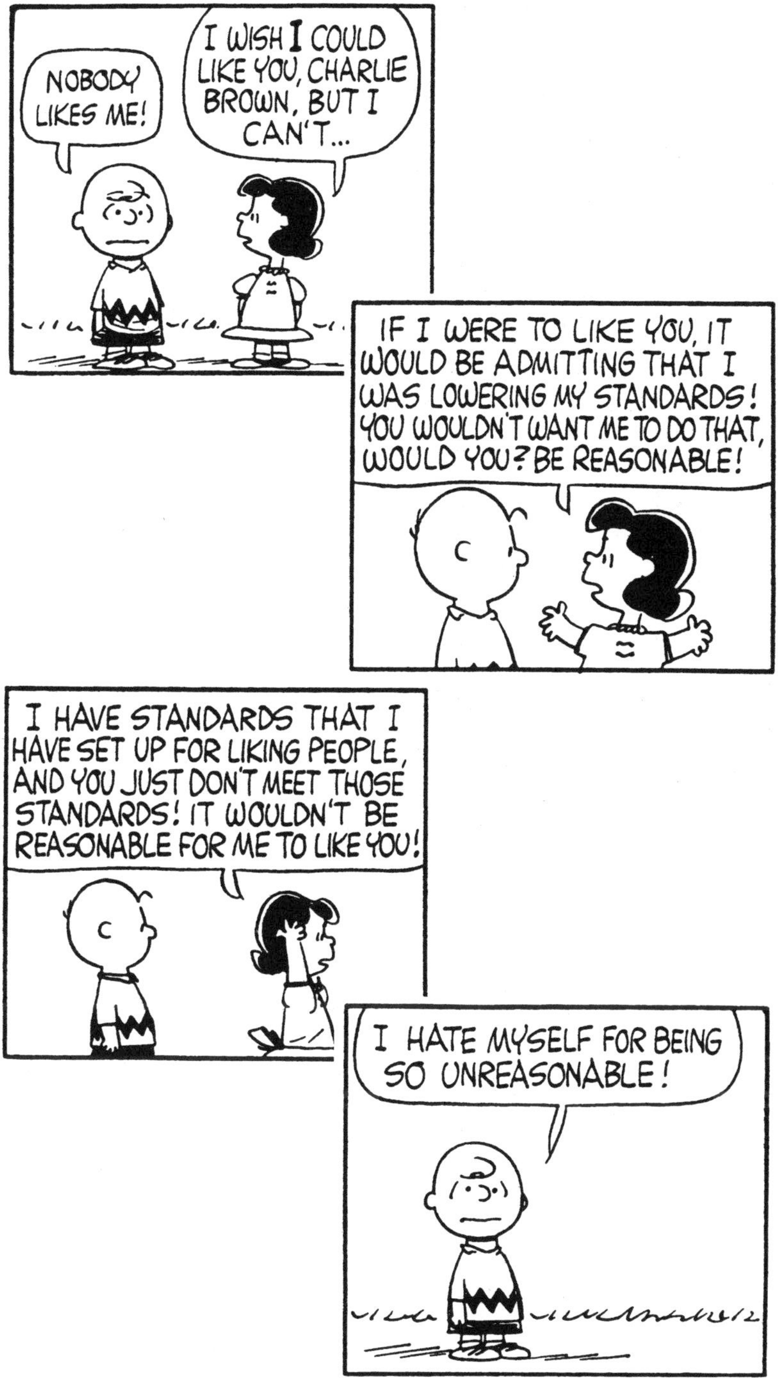
NOBODY LIKES ME!
I WISH I COULD LIKE YOU, CHARLIE BROWN, BUT I CAN'T...
IF I WERE TO LIKE YOU, IT WOULD BE ADMITTING THAT I WAS LOWERING MY STANDARDS! YOU WOULDN'T WANT ME TO DO THAT, WOULD YOU? BE REASONABLE!
I HAVE STANDARDS THAT I HAVE SET UP FOR LIKING PEOPLE, AND YOU JUST DON'T MEET THOSE STANDARDS! IT WOULDN'T BE REASONABLE FOR ME TO LIKE YOU!
I HATE MYSELF FOR BEING SO UNREASONABLE!

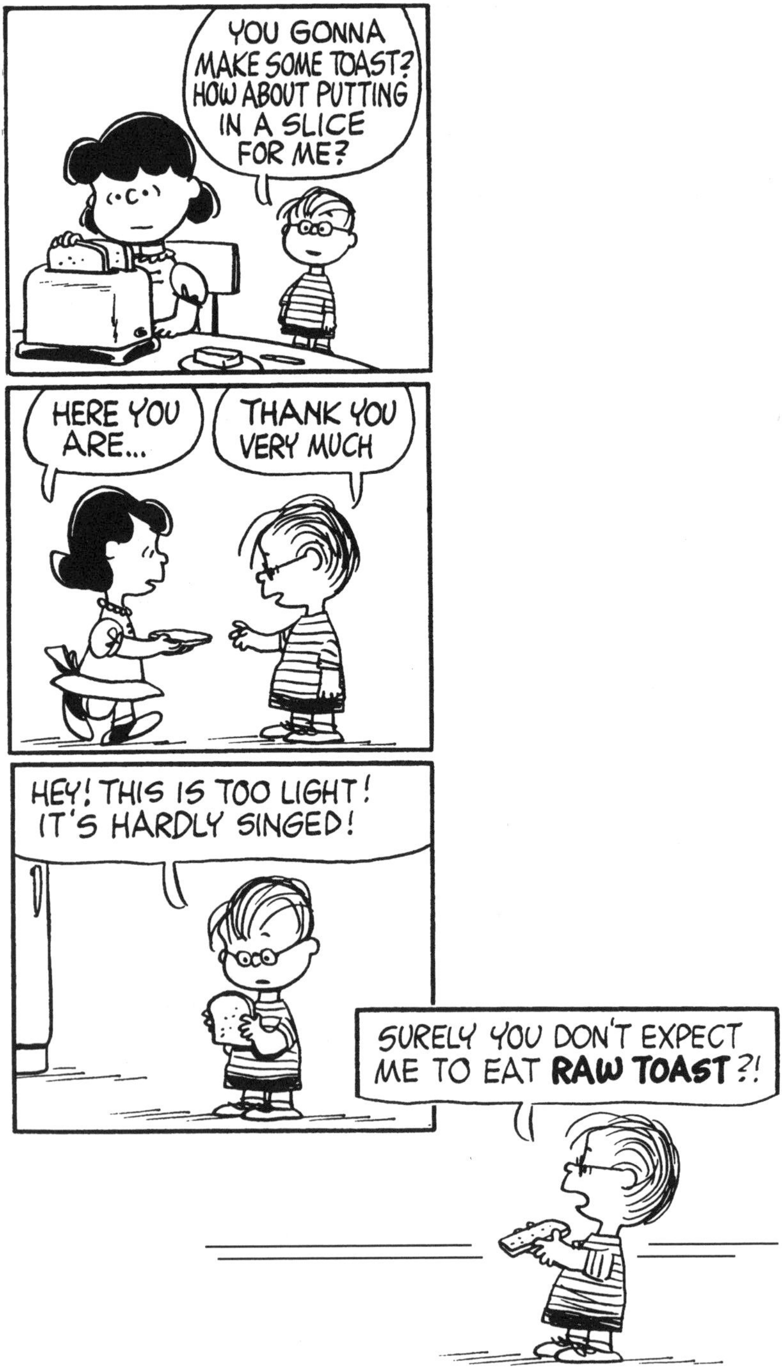
YOU GONNA MAKE SOME TOAST? HOW ABOUT PUTTING IN A SLICE FOR ME?
HERE YOU ARE...
THANK YOU VERY MUCH
HEY! THIS IS TOO LIGHT! IT'S HARDLY SINGED!
SURELY YOU DON'T EXPECT ME TO EAT **RAW TOAST**?!

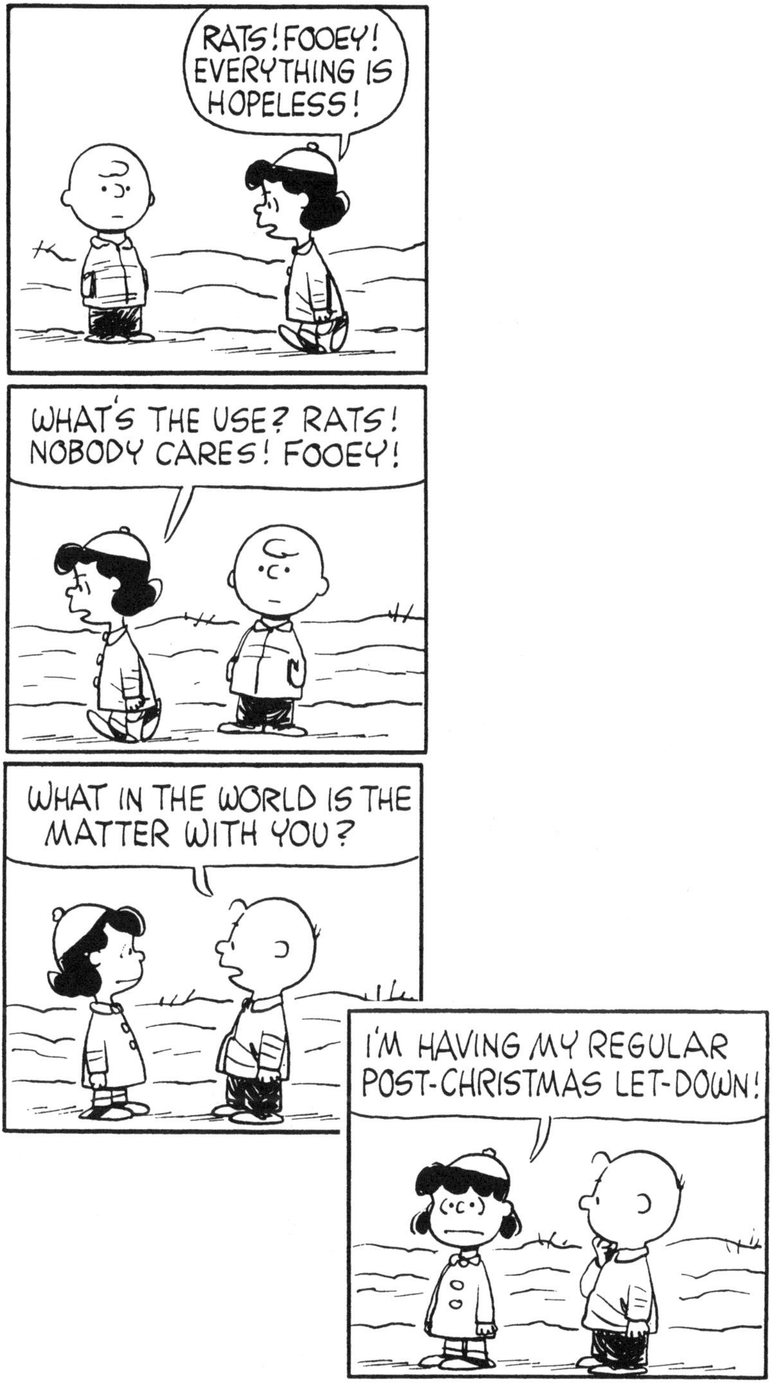
RATS! FOOEY! EVERYTHING IS HOPELESS!
WHAT'S THE USE? RATS! NOBODY CARES! FOOEY!
WHAT IN THE WORLD IS THE MATTER WITH YOU?
I'M HAVING MY REGULAR POST-CHRISTMAS LET-DOWN!

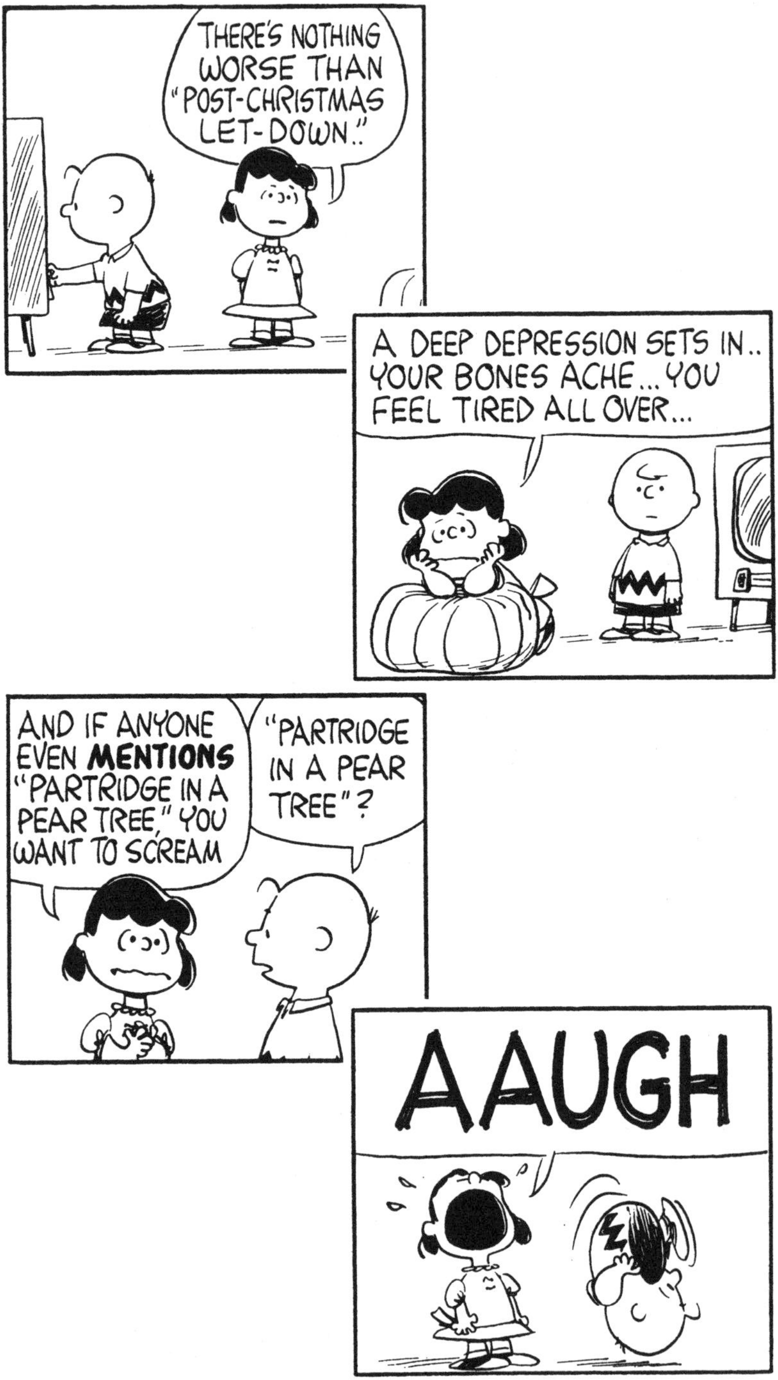
THERE'S NOTHING WORSE THAN "POST-CHRISTMAS LET-DOWN."
A DEEP DEPRESSION SETS IN.. YOUR BONES ACHE... YOU FEEL TIRED ALL OVER...
AND IF ANYONE EVEN **MENTIONS** "PARTRIDGE IN A PEAR TREE," YOU WANT TO SCREAM
"PARTRIDGE IN A PEAR TREE"?
AAUGH

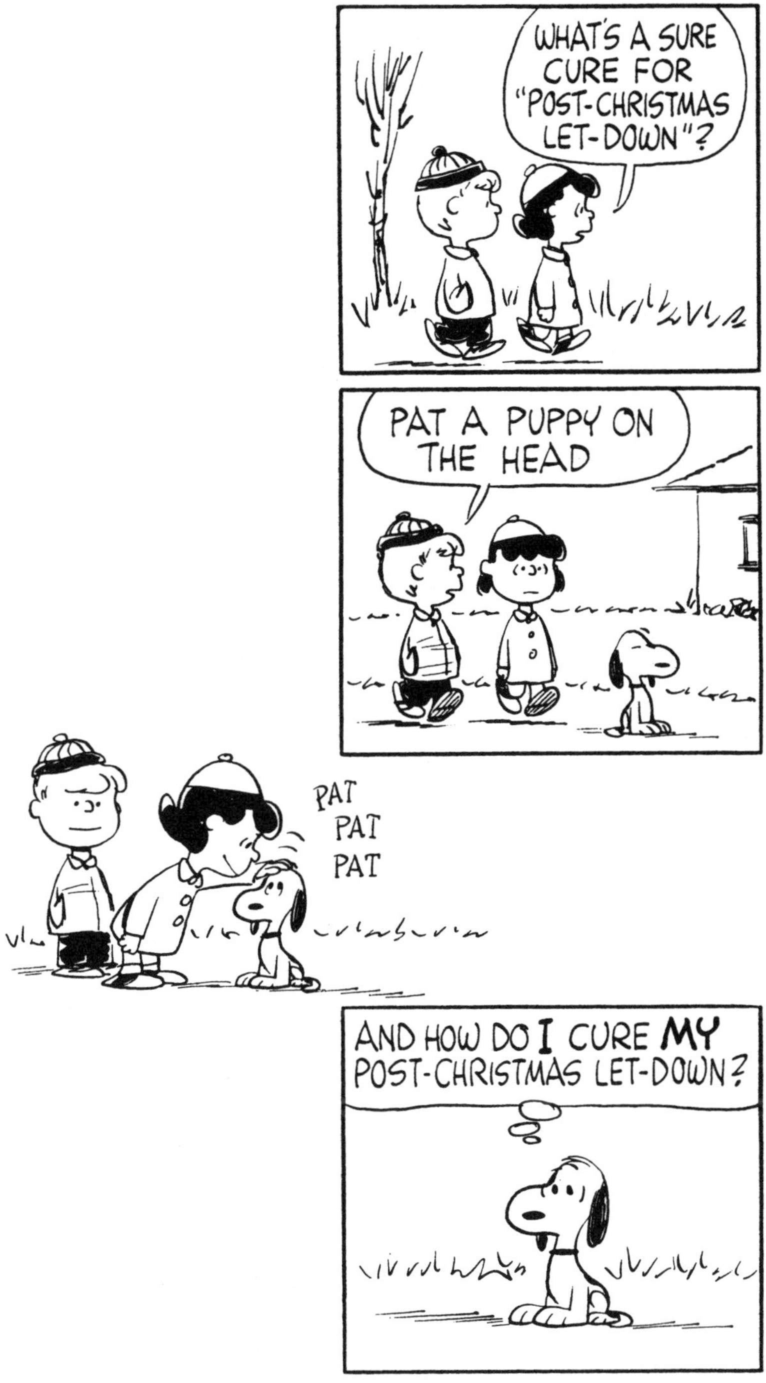
WHAT'S A SURE CURE FOR "POST-CHRISTMAS LET-DOWN"?
PAT A PUPPY ON THE HEAD
PAT PAT PAT
AND HOW DO I CURE MY POST-CHRISTMAS LET-DOWN?

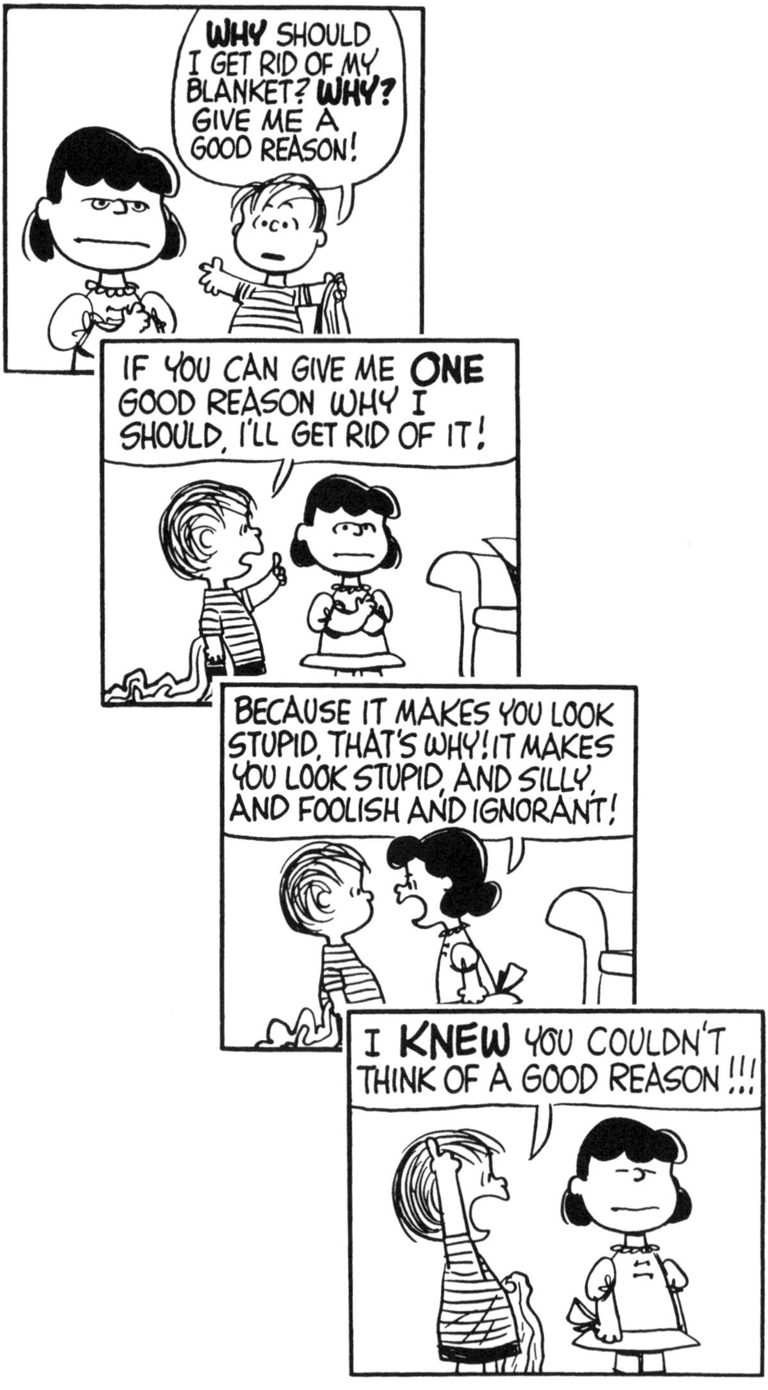
WHY SHOULD I GET RID OF MY BLANKET? WHY? GIVE ME A GOOD REASON!
IF YOU CAN GIVE ME ONE GOOD REASON WHY I SHOULD, I'LL GET RID OF IT!
BECAUSE IT MAKES YOU LOOK STUPID, THAT'S WHY! IT MAKES YOU LOOK STUPID, AND SILLY, AND FOOLISH AND IGNORANT!
I KNEW YOU COULDN'T THINK OF A GOOD REASON!!!

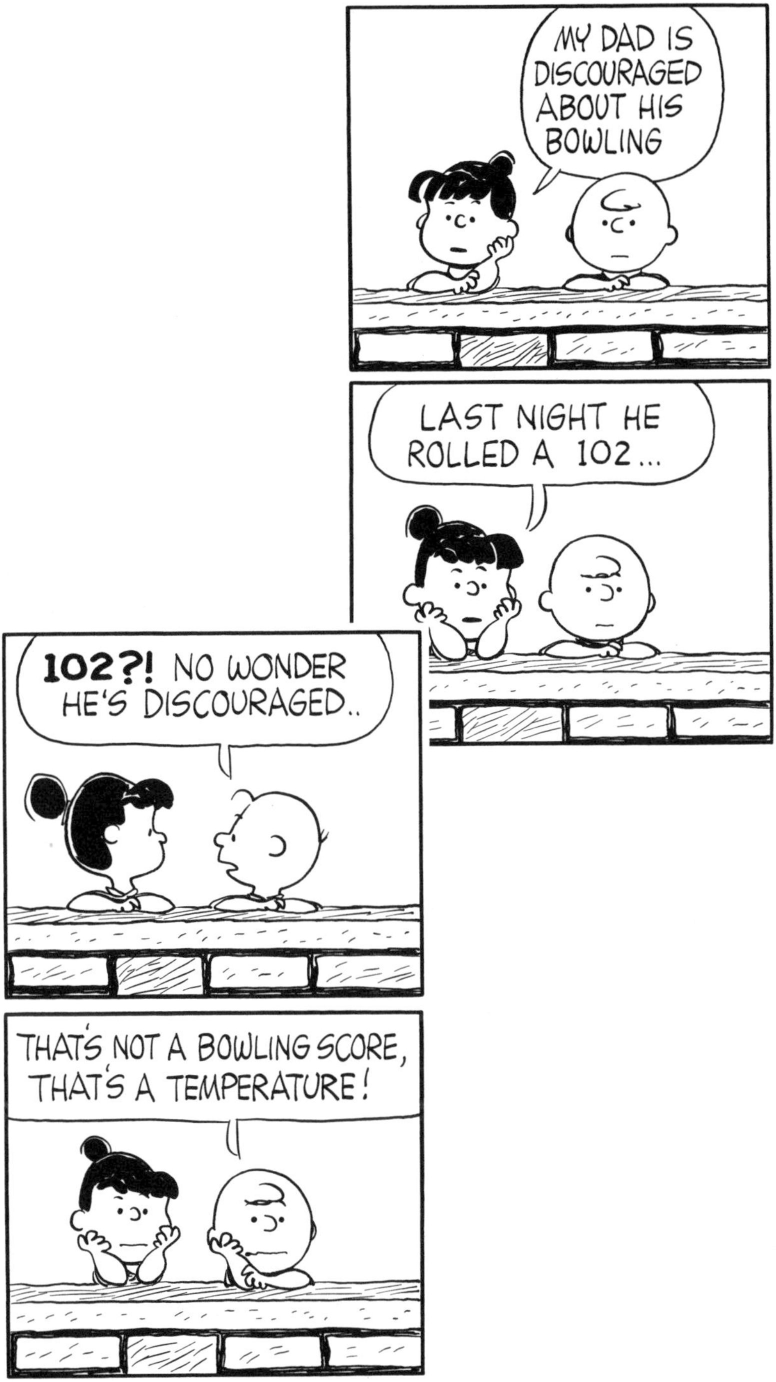
MY DAD IS DISCOURAGED ABOUT HIS BOWLING
LAST NIGHT HE ROLLED A 102...
102?! NO WONDER HE'S DISCOURAGED..
THAT'S NOT A BOWLING SCORE, THAT'S A TEMPERATURE!

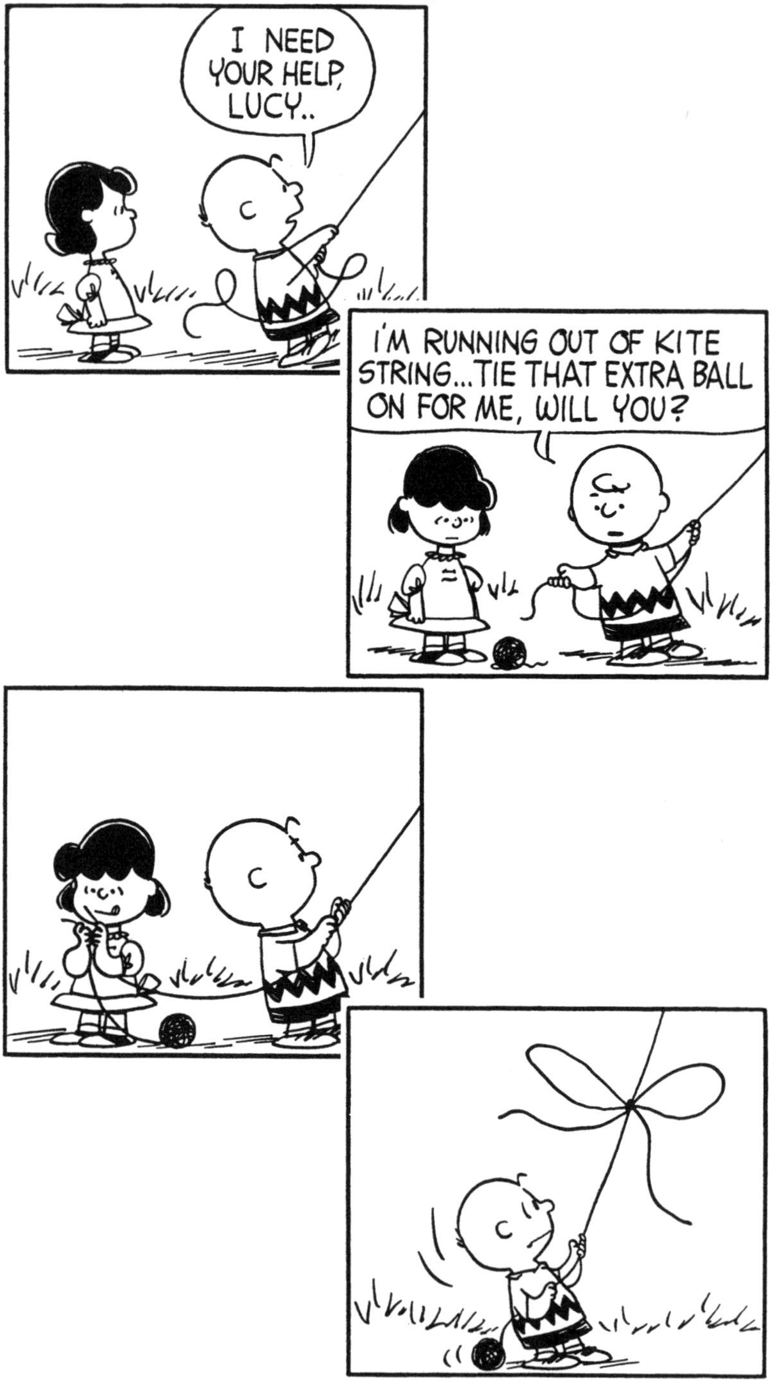
I NEED YOUR HELP, LUCY..
I'M RUNNING OUT OF KITE STRING...TIE THAT EXTRA BALL ON FOR ME, WILL YOU?

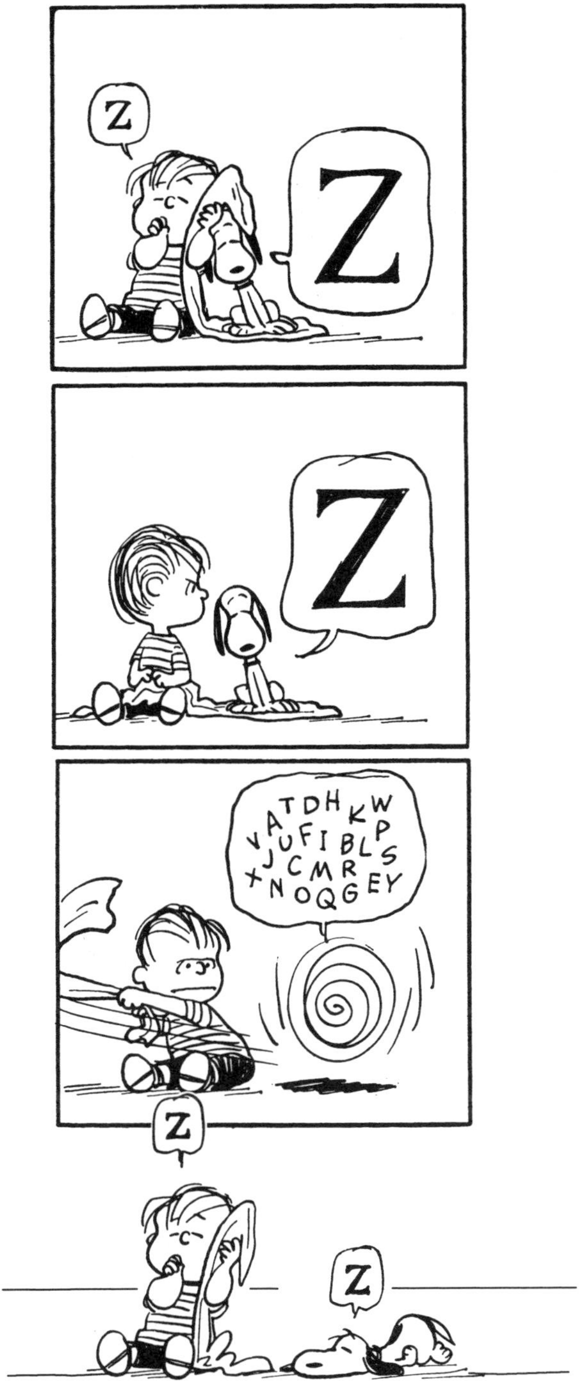
Z
Z
Z
ATDH KW
VUFIBLP
JCMRS
XNOQGEY
Z
Z

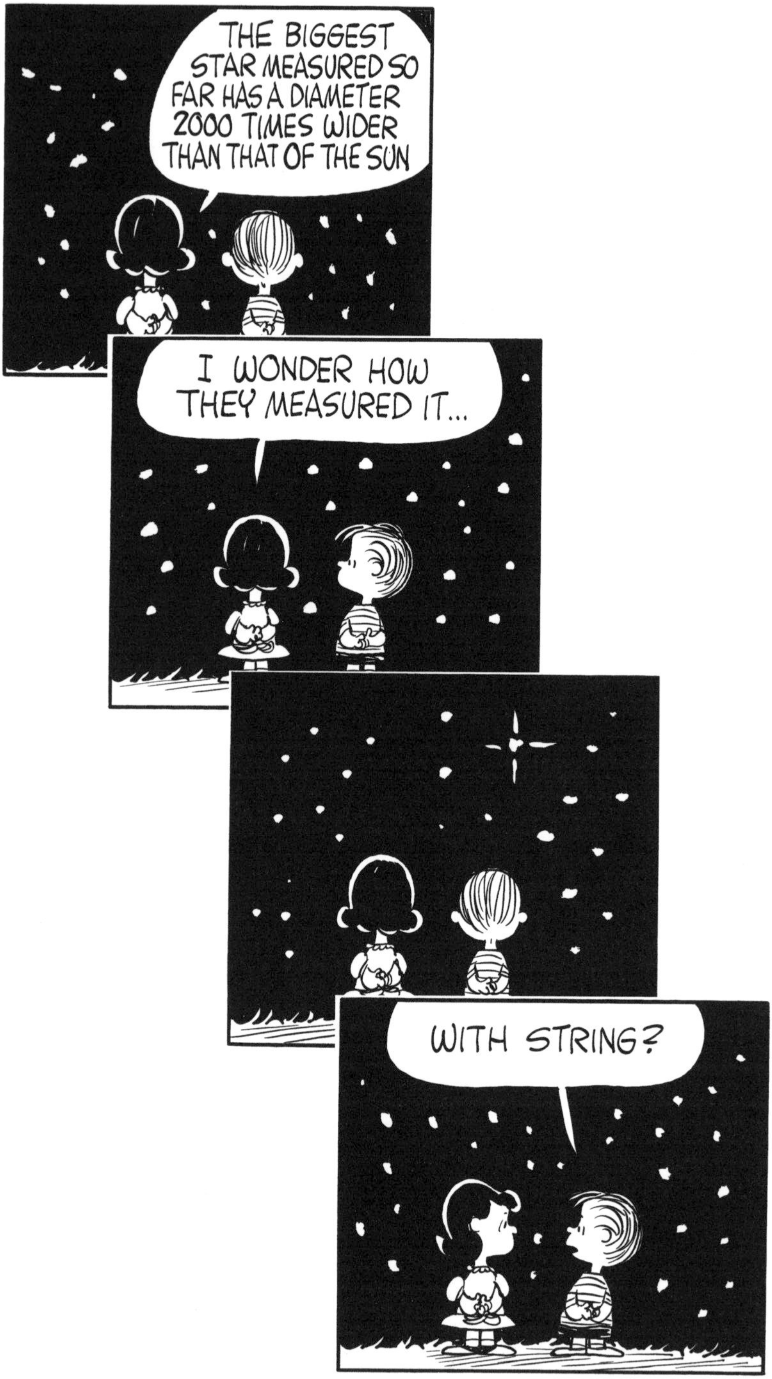
THE BIGGEST STAR MEASURED SO FAR HAS A DIAMETER 2000 TIMES WIDER THAN THAT OF THE SUN
I WONDER HOW THEY MEASURED IT...
WITH STRING?

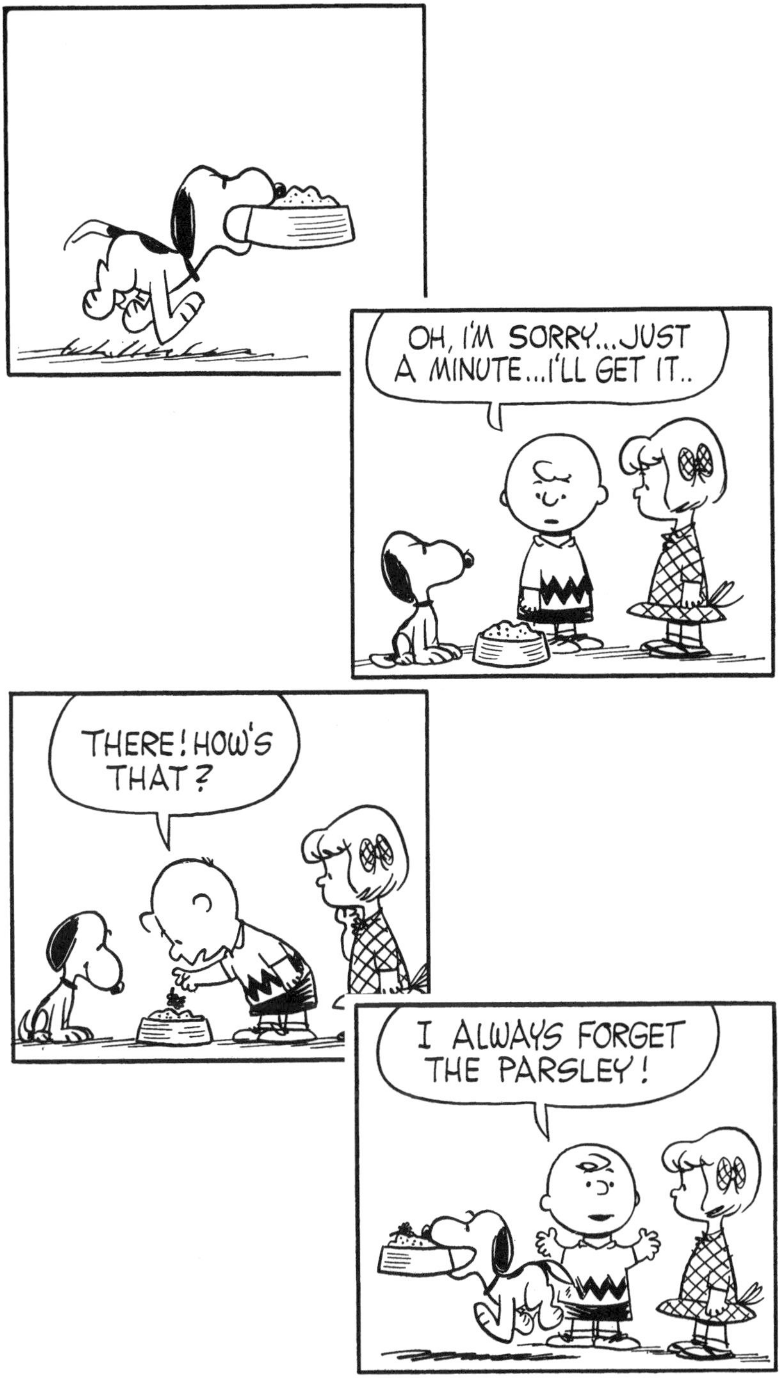
OH, I'M SORRY...JUST A MINUTE...I'LL GET IT..
THERE! HOW'S THAT?
I ALWAYS FORGET THE PARSLEY!

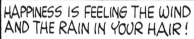

HAPPINESS IS FEELING THE WIND AND THE RAIN IN YOUR HAIR!

SORT OF!